A histo

J. JAMES &
AMMANFORD
SOUTH WALES

Including

JONES BROS. 'BRYNTEG'
UPPER TUMBLE, LLANELLY.

by Vernon Morgan

J. James & Sons Ltd.

Published by Vernon Morgan

September 2012

Designed by - Proprint, Carmarthen
Printed in Wales by - Proprint, Carmarthen

ISBN 978-0-9574045-0-2

All photographs are from the author's collection unless otherwise stated.

Photographs:

Cover picture: Captured here outside James' Bus Station in College Street, Ammanford, picking up passengers for the outward journey to Ystalyfera and Swansea in 1962 is Leyland Tiger Cub 218 (KBX997). Fitted with an 8ft. wide Weymann 44 seat bus body, it was the first 'Tiger Cub' delivered to the company in February 1955.

Roy Marshall collection

Title page: A superb official view of the company's first 'real bus' – a Leyland G7, 36h.p. 4 tonner registered BX1735. New in February 1921, carrying fleet No.1, it was fitted with this Leyland 'Edinburgh' style 32 seat rear entrance body of timber construction. The acetylene lighting and solid tyres were standard fitment in those by gone days.

Chris Taylor collection

Rear cover: Private hire was an additional source of revenue during the summer months, with heavy demand for excursions to the seaside. J. James & Sons Ltd., were given consent in 1961 to use double decker buses with driver operated doors on day and half day excursions; a feature that became commonplace on Sunday School outings thereafter. Weymann bodied Leyland Atlanteans 236/238 (UBX49/WTH114) are captured here at Aberavon beach coach park in the summer of 1961, working an excursion from Ammanford – a Sunday School outing. Aberavon in those halcyon days was a very popular seaside resort, which boasted 2 miles of golden sands, an esplanade with all the usual features, including a fun fair, amusement park, swimming pool and theatre.

Roy Marshall collection

CONTENTS:

Author's Acknowledgements

The extensive research and production of this book has taken over 7 years and I am indebted to numerous people for their sincere help and assistance in compiling it.

First of all I would like to single out and thank transport historian Chris Taylor of Cardiff, for his enthusiastic help and assistance, giving up his precious time, and allowing me access to his extensive collection of historic transport material. Chris also proof read the draft, corrected minor details and added several pieces of information. Without his valuable input, this book would not have progressed so well.

Much valuable information has also come from material in the care of Carmarthenshire County Council Cultural Services Department, The City & County of Swansea Cultural Services Department, Carmarthen Reference Library, The P.S.V. Circle, and First Cymru Ltd., (previously South Wales Transport Co.)

Special thanks are due to Roy Marshall, Alan Cross, D. A. Jones, Chris Taylor, Chris Carter, Alan Harris, T.S. Powell, Leyland Motors Ltd, (archive), the late Arnold Richardson (Photobus), Peter Yeomans and Robert Mack, for kindly allowing me to use their photographs to illustrate this book. Other photographs from my own collection are the copyright of persons unknown, as the photographs are not back stamped. No discourtesy to the photographer is intended through lack of acknowledgement, in lieu of which I trust they will accept my thanks.

Thanks also to former James employees, Wynford Prout, John and Ena Thomas, Dillwyn Richards, and the late Stan Williams, for their valuable information, and to fellow enthusiasts Andrew Porter, Paul Fox, Richard Evans, John Jones, John Martin, Byron Gage and the late Gerald Truran for their contributions and encouragement.

I would like to tender my grateful thanks to Kath, my wife, for her understanding, co-operation and tolerance over the last few years and her contribution in the production of this book – correcting my spelling and typing each page and to my daughter Katie for her contribution – correcting small grammatical errors, scanning and embedding each photo, and tidying up each page.

Finally I would like to thank Adrian and staff at Proprint, Carmarthen for their professional assistance in producing the final product.

FOREWORD

John James & Sons Ltd., of Ammanford were once Carmarthenshire's largest independent 'bus operator, employing no less than 200 people in the company's heyday.

The complex history of this fascinating company spanned a period of around 73 years, the roots of which can be traced back into the 19th century, long before the invention of the internal combustion engine.

Extensive and painstaking research into the history of John James' business has proved that previously published information stating that the business commenced in 1880 is incorrect.

Published to commemorate the 50th anniversary of the company's demise, this book is an attempt to record the true history of J. JAMES & SONS LTD., pioneers of public transport in Ammanford and the Amman Valley. To complete the picture, the turbulent history and eventual absorption of the notorious Jones Brothers' business, known as 'BRYNTEG' is separately included.

The spelling of place names referred to in this story are taken from authenticated records of that period in time, as several Welsh place names were changed to the true Welsh spelling from around 1960 onwards.

INTRODUCTION

For the reader, who may not be familiar with the area, we start the story with a brief history of Ammanford, which is situated in the Amman Valley district of rural east Carmarthenshire.

Previously known as Cross Inn, it was a village well known to weary travellers in the by gone days of stage coach and mail coach travel. Travellers frequently used the village staging post called the 'Cross Inn Hotel' for refreshments, and if necessary, a change of horses. The village had been named 'Cross Inn' after its location; a name derived from 'cross-ing' – the crossing point of two important South Wales coaching routes, and the crossing of the river 'Amman', which happened to be the county boundary between Carmarthenshire and neighbouring Glamorganshire. The river 'Amman' crossing, in those days, was made by means of a 'ford' (a crossing through the river bed), saving travellers some 20 miles on a journey between West Wales and Neath, or beyond.

With a population of around 200 in the early 1800's, the village inhabitants had earned their living mainly from farming and coal mining, until the Industrial Revolution took place changing the village scene virtually overnight. There were numerous heavy industries opening up across South Wales producing iron, steel, copper, tinplate, bricks etc., which demanded huge quantities of coal. The whole Amman Valley area, having massive reserves of top quality anthracite coal, soon had numerous collieries constructed, and working to full capacity, producing the coal required. Transportation of the coal was by means of an elaborate rail network set up in South Wales, linking all parts of the country.

Within a short space of time, these railways began carrying passengers and goods, after a large goods depot was constructed one mile from Cross Inn at Pantyffynnon Railway Station (Pantyffynnon Junction). At this location, trains from North Wales and the Midlands to Swansea; operated by the London & North Western Railway Co., (L.N.W.R.), connected with local Amman Valley trains running to Brynamman; operated by the Great Western Railway Co., (G.W.R.).

The Industrial Revolution, however, brought with it a huge influx of people into the area, brought in specifically to work the community's numerous collieries. This inevitably created rapid growth to the village of Cross Inn, and neighbouring Amman Valley villages.

In November 1880, however, the village inhabitants, unhappy with the name 'Cross Inn', held an important and historical meeting, at which they unanimously decided to rename the village. Adopting the name of AMMANFORD, it was an appropriate description of the village at the time, another name derived from its 'famous' river crossing 'Amman-ford' as mentioned earlier.

Over the next 20 years, Ammanford village rapidly expanded, becoming a market town for the Amman Valley, with the population increasing to just under 6,000 at the beginning of the 20th century. The collieries soon became Ammanford's largest employer, and in fact, Ammanford's wealth and prosperity came from the 'black gold' mined in the community.

A view of Ammanford Square, known as 'The Cross' circa 1910, showing the 'CROSS INN HOTEL' (to the left of the picture) and the newly erected commercial development of Evan Evans (Chemist), built on a site previously occupied by the Cross Inn Hotel's stables.

HOW JOHN JAMES' BUSINESS STARTED

John James, the pioneer of public transport in Ammanford, was born at Llywel, Breconshire in 1863. Llywel was a small agricultural village situated on the main West Wales to London mail coach route, known then as highway number 40, which eventually became designated trunk road A40.

At the age of 14 he left the sleepy Breconshire village to begin his working career as a labourer at Swansea Docks. Moving on from the docks he entered the grocery trade, and at the age of 21, became manager of a business owned by Messrs. Thomas & Evans (of Corona soft drinks fame) at Treherbert, Glamorganshire.

Returning again to the grocery trade in Swansea, he met Elizabeth Ann Fletcher, a butcher's daughter from Ammanford. She was the grandaughter of Mr. J. Daniells proprietor of the Rheidol Valley lead mines in North Cardiganshire. It was his marriage to Elizabeth in December 1888 that brought him to Ammanford where he opened his own grocery and provision merchants buisiness at the Golden Eagle Stores, 16 Wind Street, Ammanford. This was opposite his mother-in-law's coffee tavern at 15 Wind Street (previously the butchers shop owned by the Fletcher family)

His establishment could be regarded as a village store as he stocked china, earthenware goods, ironmongery and collier's oil, in addition to other commodities. He also provided a home delivery service for the provisions with his horse and cart, and then began door-to-door selling of salt, for which he became known locally as James-y-halen (James the salt).

Salt was a much used commodity in those far off days before the invention of fridges or freezers. Commonly used in butter making, salt was also widely used as a preservative for pork and for curing ham and bacon by many people who "bred" and killed their own pigs in back garden pig-sty's.

However, eleven years later in October 1900, the James family moved from the Golden Eagle Stores to new larger premises approximately 200 metres away at Bancyrhin on the Ammanford to Llandilo road. Their new home, 'Brynderwen' a double fronted house with lean-to cottage had great potential with its huge back garden, stables and outbuildings. From here, John James opened a 'mews' called 'Brynderwen Mews', situated only 80 metres from the famous village cross roads and Cross Inn Hotel.

Continuing with the provision merchants business, he then began a haulage business with his horse and cart, and subsequently conducted a very extensive business as posting master.

However, as the community expanded, John James' business equally expanded, firstly with the carriage of goods and later by carrying mail and passengers. Hauling goods by horse and cart or flat wagons, commonly known as 'gamboes', passengers were carried in horse-drawn wagonettes, dogcarts, traps and brakes for all occasions including weddings. Family picnics and parties were also catered for, with outings to Craig-y-nos Castle, Carreg Cennen Castle, Dryslwyn Castle, Llygad Llwchwr, Llynyfan reservoir and other places of historical and geological interest in the neighbourhood. Additionally, Mr. James bought a horse-drawn 'Shillibeer' hearse and started a funeral business.

Meanwhile, in the early 1900's, Ammanford received its Town status and all the town streets were given names by the Ammanford council. John James' premises Brynderwen Mews then became number 25 College Street, and the lean-to cottage, number 23

In 1910, John James ventured into a separate business that had no connection with the Mews. Forming a partnership with local haulier, David Evans, they had plans drawn up in March 1910 to build a roller skating rink at Margaret Street, Ammanford. Two years later they submitted another plan to the Ammanford council to alter the building into a cinema and roller-skating rink complex.

The partnership however, dissolved after a very short time and the building was sold as a going concern to Mr. J. R. Pooles of Edinburgh, from whence it was known as 'Pooles' Cinema.

Agreement made the twenty second day of October one thousand and nine hundred Between Gwilym Vaughan of Brynamman in the parish of Quarter Bach in the County of Carmarthen, printer of the one part, and John James Golden Eagle Ammanford in the parish of Llandebie in the County of Carmarthen Grocer of the other part. Whereas the said Gwilym Vaughan has agreed to sell the Leasehold Dwelling House situate on the main road leading from Ammanford to Llandilo and called Brynderwen now in the occupation of Mr William Edwards as quarterly Tenant Together with the lean-to Cottage now in the occupation of Mr E. Jones, Stables, and all out Buildings to the said John James at the price of £580 Five hundred & Eighty pounds and the said John James has paid to the said Gwilym Vaughan the sum of £5 Five pou by way of deposit and in part payment of the purch-money, and the said John James hereby agrees to complete the purchase on the 25th day of March next, the said John James to retain possession of the Stables and shall pay to the said Gwilym Vaughan the sum of £1 One pound per Calender Month as rent untill the day of Completion.

The Rents or possession of the Dwelling Houses shall be recieved or retained by said Gwilym Vaughan (Vendor) untill the purchase is completed The said Gwilym Vaughan hereby conforms the said sale and acknowledges the receipt of the said Deposit

Gwilym Vaughan
John James

Witnessed this 22nd day of October 1900

This is a copy of the original purchase agreement for Brynderwen Mews signed by John James on 22nd October 1900. Brynderwen was afterwards rented at 8 guineas a quarter until the purchase was completed in August 1905, with ALL other documentation and receipts in the name of Mrs. E.A. James

One of John James' horse and carts delivering goods around the Amman Valley district

Very much like the Killarney 'jaunting cars' of today, this 'brake' owned by John James, seated 12 passengers.

This rather modern looking brake, seated eight people.

CHANGING TO MOTOR VEHICLES

Having operated horse drawn vehicles for more than 20 years, John James decided to modernise and expand his transport business. Serious family discussions took place after which it was decided to form a partnership with his three sons, Percy, Lindsay and Angus in 1912. The new family partnership 'Messrs. J. James & Sons' soon began improving and modernising the business by adding a motor vehicle to the 'hire fleet'. The first motor vehicle purchased, a black Ford 'Model T' 20.H.P., charabanc was acquired new in September 1912. Registered (BX 234), its body was constructed to carry approximately 8 passengers by local coachbuilder, David Jones, The Garage, College Street, Ammanford. With this 'Model T' the James family started a motor charabanc business in addition to their well-established horse drawn carriage business operating from the Mews.

The first motor vehicle owned by Messrs. J. James & Sons was this Ford Model T charabanc which carried 8 passengers.

Diversifying to the new mode of transport – 'motor transport' – Messrs. J. James & Sons became Ammanford's first charabanc proprietors even though the Great Western Railway Co., had already made their presence known in the town running buses into Ammanford on rail-feeder services from Carmarthen and Neath. These G.W.R. buses however, were based at Carmarthen and Neath depots, several years later becoming outstationed at Pantyffynnon.

Messrs. James & Sons purchased a second motor vehicle in September 1914. This was a grey liveried 18 H.P. Royal Enfield charabanc, seating around 20, and was purchased through the local dealership of David Jones, the coachbuilder, in College Street, Ammanford. David Jones was also a motor agent (dealer) for Ford, Darracq, Briton, Pilot and Royal Enfield motor vehicles, in addition to his established coach building business. The third motor vehicle arrived in December 1914, an American built Maxwell 18 H.P., supplied by another local agent, G. Thomas, of Penybank Garage, Ammanford.

After adding motor cars and charabancs to the hiring fleet, the Mews then became known as Brynderwen Mews Garage in 1914, with John James' enthusiastic sons, eager to expand the business they undertook all types of repair work to motor vehicles and soon became automobile engineers.

However, several types and makes of vehicle were tried and tested during these early days, but the partnership bought a second and larger Royal Enfield with 24 H.P. engine in January 1917. This charabanc was 'champagne' in colour and like previous charabancs purchased it was basically a car-derived conversion that was relatively small, having a low seating capacity. The bodywork of these early charabancs, were built either by James themselves, at their own workshop, or by David Jones, the coachbuilder, in College Street.

Meanwhile, nearby Pantyffynnon Railway Station had the regular passenger services of two railway companies; L.N.W.R., (known locally as the 'Midland Railway') and the G.W.R., (Great Western Railway). The passenger services operated from Pantyffynnon Station were extremely popular, with regular excursions organised to destinations such as Aberystwyth, Blackpool, Cardiff, Hereford, London, etc.

Messrs. James & Sons had the foresight to see a huge potential here for their hiring business and the need for public transport from Ammanford town to the Railway Station at Pantyffynnon. As a result they began operating an unlicensed 'Taxi' service the short distance of 1¼ miles between Ammanford and Pantyffynnon Station, firstly with the 'Model T' Ford and later other charabancs.

James' business however, was faced with immense competition from the beginning even before buying their first motor vehicle. Their first competitor was local publican, Oswald David Edwards, proprietor of the famous staging post, Cross Inn Hotel, a mere 80 metres from James' premises at Ammanford. Ozzie Edwards also hired out traps, brakes, closed carriages and later cars. Ironically, only 2 weeks after Messrs. James & Sons purchased their first Royal Enfield charabanc in September 1914, Ozzie Edwards went out and purchased a 20 seater Daimler charabanc (BX 199), and even painted it in the same grey livery as James' Royal Enfield. Edwards, however, sold his Daimler during the early part of 1915, obviously due to lack of work for the vehicle after the outbreak of World War I.

Just a week after the outbreak of war, in August 1914, five of the seven largest collieries in the Ammanford area had closed owing to labour difficulties, most of the work force having been 'called up' to fight in Kitchener's army.

John James', youngest son, Angus enlisted for the army, leaving the family business within 2 months of war being declared. He served in the British Army as an officer from 1914 – 1918, and after war ended, went on to serve in the Colonial Army in Kenya for a few more years before eventually returning home to Ammanford. Angus' brother, Lindsay, enlisted some time later, serving with the British Army in France.

During the 'Great War' years 1914 – 1918 business was relatively quiet due mainly to petrol rationing. The motor vehicles were not frequently used because of the petrol shortage, causing most hirings to revert back to the more 'economical' mode of transport, the traps and brakes.

These difficult war years forced competitor Ozzie Edwards to cease trading altogether in 1918 and in May of the following year Edwards' entire 'hire fleet' of traps, brakes and gamboe's were advertised for sale along with his 3 horses.

James, however, had their regular clientele. One customer, the Ammanford Urban District Council frequently hired James' traps and charabancs for official council meetings held around the area. Noted in the Ammanford Council's Minutes Book for April 1919 was an account for the hire of a trap to a parish meeting at the cost of twelve shillings (60 pence by comparison of today's money). Amongst other council hirings noted was the hire of a charabanc to and from the Water Works near the village of Trapp in July 1919 – for five pounds and ten shillings.

However, it was only after the 'Great War' had ended in 1918, and peace signed with Germany in 1919, that the community eventually returned to a normal life. Demand in the area for public transport had now become apparent, and men who had learnt to drive whilst in Army service decided to try their hand at becoming 'bus or charabanc operators, purchasing an assortment of surplus World War 1 vehicles, buses, charabancs, lorries and cars.

The first of these enterprising operators to venture into Ammanford in April 1919 were Messrs. Jones Bros., of Brynteg Garage, Upper Tumble – known locally as 'Brynteg'. They began running an unlicenced daily service into Ammanford from the Tumble area, via: Cross Hands, Penygroes and Llandebie, with connections at Tumble for Llanelly on market days only – Thursdays and Saturdays. Their presence in Ammanford, however, was by no means interfering with James' operations, but reference to this very interesting operator is made here, as closer links were formed between the two companies in later years.

Meanwhile, in view of the fact that James' charabancs had only operated private hire work until now and an unlicenced 'taxi' service from Ammanford to Pantyffynnon

Station, it was after the World War 1 hostilities were over in 1919 that the first stage carriage service officially started.

Trading as 'Amman Valley Road Motor Bus Service', Messrs. J. James & Sons began their pioneering omnibus service:

> Pantyffynnon Railway Station to Brynamman Railway Station.
> via:- Ammanford Square (Cross Inn), Pontamman, Glanamman, Garnant and Gwaun-Cae-Gurwen.

The service started on 25th September 1919, after a national rail strike hit the Amman Valley. The Great Western Railway's train and bus crews, all members of the railmens' union ceased work in support of the stoppage leaving the community without any form of transport.

With an absence of public transport in the valley, Messrs. J. James & Sons immediately took advantage of the situation and wittingly provided a charabanc service to replace the valley's train and rail feeder bus services on the 8 miles between Pantyffynnon Railway Station and Brynamman Railway Station.

The strike however was settled in just two weeks yet James continued operating the Amman Valley route competing directly against the Great Western Railways' (G.W.R.) rail feeder bus service. The valley train times however didn't really suit the public's requirements, but James' new service having a better suited time-table soon began carrying regular passengers between the intermediate villages on route and into Ammanford Town, especially on market days.

These were the humble beginnings of Messrs. J. James & Sons' road services in 1919, making them the first Ammanford based stage carriage operator. The service however, remained unlicenced for eleven years after inauguration as the local Council were at first completely unaware of licencing regulations regarding passenger services and passenger vehicles operating within their district.

The enterprising partnership then looked for additional methods to expand their charabanc business and decided to organise and advertise excursions. One regular excursion was a trip to Swansea, for evening theatre visits when the charabancs were 'off service'. Swansea boasted 3 theatres and many cinemas in those far-gone years that attracted many visitors to the town.

THEATRE TRIPS.

For the benefit of the General Public of Ammanford.

On and after November 6th, 1919,

A MOTOR CHARABANC

Will be run from

BRYNDERWEN MEWS, AMMANFORD,

to

SWANSEA

EVERY THURSDAY.

Starting at 4 p.m. Returning after Theatre.

Fare, 6/- Return.

Seats may be booked at—

Messrs. J. JAMES & SONS,

BRYNDERWEN MEWS,

COLLEGE STREET, AMMANFORD.

N.B.—Bookings must be made not later than Tuesday of each week.

Messrs. J. James & Sons were however the first charabanc operators in the Amman Valley to introduce advertised excursions. The fare of six shillings seems rather expensive for the time yet the 'excursions' were very popular amongst the population of Ammanford. This advertisement appeared in the Amman Valley Chronicle and East Carmarthen news each week leading up to Christmas 1919.

THE ROARING TWENTIES

Over the ten years 1920 – 1930, Messrs. J. James & Sons established themselves rapidly. The 1920's however probably represented the most difficult and adventurous era in the company's history. It was the sheer willpower, determination, and hard work of the family and employees alike, that brought about their survival and success. It became a tremendous challenge to everyone involved, as it must not be forgotten that bus travel at this time was only in its infancy. The vehicles themselves were by today's standards very primitive, slow, no power, poor brakes, no self-starters, safety equipment or heaters. The chassis design and construction of some vehicles was again quite poor resulting in frequent mechanical breakdowns. The general comfort for passengers and crews alike was hardly the keynote with solid tyres, harsh springing and poor lighting. Coupled with all of this, the roads were in bad condition, with potholes and ruts abounding.

However, in 1920 when petrol was only 7d (7 pence) per gallon, (2.74 pence by today's comparison), there were as many as ten charabanc proprietors plying the Ammanford district. These were:-

STEPHEN BOWEN, 'ARIEL', LLANDEBIE.
IDWAL DAVIES, AMMANFORD.
GREAT WESTERN RAILWAY CO. (G.W.R.), NEATH.
J. JAMES & SONS, AMMANFORD.
E. ISAAC JONES, BRYNAMMAN.
REES JONES, TALBOT GARAGE, TIRYDAIL.
DAVID LEWIS, TIRYDAIL.
JACK SMITH, GARNANT.
ALBERT THOMAS (M.M.T. SERVICES), TIRYDAIL.
REES & WILLIAMS, TYCROES

With so many operators confined to a small area, competition inevitably became quite fierce from 1920 onwards, on all aspects of motor bus operation, stage service and excursions. In fact, some operators quickly followed James' procedure of organising and advertising excursions.

BOXING DAY.

A Charabanc
Will leave
Ammanford Square
On Boxing Day at
11 a.m. for SWANSEA.
Returning after Empire.
Fee - - 6/- each.

Book your Seats at Rees Jones & Son,
Talbot Garage.

Competitor Rees Jones of Tirydail quickly followed James' practice of advertising excursions. This advertisement first appeared in the Amman Valley Chronicle on 11th December, 1919.

Tradesmen's Announcements.

FOR THE
NATIONAL EISTEDDFOD.

The New 35-Seater
CHARABANC
Will run to
BARRY

MODERATE FARES.
Apply—
REES & WILLIAMS,
Garage, TYCROES.

Rees & Williams of Tycroes were more adventurous by advertising trips to Barry, for the National Eisteddfod held there in August 1920.

All but three of the aforementioned businesses fell by the wayside after a very short time, no doubt the economic depression and 1926 general strike contributed to their demise. Besides James themselves the only companies to survive that difficult period were Rees & Williams of Tycroes and the Great Western Railway Co. However, several other operators made brief appearances in the community periodically, but disappeared equally as fast.

In order to improve their business further, Messrs James & Sons decided to operate larger vehicles. This meant demolition of John James' lean-to cottage, (23 College Street) to allow a wider entrance to the mews, and the purchase of 500 square yards of extra land situated to the rear of 21 College Street next door (the famous Army & Navy Stores) upon which a garage workshop was built.

Renaming the new garage Central Garage, this became the official adopted garage name from 1920. The old name, Brynderwen Mews Garage, was inevitably phased out along with the Mews, stables, horses and horse drawn vehicles. A new motor hearse, the first in Ammanford, replaced the old horse drawn hearse for the funeral side of the business, and a dark blue Daimler Landaulette was added to the private hire fleet in October 1920 for weddings, etc.

The first motor hearse in Ammanford, owned by John James & sons.

The automobile repair side of the business became very successful, and the company had an excellent reputation as motor engineers. In fact the Ammanford Council asked the engineers for their recommendation regarding the purchase of a lorry, inviting them to tender for it also. After the Council lorry was purchased it was maintained and refuelled at James' garage for several years. Other local authorities used James' engineering skills also, including the Pontardawe Rural District Council.

The 'omnibus' side of James' business saw big improvements also. The Royal Enfield charabancs used to inaugurate their first successful services between Pantyffynnon and Brynamman had by 1921 become too small and outdated, competing against the bigger A.E.C. buses of the G.W.R. Co. Consequently, James disposed of these charabancs in due course, replacing them with larger proper service buses.

In order to compete against the 'giant' G.W.R. company, James bought their first 'real' bus, a new Leyland in February 1921. Fitted with a Leyland 'Edinburgh' style 32 seater body, it was sign written with a newly adopted fleet name 'Ammanford & District Bus Service'. Its livery of deep maroon with cream relief, became James' standard livery for some 17 years, yet the fleet name, Ammanford & District Bus Service, was phased out completely in 1933, as the company's operating area greatly increased.

The first new Leyland bus owned carried fleet No.1. Registered BX 1735 it carried a Leyland 32 seat body constructed to 'Edinburgh' design. (V. Morgan collection.)

One of the Great Western Railway Co.'s AEC charabancs that competed against James in the Amman Valley. This 28 seater was new in 1919.

CUT THIS OUT.

Amman Valley Road Motor 'Bus Service

REVISED TIME TABLE FROM MARCH 1st.

Ammanford—Brynamman.

	MONDAY TO FRIDAY.			SATURDAY SERVICE.			
	a m	p m	p m	a m	p m	p m	p m
Ammanford ...	8-15	2-0	6-30	8-15	2-0	6-30	9-15
Mount Pleasant ...	8-27	2-12	6-42	8-27	2-12	6-42	9-27
Glynmoch ...	8-32	2-17	6-47	8-32	2-17	6-47	9-32
Glanamman Square ...	8-40	2-25	6-55	8-40	2-25	6-55	9-40
Half Moon Hotel ...	8-45	2-30	7-0	8-45	2-30	7-0	9-45
Raven Hotel ...	8-50	2-35	7-5	8-50	2-35	7-5	9-50
Gwaun-cae-gurwen ...	8-57	2-42	7-15	8-57	2-42	7-15	9-57
Brynamman ...	9-10	2-50	7-25	9-10	2-50	7-25	10-10
Brynamman ...	9-30	4-0	7-45	9-30	4-0	7-45	10-30
Gwaun-cae-gurwen ...	9-40	4-10	7-55	9-40	4-10	7-55	10-40
Raven Hotel ...	9-47	4-18	8-2	9-47	4-18	8-2	10-47
Half Moon Hotel ...	9-52	4-22	8-7	9-52	4-22	8-7	10-52
Glanamman Square ...	9-57	4-25	8-12	9-57	4-25	8-12	10-57
Glynmoch ...	10-5	4-35	8-20	10-5	4-35	8-20	11-5
Mount Pleasant ...	10-10	4-40	8-30	10-10	4-40	8-30	11.10
Ammanford ...	10-15	4-45	8-35	10-15	4-45	8-35	11-15

AMMANFORD AND PANTYFFYNNON.

Leave Ammanford ...	10-20	1-30	6-0	10-20	1-30	6-0	8-45
Leave Pantyffynnon ...	10-45	1-45	6-15	10-45	1-45	6-15	9-0

Passengers picked up and set down at any point.

J. JAMES & SONS, Central Garage, Ammanford.

This was the first timetable published by Messrs. J. James & Sons in February 1921. The trading name of Amman Valley Road Motor Services was phased out soon after publication of this timetable – changing the trading name to Ammanford & District Bus Service. A short while later, competitor Phillips Bros., of Llandebie picked up a similar fleet name – 'Amman Valley Bus Service.

The Amman Valley residents were so appreciative towards James' bus service, many expressed their feelings by writing letters to the local newspaper – 'The Amman Valley Chronicle' thanking Messrs. J. James & Sons for their motor bus service and effectively calling them 'The Samaritan of the road'.

Our Letter Box.

VALLEY 'BUS SERVICE.

To the Editor, *Amman Valley Chronicle.*

Sir,—I shall thank you, in conjunction with other readers of your paper, to insert a few remarks in reference to the great competition now existing between motor-'bus services. It is well known to the inhabitants of Ammanford and the districts, and especially so to travellers following commercial duties, that they were sadly handicaped regarding opportunities of conveyances, train services were greatly curtailed, and for a length of time it seemed as though the upper parts of the Valley were deserted entirely; and the public at large in their sad plight had to grin and bear it. To relieve the tension, Messrs. James and Sons, of College Street, Ammanford, adopted the idea of running a charabanc service for a time, pending the arrival of a first-class motor-'bus, which is still at the services of the public. It is admitted and endorsed by all who have occasion to use it that it it is a boon to the Valleys. The main point of ventilating this matter to the local Press is that, at the present time, adequate provision is the order of the day. The G.W.R. are running a service as well, trains are reinstated, and the public are once more out of the difficulty. But the initiative movement is due to the enterprise of Messrs. James and Sons, who thereby deserve the patronage of all concerned. This was done when other services were so limited that it was a case of "A friend in need," &c. It is to be hoped they will retain the patronage. Thanking you in anticipation.—Yours, &c.,

HARRY EDMUNDS.

An example of a letter sent to the local newspaper- 'The Amman Valley Chronicle' by H. Edmunds dated 25th August, 1921, in appreciation of James' new bus service in the Amman Valley.

Messrs. JAMES & SONS,
The Mews, AMMANFORD,

Beg to heartily thank the Amman Valley Public for their splendid patronage of their ROAD PASSENGER VEHICLES in the past, and hope they will continue their support in the future. Despite keen competition, they are still going strong, and they feel deeply grateful to their Patrons for their stand for the OLD FIRM—

Messrs. JAMES'.

New Time Table will appear in our next issue.

Messrs. J. James & Sons' reply to these letters in the local newspaper 22nd September, 1921, thanking the public for their continued support.

With all this 'bus challenging' going on between the Amman Valley bus proprietors, a special meeting of the Ammanford U.D.C. was called on 7th September 1921 to discuss the matter. The council surveyor expressed deep concern over the amount of buses plying into the town, asking what action had been taken in other towns, and the question of having 'standing places' for them. He then contacted other local authorities and the Ministry of Transport for advice on the matter. At a later meeting, the Chairman stated that in future all bus and charabanc proprietors would have to apply to the Council's Transport Committee for:-

1. a Hackney Carriage licence for each vehicle.
2. a drivers licence for each driver operating into the town.
3. a licence to operate each route into the town.

The council, however, failed to carry out this commitment, and so the 'bus challenging' continued.

In the meantime, James' Brynamman service had become so popular the company decided to improve the service in October 1921 by introducing a timetable doubling the amount of daily journeys. At the same time they inaugurated a 'new' service from Ammanford Square (The Cross Inn Hotel) to the village of Tycroes, two miles away.

AMMANFORD AND DISTRICT.

Motor Bus Services

Between

Ammanford (SQUARE), Glanamman, Garnant, Gwaun-cae-gurwen, & Pantyffynnon & Tycroes. **Brynamman** (STATION).

AMMANFORD AND BRYNAMMAN.

	a.m.	a.m.	p.m.	p.m.	p.m.	p.m.	p.m.	Additional Service on Saturday. p.m.	p.m.
Ammanford (dep.)	8 30	11 15	2 0	3 0	5 0	6 30	7 45	9 30	10 15
Mount Pleasant ...	8 35	11 20	2 5	3 5	5 5	6 35	7 50	9 35	10 20
Glynmoch ...	8 40	11 25	2 10	3 10	5 10	6 40	7 55	9 40	10 25
Grenig Road ...	8 45	11 30	2 15	3 15	5 15	6 45	8 0	9 45	10 30
Glanamman ...	8 50	11 35	2 20	3 20	5 20	6 50	8 5	9 50	10 35
Half Moon ...	8 55	11 40	2 25	3 25	5 25	6 55	8 10	9 55	10 40
Raven	9 0	11 45	2 30	3 30	5 30	7 0	8 15	10 0	10 45
Prince Albert ...	9 3	11 48	2 33	3 33	5 33	7 3	8 18	10 3	10 48
Gwaun-cae-gurwen	9 10	11 55	2 40	3 40	5 40	7 10	8 25	10 10	10 55
Brynamman (arr.)	9 15	12 0	2 45	3 45	5 45	7 15	8 30	10 15	11 0

	a.m.	p.m.	p.m.	p.m.	p.m.	p.m.	p.m.	p.m.	p.m.
Brynamman (dep.)	9 30	12 30	3 0	4 0	5 45	7 45	9 0	10 30	11 15
Gwaun-cae-gurwen	9 35	12 35	3 5	4 5	5 50	7 50	9 5	10 35	11 20
Prince Albert ...	9 42	12 42	3 12	4 12	5 57	7 57	9 12	10 42	11 27
Raven	9 45	12 45	3 15	4 15	6 0	8 0	9 15	10 45	11 30
Half Moon ...	9 50	12 50	3 20	4 20	6 5	8 5	9 20	10 50	11 35
Glanamman ...	9 55	12 55	3 25	4 25	6 10	8 10	9 25	10 55	11 40
Grenig Road ...	10 0	1 0	3 30	4 30	6 15	8 15	9 30	11 0	11 45
Glynmoch ...	10 5	1 5	3 35	4 35	6 20	8 20	9 35	11 5	11 50
Mount Pleasant ...	10 10	1 10	3 40	4 40	6 25	8 25	9 40	11 10	11 55
Ammanford (arr.)	10 15	1 15	3 45	4 45	6 30	8 30	9 45	11 15	12 0

AMMANFORD & PANTYFFYNNON.

	a.m.	p.m.	p.m.	p.m.	Additional Service on Saturday. p.m.
Ammanford (dep.)	10 20	1 20	4 45	6 0	8 45
Pantyffynnon (dep.)	10 45	1 45	5 0	6 10	9 0

AMMANFORD & TYCROES.

	p.m.	p.m.	p.m.	Additional Service on Saturday. p.m.
Ammanford (dep.)	4 0	6 30	8 45	9 45
Tycroes (dep.)	4 15	6 45	9 0	10 0

Passengers picked up and put down at any point.

JOHN JAMES & SONS,

CENTRAL GARAGE,

AMMANFORD.

OCTOBER, 1921.

TELEPHONE: No. 35.

This was the new timetable published by Messrs. John James & Sons on 13th October, 1921, which doubled the amount of daily journeys between Ammanford and Brynamman. The increased frequency was introduced as a result of the tremendous public support for the service.

To cope with the increased passenger loadings, the company purchased their second Leyland a few months later, with a third one arriving in 1922, followed by three more in 1923. With these new Leylands, James extended the Ammanford – Brynamman service, a further 3 miles down the valley, from Brynamman to reach Cwmllynfell, situated in the upper Swansea Valley, and by 1925 extended the service by another two miles, to reach the village of Cwmtwrch.
The Leylands proved to be such a success in the development of James' business, that eventually, an association was formed with Leyland Motors, which lasted more than 41 years, until the demise of James' business in 1962.

As the 'bus war' continued in 1922, another heated council debate took place regarding buses running into Ammanford on Sundays, creating a nuisance, according to the councillors, who were asking for NO bus services on Sundays, on religious grounds. They were over-ruled by the Transport Committee, but the G.W.R. Co., nevertheless, discontinued their Sunday buses voluntarily soon afterwards. Two years later in 1924 nothing had been organised in respect of licensing buses or drivers in Ammanford. Things were then really getting out of hand regarding the amount of unlicensed buses using Ammanford Square. Messrs. James & Sons asked the council for a standing place for their services at Wind Street, in Ammanford, but were refused on the grounds of local by-laws, yet other towns provided ample bus stands for all bus services. Neighbouring Llandilo R.D.C., and Cwmamman U.D.C., found themselves in the same situation as Ammanford, regarding bus traffic in their districts, and it was therefore suggested that a meeting should be held between all the local authorities in the area, with the intention of bringing the 'bus war' to an end.

At the height of the Ammanford 'bus war' in 1923, Angus James, youngest son of Mr. John James, founder of the James business, returned home from the Colonial Army in Kenya after 9 years army service. Rejoining the family business he soon took an active part in the company management becoming company secretary and latterly General Manager. Angus, however, was a well-respected gentleman amongst the company employees and public alike, which undoubtedly attributed to the company's continued success.

By January 1923, the Tycroes based Rees & Williams company, now trading as Tycroes & District Bus Service, began seriously challenging James, by running a service from their home village of Tycroes into Ammanford, and later that year extended the service beyond Ammanford to include the Amman Valley reaching Gwaun-Cae-Gurwen and Cwmgorse. A short while later in 1924, Rees & Williams were again following James, by running from Ammanford to Brynamman. This inevitably caused a lot of friction between the two companies, which often led to 'fighting' between rival crews. Even Angus James himself got involved in a fistfight with a Rees & Williams driver!

With James seriously concentrating their 'bus operations to the east of Ammanford Town, the North and West sides of Ammanford, so far untouched by James' services, were plied by several other operators including the aforementioned Jones Bros., 'Brynteg', Upper Tumble. In addition to Jones' Ammanford to Llanelly service, they introduced an ambitious new daily service in August 1923 from Ammanford to Lampeter (Railway Station). Having connections from Tumble and Cross Hands the 2 hour; 32 mile journey from Ammanford to Lampeter ran via: Llandebie,, Llandilo, Llanwrda, Pumpsaint and Cwmanne. Jones Bros., however were soon experiencing difficulties that included financial problems. Adding to their difficulties, six other operators challenged them on the first section of the route between Ammanford and Llandilo, all unlicensed. One competitor, the South Wales Transport Co., of Swansea, were running two services into Llandilo in 1924, one from Swansea via the Amman Valley, the second from Llanelly via Pontardulais and Ammanford.

In 1924, there were several improvements and additions to James' business. First of all, they accepted an agency for Henley tyres and Mackintosh N.A.P. pneumatic tyres, in February 1924; and one month later, accepted a dealership for American built Dodge cars and light vans, along with a dealership for Trojan light vans. Trojan, described as a genuine utility vehicle, with its unusual 4 cylinder horizontal engine, were built by the bus and lorry manufacturer, Leyland Motors' associate company – Trojan Ltd., at Leyland's Kingston-Upon-Thames factory.

As the company were appointed sole agents for the Mackintosh N.A.P. 'commercial vehicle' pneumatic tyres, they were one of the first bus operators locally to introduce pneumatic tyres to their buses in the mid – 1920's. Changing to pneumatics' brought with it, an improved ride and better road holding, with an added incentive (introduced in 1928) of a reduction in licence fee by 20% for vehicles fitted with the softer tyre. This was an added bonus for the enterprising company.

This particular advertisement for Messrs. J. James & Sons' business appeared in the Amman Valley Chronicle dated 13th March, 1924. The advert included their recently acquired tyre agency along with the Trojan van, Dodge car and van agencies. Exactly two years later the Dodge agency passed to Castle Garages, Ammanford.

The association with Trojan came to an end in 1928 when Leyland Motors concentrated solely on bus and lorry manufacturing.

Meanwhile, with the vast amount of buses running in the Amman Valley, what had originally been a 'boon' had become a nuisance and serious menace to public safety with up to 45 buses a day using the Ammanford Square. Ammanford Square and the Amman Valley became famous for its 'bus racing' with regular newspaper reports of incidents and accidents alike between the rival companies. Some accidents were extremely serious, with wheels coming off or even brake failure. There were also reports of buses overturning and vehicles catching fire whilst in service.

Three 'Buses Involved in Collision.

ONE TOPPLES OVER

Three motor-'buses were involved in a serious collision between Garnant and Gwaun-cae-gurwen on Tuesday night, one of them toppling over an embankment with several passengers inside. The driver of another, which was forced into an electric light standard, was rendered unconscious.

It appears that about 11 o'clock on Tuesday night a G.W.R. 'bus driven by B. Langley and a similar vehicle owned by Messrs. John James and Sons, Ammanford, and driven by Dai Morris, were coming from the direction of Neath, when on the Gwaun-cae-gurwen Hill they met another 'bus owned by Messrs. James, driven by F. Baker. The G.W.R. 'bus endeavoured to cut in between the two, with the result that the vehicle driven by Baker was forced into the side of the road, mounted a small bank and toppled over on its side. The other, driven by Morris, as stated, crashed into the electric light standard, and the force of the impact was such that Morris was knocked out. But for the standard, this 'bus would also have toppled over. The G.W.R. 'bus swerved into the side, and when brought to a standstill had one of its wheels dangling over a precipice higher up the hill. A step further, the 'bus and its human contents would have been hurled into eternity. The passengers in the 'bus which toppled over had miraculous escapes, and only one is known to have had injuries. He received cuts about the nose. A little girl, the daughter of Robinson, a conductor of one of the 'buses, received nasty cuts on the hands. A large number suffered extensively from shock. The three 'buses were badly damaged.

Kamikazi Driving?

Bearing in mind that driving tests had not been introduced at this time it was a miracle that no one was killed during the long period of furious bus driving. Licences to drive a public service vehicle at this time were merely permits to drive for hire and reward in a particular council district.

Accidents and incidents were so numerous a separate chapter could be written listing each one individually. This newspaper cutting refers to just one particular serious accident which occurred on the 22nd September, 1925.

The sequel to this mishap was that the driver of the G.W.R. bus, B. Langley was fined £10 plus costs 'for driving to the danger of the Public'.

Several bus drivers were prosecuted for varying offences, which included obstruction, negligent driving, dangerous driving, reckless driving, and speeding (exceeding the 12m.p.h. speed limit). Speeding in those days was not recorded by means of a radar gun or speed camera, a vehicle was timed over a measured distance of highway. Some of James' employees were prosecuted also, including Angus James who was fined ten shillings (50 pence by today's comparison) for obstructing the highway with his Trojan motor car and deliberately impeding the progress of a G.W.R. bus; driver E. W. Greyland was fined for reckless driving and Dominic Impanni on two occasions for reckless driving with a bus appropriately named 'The Whippet'. The transport magazine 'Motor Transport' commented in 1924 on Ammanford council's 'strange tactics' regarding buses creating a nuisance at Ammanford Square. The Deputy Police Chief publicly warned bus proprietors that the rival bus racing had to stop before someone was killed, and a doctor at Cwmamman also expressed his concern about the buses racing through the villages.

Besides this bus racing, 'bully boy tactics' were used by some crews, as they literally fought over passengers. By 1924, competition in the Amman Valley villages had become so fierce it could be termed as piracy. There were as many as six bus operators plying the valley route at this time. They were:-

GREAT WESTERN RAILWAY CO., NEATH
J. JAMES & SONS, AMMANFORD
IDWAL DAVIES, AMMANFORD
R. W. THOMAS, CWMLLYNFELL
REES & WILLIAMS, TYCROES
SOUTH WALES TRANSPORT CO., SWANSEA.

The Great Western Railway Co., who were obviously having a difficult time, had every intention of squeezing out all of these competitors on the Amman Valley route, when they decided to move into Ammanford, building a new depot adjacent to Tirydail Railway Station, half a mile from Ammanford Square, late in 1924. Despite this threat, Messrs James & Sons 'dug their heels firmly in', and challenged the G.W.R. Co., even further by running on their Neath – Pontardawe - Ammanford route also. The route, incidentally, followed along the old stage coach route to Neath, as mentioned earlier.

Using their new Leyland buses, James vigorously challenged the G.W.R., on the Neath route from 1924 onwards, and cunningly made sure that all councillors and their wives held free passes to travel on James' buses. Six months later, there were six or seven operators plying the Neath to Ammanford route, and the Glamorganshire County Council were complaining that there were too many bus companies operating that route, chasing each other for passengers, and publicly warned proprietors that the Police would prosecute any offending speeding drivers.

By now it was obvious that the James family were extremely shrewd business people, yet, were regarded as being quite generous when supporting charity events. James' generosity extended to treat all the unfortunate inmates of Llandilo Workhouse to an outing each year. The first such outing took place in September 1924, with 60 adults and children travelling in two buses, to the seaside village of Llanstephan, where lunch and tea was provided for all. Mr. James provided an extra surprise for the 23 children on board by treating them all to sweets and fruit upon arrival at Carmarthen. Furthermore, it was an added privilege for them to travel in James' brand new Lancia Pentaiota bus, (BX 4914) fleet No.6. It has also been said that whenever a new bus arrived at James' premises, all the local school children were taken for a short ride around the town to try it out.

Bodied by Northern Counties, this 'all weather saloon' 20 seater Lancia Pentaiota, No. 6 BX4914) was the only Lancia ever owned by Messrs James.

As the bus rivalry worsened in the Amman Valley, the Ammanford U.D.C. Transport Committee called a meeting in September 1924 for all bus proprietors plying into the Town. Ten proprietors were asked to co-operate with the council, compile a timetable approved by all parties, and to adhere to it; and to additionally run on routes only approved by the council. The proprietors agreed to comply with the committee's request, meeting them a week later, submitting a provisional timetable that they had agreed upon for the Amman Valley route only. At another meeting held on 12th November, 1924, the Transport Committee finally issued Hackney Carriage licences – at long last – for all passenger vehicles operating within the town. Messrs. James & Sons applied for 12 vehicle licences at this meeting, when only 6 vehicles were owned, stating that they had six more new buses on order. The vehicle licences, however, were all granted and the Transport Committee resolved that no more licences would be issued other than licences for vehicles actually owned by the applicants. Additionally, omnibus drivers were issued with their first driving licences at this meeting, which were merely driving permits for the Ammanford Council district.

At another meeting held just two weeks later on the 26th November, the bus operators came to a deadlock on the proposals for a co-ordinated timetable, sadly resulting in the bus rivalry continuing. However, in December 1924, all the Amman Valley bus operators applied to neighbouring Cwmamman Urban District Council at Garnant for licences to run services through their district also. Their applications were, unfortunately, ignored, and the services continued to run without licences.

In January 1925, after only five months use, James exchanged their normal control Lancia bus (BX 4914) for another Italian manufactured vehicle. The replacement vehicle had a chassis built by Societa-Ligure Piemontese Automobili (S.P.A.) of Turin and was purchased through the dealers A. G. Morse at Cardiff. Registered (BX5196) this was again allocated fleet No. 6, the number previously carried by the Lancia. The S.P.A. was another, somewhat, unusual vehicle. Remaining with the company for only two years, it appeared to have many problems, which included the front axles snapping. The S.P.A. happened to be the first bus delivered from the batch of six buses mentioned earlier, being on order during the first licensing committee meeting in November 1924. The other buses mentioned at the Transport Committee meeting, finally emerged in early 1925, as four new Leylands, made a total of five new buses, and not six as the company had stated. The new Leyland buses, Nos. 7/8 (BX5197/8) were forward control SG9's fitted with larger 40/48 h.p. engines and Leyland 38 seat dual door 'Ribble' style bodies, together with Nos. 9/10 (BX5204/5) a pair of normal control 36 h.p. Leyland C9's fitted with pneumatic tyres and Leyland 26 seat rear entrance bus bodies.

This forward control Leyland SG9 (BX5197) was numbered 7 in James' fleet. Registered in `January 1925 it carried a 2 door 'Ribble' style body with unusual arched doorways built by Leyland Motors, to seat 38 passengers.

(BX5205) bus No.10 was one of a pair of normal control Leyland C9's delivered in February 1925 with Leyland 26 seat rear entrance bodies. Fitted with these 'luxurious' pneumatic tyres from new it probably represented the first James' bus fitted with pneumatic tyres.

In February 1925, a combined meeting was held between Ammanford U.D.C., and neighbouring local authorities regarding bus traffic in Ammanford, at which the Chairman of the Transport Committee stated he did not have co-operation from the bus proprietors regarding adherence to timetables. The Committee had asked the Ministry of Transport for guidance on the matter to which they replied – The local authority should use the powers vested in them under the provision of the Town Police Act, as it was the Council's discretion to refuse or revoke a licence to any offending bus operator. The bus war, nevertheless, continued, and in February 1925, due to financial difficulties, competitor Idwal Davies of Ammanford sold his one bus and Brynamman to Ammanford service to Mrs. Anne Morgan of Maesyquarre Road, Bettws, Ammanford. Mrs. Morgan acquired the business for her two sons, Thomas L., and David Rees Morgan. Trading as Morgan Bros., they became another challenger on the busy Amman Valley route, soon to be followed by Vaughan Saloon Services of Tycroes, operating Ammanford to Brynamman, and later Ammanford to Tairgwaith, both via the Amman Valley.

1925 also saw the beginning of another ambitious bus operator within James' operating area. Trading as Eclipse Saloon Services, and owned by the Griffiths family from Graig-Cefn-Parc, Clydach, their business expanded rapidly, acquiring several routes in the Swansea Valley area, which inevitably clashed with James' routes.

By 1926, however, Rees & Williams had stepped up their challenge in the Amman Valley by running a new through service from Ammanford via Gwaun-Cae-Gurwen to Clydach in the Swansea Valley. The service ran only for a short while, until 19th August,

1926, when a second disastrous fire at their depot destroyed four of their five buses and seriously damaged their new garage. With a shortage of buses after the fire, Rees & Williams withdrew their Ammanford to Clydach service, terminating it at Gwaun-Cae-Gurwen.

Meanwhile, on the night of 13th May, 1926, a mysterious fire occurred at the premises of rival Amman Valley operator; R.W. Thomas of Cwmllynfell. Thomas' garage containing the entire fleet of four buses, (2 Lancia and 2 Commer) burnt to the ground. The damage estimated at £5,000 was only partly covered by insurance, resulting in the complete failure of Thomas' service, Ammanford via Brynamman to Ystalyfera. James, already competing along 90% of Thomas' route:- Ammanford, Brynamman to Cwmtwrch, took the opportunity of Thomas' misfortunes to extend their service another 3 miles down the Swansea Valley to reach Ystalyfera, a village previously served by R. W. Thomas. Taking over this service meant outstationing one bus at Ystalyfera each night. Manned by crews living in the Ystalyfera area, the bus would then work the first trip each morning from Ystalyfera back to Ammanford, at 5.50.a.m.

At the time, neighbouring Pontardawe Council were experiencing the same problems as Ammanford Council, with too many bus operators plying in their district, also. However, Pontardawe R.D.C. wasted no time in applying to the Ministry of Transport, through the Ministry of Health, for the necessary powers to licence all passenger service routes, omnibuses and drivers plying in their district. The council were granted these powers as requested, taking effect from October 1st, 1926. Cited as the Pontardawe Rural (Urban Powers) Order 1926, J. James & Sons were granted two Road Service Licences (R.S.L.'s) and 10 Hackney Carriage (vehicle) licences to legally operate their services through the district. The R.S.L.'s issued to James by the Pontardawe Council were Brynamman to Ystalyfera, and Gwaun-Cae-Gurwen via Pontardawe to Fforestgoch, (the council's boundary) on the Neath route. Both services emanating from Ammanford and the Amman Valley, they remained unlicenced on the Amman Valley section of the route, as it was the responsibility of the Ammanford and Cwmamman councils to issue those relevant licences. Several of James' competitors in the Pontardawe district received licences also, namely: South Wales Transport Co., Great Western Railway Co., J. W. Davies of Pontardawe, and Davies & Williams of Trebanos. On the other hand, there were 3 applicants for Road Service Licences on James' Brynamman to Ystalyfera route:- J. James & Sons; L. J. Davies; and Morgan Bros. After careful consideration, the Council's Transport Committee decided that as a consequence of the narrowness of the roads and the very dangerous hills, the public would be best served by granting a licence only to Messrs James & Sons. L. J. Davies however disappeared quietly, Morgan Bros., accepted their refusal and continued running from Ammanford to Brynamman only.

Two months later, in November 1926, another new operator, John Rees, from Ystalyfera, applied to Pontardawe R.D.C., for a licence to ply the Brynamman to Ystalyfera route which was immediately rejected. Rees, however, was extremely determined, and ran the service illegally for an entire year, unlicenced, challenging James, and inevitably caused a lot of friction. He continually re-applied for a licence during that year, until the Council finally granted him a licence for 4 buses to ply the route in October 1927, with a proviso that timetables be mutually arranged with Messrs. J. James & Sons. The Transport Committee also decided that as James was the established operator of this route, they were entitled to preferential consideration, and shared the licences on a ratio of 4 to 3 in favour of Messrs. James.

This sparked off another lengthy battle, with both proprietors failing to arrange a co-ordinated timetable, Rees then ran illegally beyond Brynamman to Gwaun-Cae-Gurwen. The irregularities eventually led to an enquiry involving the Ministry of Transport in 1928, who recommended that James have 24 through trips each day, and Rees have 12 trips each day between Ystalyfera and Gwaun-Cae-Gurwen. This was granted in July 1928 for a trial period of 3 months only. The licence was later renewed for a further 3 months on condition that the two proprietors, J. Rees and J. James & Sons install Bus Timing Recorders (clocks) along the route for the purpose of timing their buses. Nevertheless, the rivalry continued with many complaints against Rees' irregularities, which included a prosecution for 'fraudulently' using the same registration plate on 2 buses' in October 1929.

Despite all this activity, James were continuously in the lead making improvements to their business. One such improvement (in 1926) with the intention of gaining all travellers during the hours of darkness, was to fit a small green light to the front near side of all their buses so that passengers could distinguish an approaching James' bus. Rees & Williams followed suit, and equipped their buses with a small blue light mounted on the front near side. James also maintained their excellent reputation by updating and modernising their bus fleet regularly; purchasing the most modern up to date vehicles secured regular clientele. In November 1926 they purchased their first Leyland 'Lion', No. 12 (BX 7333) for use on the busy Neath route, followed a year later by three more 'Lions' Nos. 14 – 16 (BX 8220 – 2). As can be seen, fleet No. 13 was not used, as the family were extremely superstitious.

J. JAMES & SONS LTD. AMMANFORD

This SINGLE TICKET which is NOT TRANSFERABLE must be retained for inspection and is issued subject to the rules and regulations of the Company.

PASSENGER SHOULD NOTE PRICE REMAINING ON TICKET

"Willebrew" System Patents 321939 & 567262 — Williamson, Ticket Printer, Ashton-under-Lyne

SINGLE 2/1

2/2 2/3 2/4 2/5 2/6 2/7 2/8 2/9 2/10 2/11 3/- 3/1 3/2 3/3 3/4 3/5 3/6 3/7 3/8 3/9 3/10 3/11 4/-

0702

4/-Aa

This was the first Leyland Lion purchased by Messrs James & Sons in 1926. The body built by Leyland Motors seated 29 and was built to this configuration of dual entrance for quicker loading and unloading on the Neath route, whilst challenging the G.W.R. Co. (V. Morgan collection.)

Surprisingly, the company's fierce challenging against the G.W.R. Co., on the Ammanford to Neath route, eventually paid off. In April 1927, after extreme pressure from Pontardawe R.D.C., joint running arrangements were agreed upon between the two companies. Timetables and schedules were mutually arranged, and return tickets became inter-changeable between the companies. This, however, was an extremely unusual arrangement to be made between a large company and a small private operator, an obvious reflection of the James family's sheer willpower and determination. Within 6 months of the co-ordination agreement being made between James and the G.W.R. Co., the South Wales Transport Co., seriously challenged them by introducing a new timetable, increasing their service frequency on the Ammanford, Amman Valley to Swansea route, and reduced the cost of return fares to Swansea to three shillings 3/- (15 pence).

In October 1927, Leyland Motors Ltd. introduced two new passenger vehicle chassis which were exhibited at the 1927 Commercial Motor Show held at Olympia, London.. The single decker chassis; for buses and coaches was named a 'Tiger' and the double decker chassis was named a 'Titan'. Designated as TS1 and TD1 respectively they were both fitted with newly developed more powerful 6.8 litre (6792cc) 6 cylinder engines. Leyland Motors had not yet developed a diesel engine but James were amongst the first customers to order these 'Tigers', purchasing two of the earliest production models, which evoked widespread praise from the travelling public. Having consecutive chassis numbers 60013 and 60012 they were registered in December 1927 and April

1928 as (BX 8400/8530) respectively, and were fitted with 32 seat Leyland bus bodies. The only other new vehicle purchased in 1928 was the last Leyland 'Lion' acquired, No.19 (BX 9119).

Bus No. 17 (BX 8400) happened to be the first in a long line of Leyland Tigers operated by James. This TS1 Tiger, fitted with Leyland rear entrance 32 seater body was registered on 31st December 1927 and licensed on New Years Day 1928. In 1933 however, it was completely rebuilt receiving a new Beadle 31 seat one and a half decker coach body and a diesel engine. It was then re-numbered 40 and later 140.
(V. Morgan collection.)

An Enterprising Firm.

Messrs. John James and Sons, 'bus proprietors, Ammanford, can be ranked amongst the most enterprising firms in South Wales. The installation on the Ammanford-Neath service of a Leyland Motors' latest product certainly substantiates the claim, and, despite the deplorable state of the roads, "(potholes)" are not felt, so perfect is the running. The Tiger Six-Cylinder Passenger Coach, by which the vehicle is known, has the remarkably low loading line of 10 inches from ground. The low-pressure balloon tyres, combined with the pneumatic cushions on the seats, which have spring back-rests, give a "ride on air" feeling. There is no bumping, and the interior is heated, but with special ventilating giving fresh air and adding to the comfort of the passengers. Apart from all these facilities, the 'bus is noiseless and vibrationless. There are racks provided for light luggage and a carrier at the rear (inside) for cases and handbags. The driver's cab is as luxurious as any first-rate limousine. To sum up, it is a perfect de-luxe model.

It appears that Messrs James & Sons were extremely proud of their newLeyland Tiger working the Neath route. This particular newspaper cutting appeared in the Amman Valley Chronicle on 19th January, 1928.

As the bus war continued in the Amman Valley, a Swansea newspaper – The South Wales Evening Post, was reporting about the lackadaisical attitude of local authorities in the Amman Valley regarding their method of dealing with the bus problem that was still "merrily going on". Additionally, another operator, Daniel Jones of Carmarthen, ventured into Ammanford in late 1927. By extending his well-established Carmarthen to Llandilo service, Dan Jones began serving Ammanford town also, competing against nine other operators on the busy Llandilo to Ammanford route. Due to the continuous rivalry on the Llandilo road, coupled with numerous accidents and the economic depression, long standing operator, Albert Thomas (M.M.T. Services) of Tirydail, Ammanford, sold his business, three buses and garage at Tirydail, to the South Wales Transport Co., in December 1927. This gave S.W.T. a greater foothold in the Ammanford area, having already reduced fares and increased their service timetable to Swansea.

By early 1928, Rees & Williams had overcome their problems, caused by the garage fire, and began seriously challenging James again in the Amman Valley. Inaugurating two new services, Rees & Williams began running direct buses in 1928 from Brynamman to Carmarthen, and Brynamman to Llanelly, both via Ammanford Town and the Amman Valley.

In the meantime, however, as the economic recession worsened, Carmarthenshire's largest passenger vehicle operator, Jones Bros., Brynteg Garage, Upper Tumble, were experiencing serious financial problems and unfortunately their business eventually collapsed in bankruptcy in October 1928. The Jones brothers, operating some 25 buses at the time, were by now trading as 'The Llanelly Express Motor Service Co.,' and had acquired a bad reputation for unreliability, due to poor maintenance and unsuitable vehicles. After the company's failure the Llanelly Borough Council shared their road service licences between the G.W.R., Co., David Lewis of Cross Hands and the newly formed syndicate of West Wales Motors from Llanelly. West Wales Motors was a partnership of directors from the defunct Llanelly Express Co., and C.B. Williams, a partner of the Rees & Williams business at Tycroes, who had left that partnership after a disagreement.

In 1928, the Minister of Transport, Sir Henry P. Maybury, made an announcement that was long awaited in the Transport business. He permitted buses fitted with pneumatic tyres all round to have an increased speed limit of 20 m.p.h. from 1st October, 1928. Two years later the maximum speed was once more increased to 30 m.p.h. This new regulation was an added bonus to James' business, as their buses were already equipped with the softer tyres, it enabled shorter running times on all their services.

Messrs. James in the meantime being more than pleased with their choice of Leyland 'Tigers' delivered in 1928, went ahead to purchase three more during 1929, Nos. 20 – 22 (BX 9850, TH 120, TH 260) respectively.

Bus No. 22 (TH 260) was the third Leyland TS2 'Tiger' delivered in 1929. This Leyland 32 seat body was replaced in 1937 with a new Beadle body. (V. Morgan collection / Leyland Motors Ltd.)

In 1929 however, the Great Western Railway Company purchased a majority shareholding in the Cardiff based company 'South Wales Commercial Motors' who were passenger vehicle operators in South East Wales and also motor vehicle dealers. The eventual absorption of South Wales Commercial Motors led to an amalgamation of G.W.R. and S.W.C.M.'s omnibus services in South Wales. The combined bus operation was then renamed Western Welsh Omnibus Company Ltd., having their headquarters at Cardiff. The co-ordination agreement previously held between James and the G.W.R. Co., nevertheless was honoured and continued after the formation of Western Welsh on 1st August 1929.

By now, almost a year had passed since the demise of 'The Llanelly Express Motor Service Co., in 1928, when William Jones, a member of the Jones Bros., partnership, former proprietors of Llanelly Express restarted the business from the same premises at Upper Tumble. Trading as 'BRYNTEG', he purchased two new buses in 1929, and eventually took over the small business of Phillips Bros, at Llandebie (T/A: Amman Valley Bus Service) in late 1930 with their three buses and Ammanford to Burry Port service. Additionally, Wm. Jones successfully obtained the Road Service Licences, previously held by the defunct Cross Hands operator, David Lewis. The licences included a share of the Llanelly, Cross Hands to Ammanford route, together with the long distance Llanelly, Ammanford, Lampeter, Aberystwyth route.

Ironically, there were several other operators running express services from the South Wales area via Ammanford, to the popular Victorian seaside resort of Aberystwyth besides William Jones 'Brynteg'. The operators included Western Welsh Omnibus Co., Gough's Motors of Mountain Ash, South Wales Transport Co. of Swansea (Saturdays only), Jones Bros., of Aberayron and Aberystwyth; J. D. Evans, Llanybyther and L.C.W. Motors of Talley. However, most of the services were short lived and soon abandoned.

In the meantime, James' only competitor on the Brynamman, Ystalyfera route, John Rees, gave up his challenge in January 1930, selling his share of the route to Eclipse Saloon Services of Clydach. The rivalry that had existed between John Rees and Messrs James, however, had not ended: it continued for yet another year, against the new competitor - Eclipse Salon Services.

South Wales Transport, on the other hand, introduced a new direct daily service from Brynamman to Swansea, also in January 1930, and for the second time, reduced fares on their Llandilo, Ammanford to Swansea route, when their financial position was poor, in an attempt to gain all Swansea bound passengers from the Amman Valley.

Messrs. J. James & Sons, unhappy with Eclipse and S.W.T.'s encroachment into Brynamman, soon decided to apply for a licence to run into Swansea, and challenge both rival operators. Their application to Swansea Council for a licence was unfortunately rejected, but the enterprising James concern still maintained their challenge.

WHY RUN RISKS?

STEPNEY TYRES

ARE GUARANTEED FOR ONE YEAR IN PRIVATE USE, SIX MONTHS IN COMMERCIAL USE.

AVAILABLE IN ALL SIZES FOR MOTOR CARS, MOTOR CYCLES, LORRIES AND BUSES.
OBTAINABLE FROM ALL MOTOR DEALERS.

SOLE MANUFACTURERS

STEPNEY TYRES, Ltd., LLANELLY.

Factories: WALTHAMSTOW, LONDON, E.17.

TIME FOR CHANGE

By late 1929, there were seventeen bus companies operating in and out of Ammanford, and the need of controlling these buses had become crucial. In order to solve the town's bus traffic problem, the Ammanford council held combined meetings with other local authorities in the area from December 1929 to March 1930, when it was finally agreed the time had come to call upon those operators plying for hire in the district to apply for Road Service Licences from the Ammanford council, and that Hackney Carriage licences would then be issued in respect of all buses currently running into the town. The council then placed a public notice in the local newspaper inviting operators to apply for their licences by 20th March, 1930. This decision to licence all omnibuses and routes was taken soon after the Government had announced their intention of controlling all omnibus licencing matters themselves, via the Ministry of Transport, removing the responsibility from local authorities under the proposed 1930 Road Traffic Act.

At the time, in March 1930, there were still seven operators plying the Amman Valley route: J. James & Sons, Western Welsh Omnibus Co., Rees & Williams, South Wales Transport Co., Morgan Bros., Phillips Bros., and Vaughan's Saloon Road Coach Services of Tycroes.

However, the bus challenging on this route and all other routes into Ammanford came to an abrupt end in April 1930 when the council finally granted Road Service Licences to all operators plying into the town. The licences were issued with special conditions attached: - that mutually agreed upon, co-ordinated timetables were arranged and adhered, to by all bus companies concerned. Sharing these services finally ended the lengthy battle between the rival bus operators, but ironically, the council had still not provided standing places (bus stops) in the town. That took a further 4½ years to organise. The Hackney Carriage Licences (vehicle licences) issued to the Ammanford bus operators in March 1930 were as follows:

J. James & Sons	13	Morgan Bros, Bettws.	3
Western Welsh O.C.	25	Rees & Williams, Tycroes	6
South Wales Transport	36	L.C.W. Motors, Talley	5
Jones Bros, Brynawel' Penygroes	3	Phillips Bros. Llandebie	3
Wm. Jones, 'Brynteg', Upper Tumble	5	D. Williams, Garnswllt	1

These figures given were the number of vehicles licensed by the council, not the amount of vehicles operating at any one time into Ammanford. Other operators plying into the town at the time – West Wales Motors; Petters of Carmarthen; D. Jones, Abergwili; D.

J. Davies, Garnswllt; M. Vaughan, Tycroes, Jones Bros, Aberystwyth and J. D. Evans, Llanybyther, were all invited to apply for licences also. They all applied as requested and were issued with their relevant licences by October that year, including D.J. Davies, who had by now become Bevan & Davies after forming a partnership with his second cousin John Higgs Bevan at Maerdy Farm, Garnswllt, in October 1930. A month later, Bevan & Davies absorbed the struggling business owned by Morgan Vaughan of Tycroes, with his share of the Amman Valley route; services from Pantyffynnon to Brynamman and Tycroes to Tairgwaith, both via Ammanford. Neighbouring Cwmamman U.D.C. at Garnant in the Amman Valley suprisingly followed the Ammanford council's policy and issued all seven Amman Valley route operators with Road Service Licences in September 1930 for a 6-month period only, after which, it would become the Ministry of Transport's responsibility.

Inevitably, several operators were unhappy with Ammanford council's method of granting and issuing these licences, which resulted in several public hearings after the licences had been issued. Some of these operators applied for extra licences from the council soon afterwards, all of which were deferred pending introduction of the 1930 Road Traffic Act, in April 1931. This was on specific instructions from the Ministry of Transport.

Phillips Bros., nevertheless, appealed in vain to the Ministry of Transport in April 1930 against Pontardawe and Neath Council's decision to refuse renewal of their Road Service Licence for Burry Port to Neath via Ammanford and the Amman Valley. The licence had been refused on the grounds that they no longer maintained the route. As the route ran in common with J. James and Western Welsh from Ammanford to Neath, Phillips Bros. negotiated an arrangement with them regarding a connection to transfer intending passengers for Neath. Phillips Bros., then continued to operate their Burry Port, Gwendraeth Valley, Cross Hands, via Ammanford to Brynamman route, but six months later abandoned the Ammanford to Brynamman section of the route and sold the remaining business to Wm. Jones & Sons, 'Brynteg' in December 1930.

Regulating the buses, however, brought with it another problem for the Police; that of overloading caused by infrequent services. It became a regular feature in the newspaper at the time; bus conductors being fined from £1 to £5 for overloading the buses, sometimes to the extent of more than double the vehicle's seating capacity. There is no evidence as to who paid these fines, but presumably they were paid by the bus proprietors, as wages were comparatively small. The standard rate of pay, nationally, for bus drivers operating in rural areas at this time was 58-shillings for a 48-hour week (£2.90), and conductors earned approximately 5 per cent less than the driver.

Meanwhile, the recession in South Wales continued. Coupled with on going colliery disputes in the Amman Valley, there were large numbers of unemployed in the community. Bearing this in mind, together with scepticism over the proposed Road Traffic Act, the James family decided to register their business as a limited company in order to safeguard themselves from any heavy losses in the event of business failure. After forming the limited company; J. James & Sons Ltd., on 1st April, 1930, (registered No. 247071) the four partners and their wives all became directors of the company. The founder, John James became Managing Director; Angus R. James, Company Secretary, later General Manager; R. Lindsay James, Mechanical Engineer; and J. Percy James, Traffic Manager.

Nevertheless, Messrs James maintained their excellent reputation and updated their fleet regularly, as the effective life of an omnibus at this time was only about 6 years. Modernising the fleet again in 1930, James purchased two more Leyland 'Tiger' 32 seater buses and acquired their first double decker buses. Purchased for the busy Neath service, the new deckers registered (TH 800/1) were numbered 24/25 respectively by the company, and were a pair of Leyland TD1 'Titans' with 6.8 litre, 6 cylinder petrol engines and Leyland lowbridge type bodies, exactly 13 feet high. They were the forerunners of a long line of lowbridge bodied deckers owned by the company. It was an absolute necessity for all double deckers purchased by the company to be built to lowbridge configuration, due to the numerous low railway bridges situated within the company's operating area. The bridges reflected the large rail network set up around the area during the Industrial Revolution, to serve the numerous collieries and heavy industries. Some bridges around the area had so little headroom, only single decker buses could pass under them - one such example was situated at Upper Cwmtwrch, on James' Ammanford to Ystalyfera route.

As the local inhabitants had never seen a double decker bus before, they were such a novelty, that they proved to be extremely popular, and everyone wanted to ride on them. In fact, one Saturday evening a local police constable on duty in Ammanford Square, stopped one of these new deckers and summonsed the bus conductor for overloading it. In court, P.C. Prout stated that there were a total of 104 passengers on board the 48 seater, 13 of which were riding on the open rear platform and staircase. The company secretary, Angus James in this instance, was prosecuted also, for aiding and abetting the bus crew. The company's profits must have been tremendous in those far off days with such large passenger loadings. James, however, were not the only company being prosecuted for overloading, as Rees & Williams were also prosecuted for carrying 78 people on a 32-seat single decker bus, as were several other local operators. As a point of interest, buses at this time were only permitted to carry 5 standing passengers, on the lower deck only.

This Leyland 'Titan' TD1 was the first double decker bus purchased by the James concern in May 1930, at the princely sum of £1,778-12s-0d complete with body. Carrying fleet No.24 (TH 800) this was the first of a pair delivered that year with Leyland 48 seat lowbridge bodies and closed staircases. Seven years later, under a modernisation programme it was rebodied by Beadle coachworks at Dartford, Kent, and fitted with a diesel engine in place of petrol unit and renumbered 124. (R. Marshall collection.)

Receiving continual harassment from the South Wales Transport Co., Messrs J. James & Sons were desperate to challenge them by running into Swansea. Swansea Borough Council however, had refused ALL Carmarthenshire based omnibus proprietors licences to ply within the Borough, saying their streets were too narrow and that more buses would cause congestion. This was probably an excuse to safeguard the services of the Swansea trams running within the Borough.

Nevertheless, in an attempt to gain access into the centre of Swansea, and to challenge the South Wales Transport, J. James & Sons Ltd., negotiated and purchased the greater half of an omnibus service owned by William Llewellyn Davies (Cambrian Express) from Clydach. Acquiring 55% of Davies' licences in May 1930 brought with it a route from Ystalyfera to Clydach, and a route from Varteg, via: Ystalyfera to Clydach which was the boundary with the Swansea Borough. Only one bus, No. 23, a Tilling Stevens (T.S.M.) was acquired with the takeover.

This 1928 Vickers bodied Tilling Stevens B10A2 (TX 5630) was acquired with the Ystalyfera – Clydach service of W. L. Davies, Clydach in May 1930. During its brief stay with James it was allocated fleet No. 23, but was quickly exchanged for a new Leyland Tiger – the Company's preference.

Purchasing Davies' Ystalyfera to Clydach route and incorporating it with their own Ammanford to Ystalyfera route, allowed a through service from Ammanford to Swansea (Borough boundary at Clydach). This brought them another step nearer Swansea town centre, but the final step to ply into Swansea proved to be the most difficult to achieve, bearing in mind the Council's policy of refusing buses access into the Borough.

Inevitably there were some bus operators that 'pirated' (ran unlicenced) into Swansea and were summoned when caught. Ironically James was summoned by the Ammanford Council, for allegedly plying into Swansea unlicenced five times during December 1930. They were proceeded against a month later, and awarded 10 guineas costs after the hearing was dismissed.

Within days of W. L. Davies' takeover, S.W.T., complained to Pontardawe council about James running unlicenced buses on the route. This resulted in James receiving 3 extra Hackney licences. W. L. Davies on the other hand, sold the remaining part of his omnibus business in September 1930, to the S.W.T. Co.,

Inaugurating another new service in September 1930, Messrs. J. James & Sons., were granted a licence by Pontardawe council to run a Saturdays only service from Cwmllynfell to the village of Rhiwfawr (meaning – Big Hill). The village situated 1000 ft. above sea level, on top of the Penller-Fedwen mountain range, 3 miles from Ystalyfera had never been served by a bus service before, even though a certain W. H. Hughes from Ystalyfera had unsuccessfully tried for a licence to ply the route in 1927 and 1928.

However, when James renewed their annual licences with the Pontardawe council just two weeks later, the service from Cwmllynfell to Rhiwfawr was modified to run on Fridays and Saturdays only, and extended beyond Cwmllynfell to start from Ystalyfera (New Swan).. These licences were the last renewals issued by the Pontardawe Council before the 1930 Road Traffic Act was implemented.

Meanwhile, the 'West Wales Motors' company moved from their temporary Llanelly premises in December 1930, to a new garage at Tycroes, Ammanford. West Wales, as previously mentioned was a new company formed by a partnership that included C. B. Williams, a director of the Rees & Williams business at Tycroes. Their unexpected move from Llanelly unfortunately meant another operator in the community competing against James for a share of local private hire work. They even applied for a licence to run the Amman Valley route to Tairgwaith in April 1931 without success.

Pictured here before delivery to James in 1930 is this Leyland bodied TS3 'Tiger', 27(TH 1280). Only two new TS3:s were purchased by the company - this was the second. Six years later it was fitted with 8.6 litre oil engine, rebodied by Beadle coachworks and renumbered 127. (R. Marshall collection.)

INTRODUCTION OF THE 1930 ROAD TRAFFIC ACT

After eleven years challenging and literally fighting with rival competitors, it came as a blessing to the enterprising James company, when the new Minister of Transport, Mr. Herbert Morrison, announced the introduction of the aforementioned Road Traffic Act (1930). This Act of Parliament passed in August 1930 gave the Ministry of Transport's Traffic Commissioners full control of public service vehicles (P.S.V.'s), passenger services and their licencing in Great Britain.

These Traffic Commissioners, with the power vested in them, brought about improved operating conditions, an adherence to timetables and stability of fares. All stage carriage and express service routes had to be licensed, and the granting of such licences, which had previously been under the jurisdiction of the local authorities, were then only obtainable through the Ministry of Transport's Traffic Commissioners. Licences to drive and conduct a public service vehicle also became the Commissioners responsibility. Under this new licensing system all public service vehicle operators (P.S.V. operators) were issued with operator reference numbers, by which they were identified. Consequently, the number issued to Messrs J. James & Sons Ltd., was TGR 347, with each Road Service Licence applied for thereafter being given licence application numbers beginning with the operators reference number.

After implementing the new Traffic Act fully in April 1931, every bus operator had to re-apply to the new authority for renewal of each Road Service Licence held, and re-apply annually, thereafter. Likewise, any changes to services, times, fares or new routes all had to be applied for and the licences would only be granted when approved by the Traffic Commissioners. However, the first licences Messrs. J. James & Sons Ltd., applied for under the new traffic act in March 1931 were renewals of licences previously held:

TGR 347/1:	Ammanford to Swansea	via	Brynamman and Ystalyfera
TGR 347/2:	Ammanford to Neath	via	Gwaun-Cae-Gurwen and Pontardawe.
TGR 347/3:	Varteg to Swansea	via	Ystalyfera and Clydach
TGR 347/4:	Rhiwfawr to Ystalyfera	via	Cwmllynfell. (Fridays and Saturdays only)

As mentioned earlier, licences were only issued after a public hearing. At the first hearing held at Swansea's Guildhall on the 9th June, 1931, licence applications TGR 347/2 and TGR 347/4 were granted immediately. Licence applications TGR 347/1 and TGR 347/3 had been applied for with modifications (an extension of the service through into Swansea town centre, from the Swansea Borough Council's boundary at Clydach). These licence applications were deferred pending an inquiry, due to objections from Swansea Borough Council; Swansea Improvements & Tramways Co.; South Wales Transport Co.; Eclipse Saloon Services; and the L.M.S. Railway, even though representation had been made backing the applications from the Carmarthenshire County Council and Ammanford U.D.C.

On 24th November, 1931, the Ministry of Transport held a public inquiry into the matter, with representation again from Carmarthenshire and Ammanford councils. Over-ruling the Swansea Borough Council's 'Watch Committee', the above licence applications TGR347/1 and TGR347/3 were finally granted by the Traffic Commissioners, with the modification allowing James' buses access into Swansea (Trinity Place). Both licences were granted with special conditions:-

1). *The licencee shall not on the inward journey from Ammanford to Swansea be entitled to take up any passengers after reaching the boundary of the Borough of Swansea at Clydach, and shall not on the outward journey be entitled to take up any passengers before reaching the said boundary at Clydach except passengers for a destination beyond such boundary.*

2). *The standing places, route, (except in so far as already set out in condition No.1 of the general conditions), and the stopping places for this service shall be those agreed between the licencee and the local authority concerned, or, failing agreement, decided by the Traffic Commissioners for the South Wales Area upon a reference to them of the matter in dispute.*

After introduction of the R.T.A. in 1931, the company's vehicle purchases slowed down a little, only acquiring one new 'Tiger' No.28 (TH 1850) in 1931. The 1932 deliveries only amounted to two, which were No.s 29/30 (TH 2300/2727) Leyland 'Titan' TD2 and 'Tiger' TS4 respectively. These re-designated chassis models TD2 and TS4, were fitted with larger capacity 7.6 litre petrol engines, which were real 'fuel guzzlers', consuming petrol at the rate of 4 m.p.g. in the 'Titan'.

Vehicle No. 29 (TH 2300) happened to be the first and only all Leyland TD2 'Titan' acquired new by the company. Registered in February 1932, it gave the company 13 years service before passing to another operator in Essex. (R. Marshall collection.)

On the 17th February, 1932, John James, founder and Managing Director of the company sadly passed away following a very lengthy illness of some 4 years. A tribute to Mr. James, published in the Amman Valley Chronicle newspaper immediately after his death, read:

"PIONEER OF MOTOR BUS SERVICE"

Death of Mr. John James, Ammanford

We regret to announce the death, which occurred on Tuesday morning, in his 69th year, of Mr. John James, Central Garages, College Street, Ammanford. Mr. James had been ailing over a long period and his illness he bore with great fortitude. He was an exceedingly popular and familiar figure in the town, not only that, but he was a fine personality and a man of acumen in his business affairs.

Mr. James had had a varied and interesting career, and it was he who, anticipating the development of road traffic, introduced the first omnibus service into the district after the war. His chief characteristic was an ambition to cope with the times and by this he succeeded in establishing one of the finest omnibus services in West Wales. He too was the first to introduce the double decker to the travelling public in the Amman Valley, and his fleet of 'buses was of the most modern and up-to-date type.

Mr. James was a native of Llywel, Breconshire, and he left his native heath at the early age of 14 years to work at the Swansea Docks.

Later he entered the grocery trade, and at the age of 21 he became manager of a business owned by Messrs. Thomas and Evans at Treherbert. He again returned to Swansea and managed different businesses there. In 1889 he married Miss Elizabeth Fletcher, an Ammanford lady, who with three sons survive him, and he opened a grocer and provision merchants business at the Golden Eagle Stores, Wind Street, Ammanford. Ten years later he established The Mews, Ammanford, now the Central Garages, and subsequently conducted a very extensive business as posting master. Among his clientele were the best known of commercial travellers in South Wales.

On the introduction of the motor car, Mr. James moved with the times and as stated; eventually became the pioneer of the motor omnibus service in the Amman Valley. He was joined in this venture shortly after the war by his three sons, Messrs. Percy, Lindsay and Angus James.

He was one of the oldest members in the country of the Motor Trade Association, and a member of the Executive, a member of the Motor Agents Association and Motor Hirers' Association, one of the biggest associations of its kind in the country.

Mr. James had travelled extensively, and had accompanied religious pilgrimages to Canada and America. Several of the leading places on the Continent had also been visited by him.

He was a faithful member of the Christian Temple and of the Christian Temple Choral Society.

The funeral (for gentlemen only) will take place on Saturday, leaving the house at 4.15.p.m. for internment at the Christian Temple burial ground.

The obituary published a week later listed all the mourners, floral tributes, along with all representatives, trades people, and the town's chief citizens who attended the funeral. Amongst the representatives of other bus companies were: T. John (Enterprise M.S.), Gorseinon; Bassett Bros, Gorseinon; Johns Bros., Grovesend; J. M. Bacus, Burry Port; Mr. Griffiths (Eclipse M.S.), Clydach; Mr. Williams (West Wales M.S.) Tycroes; Mr. T. Williams (Blue Bird Motors), Neath; Mr. Willett and Mr. Edwards (Western Welsh Omnibus Co); Mr. W. E. Gough (Goughs Motors) Mountain Ash; with floral tributes that included the Managing Director and staff of Leyland Motors Ltd.

It was noticed that no representation or floral tributes were received from local competitors; Rees & Williams; South Wales Transport; L.C.W. Motors, and Morgan Bros., indicating how much bitterness still existed between these operators even after the 1930 Act had co-ordinated and shared their services.

In John James' will, (published in July that year) he left all his property including his estate with a gross value of £2,068, upon trust for his wife Elizabeth Ann and then equally between his 3 sons on their issue.

However, after John James' death in 1932, his youngest son Angus took full control of the business and became the company's general manager. With Angus at the helm the company expanded rapidly.

Also plying into Ammanford in 1930 were Jones Bros. of Brynawel
with this 20 seater Thorneycroft A1 (WN1808).
This company was absorbed by James in 1945.

EXPANSION

The economic depression that followed the 1926 General Strike continued throughout the 1930's. This inevitably caused the failure of several small P.S.V. operators due to financial problems. The Ministry of Transport on the other hand encouraged larger bus companies to absorb the smaller operators all over the country.

Consequently, on the 4th July, 1932, Angus James made an agreement with Mrs. Anne Morgan, proprietor of the Morgan Bros' Bus Service from Maesyquarre Road, Bettws, to purchase her complete business for £1750, pending the Ministry of Transport's approval of the licence transfer. The Morgan brothers had failed to make a decent living ever since the co-ordination arrangement had been enforced upon the Amman Valley operators two years earlier.

James applied for Morgan Bros' licences, which included a small share of the Ammanford to Brynamman route, on 28th September, 1932. The licences were granted on 2nd November, 1932, allowing the deal to be finalised by 1st December that year. The two Road Service Licences taken over with Morgan Bros' business were:

TGR 347/5: Ammanford to Brynamman, via: Glanamman, Garnant and Gwaun Cae Gurwen.

TGR 347/6: Excursions and Tours starting from Ammanford.

Three buses acquired with the Morgan Bros., businesses: 2 Thorneycroft 20 seaters (BX 8638 and TH 396) and a 20 seater Commer Invader (TH 2515) were regarded as being too small for James' requirements and were soon disposed of.

After selling her omnibus business to James, Mrs. Morgan used the proceeds to purchase a motor garage business for her 2 sons, Thomas and David Rees Morgan. The business was that of Castle Garages at High Street, Ammanford.

As mentioned earlier, James were the oldest serving motor bus operator in the Amman Valley, yet were very late applying for their first 'Excursions and Tours' licence. With the exception of applying for Anne Morgan's E & T's licence (above), their first Excursions and Tours licence was not applied for until 28th September 1932. This licence, granted on 2nd November 1932 was:

TGR 347/7: Excursions and Tours starting from Brynamman.

This was probably one of the Thorneycroft 20 seaters acquired with the Morgan Bros., business in December 1932.

Meanwhile, in 1932 the business of William Jones & Sons, 'Brynteg', Upper Tumble, began facing problems. Having earlier in the year been the subject of an inquiry with the Ministry of Transport (the first of its kind), regarding a breach of the Road Traffic Act due to bad maintenance, they were now facing financial problems. When their situation worsened in October 1932, J. James & Sons Ltd., stepped in with financial assistance and cunningly formed a subsidiary company - Wm. Jones & Sons (Brynteg) Ltd., - in December that year. Jones' official address was then changed to Central Garages, Ammanford; Messrs. James' legal address.

This subsidiary company was set up to control 'Brynteg's' finances, act as guarantor to Jones' creditors, maintain their services and safeguard their Road Service Licences for services to Aberystwyth, Llanelly and Burry Port. After re-organising and incorporating the former Morgan Bros. service with their own services, James were able to loan 'Brynteg' two surplus vehicles in order to maintain their services.

With James officially controlling the 'Brynteg' business from December 1932 they soon introduced weekly and season tickets on all 'Brynteg' services as an incentive to attract regular passengers. Furthermore, inter-available return tickets were introduced on the Ammanford to Aberystwyth and Ammanford to Llanelly services between the relevant joint operators of these services.

Under James' control, 'Brynteg' applied for a new Road Service Licence in May 1933 to run a daily service from Pontyberem to Swansea via, Cwmmawr, Cross Hands, Pontardulais and Fforestfach. This, however, was refused by the Traffic Commissioners.

James then decided to run more reliable and comfortable buses on 'Brynteg's' 61 mile, 3 hour journey to Aberystwyth. Consequently, five year old Leyland 'Tiger' TS1, No 17 (BX8400) had its Leyland bus body replaced in 1933 with a new and unusual 'one-and-a- half decker' observation coach body with centre entrance doorway, built by J. C. Beadle of Dartford, Kent. At the same time it was retrofitted with a more economical 8.6 litre Leyland diesel engine and a few months later sister vehicle No. 18 (BX 8530) was similarly treated. After their rebuilding they received new fleet numbers 40/42 respectively and lettered with the 'BRYNTEG' fleetname on both sides in order to operate Brynteg's Aberystwyth route.

Fuel economy was now of paramount importance to the expanding company. With fuel oil approximately 70% cheaper than petrol, combined with an improved fuel consumption from diesel engines, financial savings on fuel would far outweigh the initial cost of purchasing new diesel engines at £485 each, compared to petrol engines at £285 each. Bearing this in mind the company began a modernisation plan to re-engine with diesel engines and rebody all the 'Tigers and Titans' after only six years use. Rebodying of these comparatively young buses was necessary due to the fact that their ash framed bodies were vulnerable to dry rot and decay and had weakened through over-loading. The pair of rebuilt 'Tigers' mentioned above, Nos. 40/42 were the forerunners of this modernisation plan.

In its new guise after rebodying in 1933 is James' Leyland 'Tiger' No.18 (BX 8400) by now renumbered 40. The very low ' one-and-a-half decker' 31 seater observation coach body was built by J. C. Beadle of Dartford. Built for James' associate company Wm. Jones (Brynteg) Ltd., it worked their Aberystwyth service and was signwritten 'BRYNTEG' using the same style of letters as JAMES' logo.

The last 'new' petrol engined Leyland acquired by the company was this 7.6 litre 'Tiger' TS4, No.31 (TH 3060) delivered in January 1933. (Roy Marshall collection.)

Consequently, the last 'new' petrol engined Leyland purchased by the company happened to be a 'Tiger' TS4, No. 31 (TH 3060) arriving in January 1933 shortly before Leyland Motors introduced the 'heavy oil engine' (diesel engine). However, their next purchase of new Leylands and all subsequent new Leylands were fitted with diesel engines. Their first new diesel engine vehicles arrived later in 1933. Fitted with the new 8.6 litre Leyland power unit they were very smart Beadle bodied 32 seater coaches, No.s 33 – 36 (TH 3580/1 and TH 3636/7) on Leyland 'Tiger' TS6 chassis.

This splendid looking coach No. 34 (TH 3581) was one of four Beadle bodied Leyland TS6's delivered in 1933. These Leyland 'Tigers' were the first diesel or 'heavy oil' engined vehicles owned by the company. They were also the first vehicles in service without the company's fleetname 'Ammanford & District' which had by now been discontinued.

Rapid expansion of James' omnibus business in 1933 inevitably resulted in the closure of their Automobile repair workshop along with their tyre dealership and petrol sales. Additionally, as the company's operating area expanded during the early 1930's, their fleetname Ammanford & District' became unsuitable and was subsequently abandoned in early 1933.At the same time the company made several changes to schedules, fares and ticketing. Firstly, they withdrew their discounted tickets and alternatively introduced weekly and season tickets in line with other local operators, and in conjunction with The Mumbles Electric Railway Co., offered through ticket bookings to the Mumbles Pier from the Amman Valley and Swansea Valley areas. Additionally, by June 1933, after continuing pressure from the Ammanford and Cwmamman councils, all Amman Valley route operators agreed to a maximum 1 penny fare for passengers travelling within 'one council area' only. In return the Ammanford council finally allocated bus stops throughout the town, and fixed up Bus Stop signs by November that year.

As they owned some of the finest motor coaches in West Wales, the company subsequently decided to concentrate more on private hire, excursions and tours. Having already operated tours to Malvern and Birmingham in 1933, permission was sought for 12 more Excursion and Tours Licences in 1934, in addition to the 2 licences already held.

These licences applied for between January and May 1934 were:

TGR 347/8	Excursions and Tours, starting from Cross Hands, including Drefach, Tumble, Penygroes and Blaina.
TGR 347/9	Excursions and Tours, starting from Ystalyfera.
TGR 347/10	Excursions and Tours starting from Llandilo (Central Square) and Ffairfach.
TGR 347/11	Excursions and Tours starting from Neath.
TGR 347/12	Excursions and Tours starting from the Llanelly area.
TGR 347/13	Excursions and Tours starting from Pontardulais, including Pontlliw, Llangyfelach and Llangennech.
TGR 347/14	Excursions and Tours starting from Cwmllynfell.
TGR 347/15	Excursions and Tours starting from Pontyberem and Ponthenry.
TGR 347/16	Excursions and Tours starting from Swansea.

TGR 347/17	Excursions and Tours starting from Clydach.
TGR 347/18	Excursions and Tours starting from Cwmtwrch.
TGR 347/19	Excursions and Tours starting from Pontardawe, including Trebanos and Ynysmeudwy.

There were several objectors to these applications, namely, South Wales Transport Co., Western Welsh O.C., Eclipse Saloon Services, Swansea Corporation and the L.M.S. Railway. Applications TGR 347/8, 9, 10, 13, 14, 17, 18, and 19 were all granted between May and November 1934, TGR 347/11 was refused, and applications TGR 347/12, 15, and 16 were withdrawn.

Meanwhile, in March 1934, James submitted plans to the Ammanford council for a proposed new garage and bus station complex to be built at their Central Garage establishment. The proposed plan basically was to enclose the whole back yard and garden area of the late John James' residence at 25 College Street, converting the open yard into an undercover bus station. After careful thought and consideration the council decided that a bus station would ease congestion on the Ammanford streets and finally gave their consent in July 1934, after several technical items on the plans were modified.

Construction work on the 1000 sq. yard bus station commenced almost immediately and when completed several months later could house James' entire fleet of 28 buses, hire cars and funeral hearse. The bus station became the terminus and starting point of all James' services, where the travelling public waited and caught their buses in comfort, protected from the elements. This was a tremendous advantage in the company's favour compared with their competitors' services.

An eye-catching feature of the new bus station was the neon sign erected above the entrance doorway in College Street. The neon sign illustrated an outline of a red double decker bus fitted with spoked wheels. The illuminated spokes flashed in rotation giving an impression of the wheels turning – to represent perpetual motion.

James' modern bus station soon became the envy of all their competitors with Western Welsh Omnibus Co., asking the Ammanford council for assistance in locating a suitable site to build themselves a new depot of approximately 1000 square yards.

This is the only photograph available of the decorative neon sign erected above the Bus Station doorway in College Street. Note the outline of the red double decker bus and the name – 'JAMES BUS STATION'.

After James' bus station was completed in 1935, the double fronted house; 25 College Street, former residence of the James family, was converted into the company's registered offices. The house, which had been occupied by Mrs. E. A. James, widow of the company's founder, and her brother George Fletcher, had by now been partially vacated after Mrs. James bought a new house on the seafront at West Drive, Porthcawl. Her brother George Fletcher, employed as a traffic supervisor with the company, continued to live in the house until his death in February 1939. After his death, the house became an office block entirely.

Meanwhile, continuing with their policy of investing large amounts of money into the improvement of the company, 2 more new Leylands arrived at Central Garages in June 1934. The pair, 43/44 (TH 4501/2) were 32 seater Beadle bodied Leyland LT5A 'Lions', fitted with 'under powered' 4 cylinder 5.7 litre 'oil engines'.

The only photograph available of the Leyland Lions operated by the company, is this view of 44 (TH4502), taken several years after disposal, and owned by a showman in Cardiff at this time. (Chris Taylor collection)

Having controlled the 'Brynteg' business for 2 years, James eventually applied to the Traffic Commissioners for transfer of the 3 Road Service Licences held by the associate company in November 1934. After a public hearing, the licences were granted to James in late June 1935. The licences were:

TGR 347/20: Ammanford (Square) to Llanelly (Railway Station).

TGR 347/21: Ammanford (Square) to Aberystwyth (Railway Station).

TGR 347/22: Ammanford (Square) to Burry Port (Railway Station)

In more detail, the content of the above licences were:

TGR 347/20: Ammanford (Square) to Llanelly (Railway Station) via:- Llandebie, Penygroes, Gorslas, Cross Hands, Drefach, Lower Tumble, Upper Tumble, Llannon, Felinfoel and Llanelly.

Service of stage carriage to operate daily throughout the year including Sundays.

Special Conditions:

(1) Subject in all respects to the provisions of the Llanelly & District Traction Act 1930, regarding no picking up of passengers between Felinfoel Vicarage and Llanelly Railway Station.

(2) No double decker vehicles shall be used on the portion of the authorised route between the Post Office and Workmens Hall at Tumble.

(3) To operate jointly with Western Welsh O.C. and West Wales Motors Ltd.

(4) Inter availability of return tickets between the 3 licensed operators.

A journey time of 1 hour 10 minutes was given for the 19.5 mile route. Condition (2) was only applied to the licence as a safety precaution, owing to the height restriction beneath a railway bridge at Tumble, that was only negotiable by single deck vehicles.

TGR 347/21: Ammanford (Square) to Aberystwyth (Railway Station) via:- Llandilo, Llanwrda, Pumpsaint, Cwmanne, Lampeter, Temple Bar, Aberayron, Llanon and Llanrhystyd.

Service of stage carriage to operate daily throughout the year including Sundays.

Special Conditions

(1) *The licensee shall not on the journey from Ammanford to Aberystwyth be entitled to take up any passengers after leaving the Cross Roads at Temple Bar and shall not on the journey from Aberystwyth to Ammanford be entitled to take up any passengers before reaching the Cross Roads at Temple Bar except passengers bound for a destination beyond that point.*

(2) *To operate the service jointly with Western Welsh O.C.*

(3) *Inter availability of return tickets between the 2 licensed operators.*

The following cutting taken from the company's 1935 timetable illustrates how well they promoted the Aberystwyth service.

Attention is respectfully directed to the excellent facilities available by Summer Services.

EIGHT HOURS BY THE SEA DAILY IN

ABERYSTWYTH

Arriving 11.30 a.m. Depart 7.30 p.m.

ALSO SEVEN HOURS BY THE SEA ON SUNDAYS.

Arriving 12.40 p.m. Depart 6.30 p.m.

The most beautiful Coach Cruise in Wales, through the Country and along the Cardigan Coast.

PRIVATE HIRE.

The Roads are yours. Our Observation Sunshine Coaches and Saloon Coaches are for Hire. Use them both for your next Outing, Tour, or Long Distance Excursions, and enjoy the comforts of travelling by road. Your day's enjoyment begins when you first take your seat in the Coach.

The 61-mile journey from Ammanford to the popular Victorian coastal resort of Aberystwyth had a running time of 3 hours, travelling through hilly and picturesque coastal, and rural West Wales countryside. The route, which could have been classed as a marathon journey in those far off days, proved to be so popular with the adventurous day trippers, the company were granted permission to run 1 extra journey daily during the summer season. Additionally, at the height of the summer season; the Miners' holidays, it was commonplace to see as many as 8 duplicate vehicles running the service, sometimes on hire from other operators. Complexity of the timetable, coupled with the length of this route required one vehicle to be out stationed overnight at Cwmanne, Lampeter. The vehicle based at Cwmanne was manned by crews living in the Lampeter area, a practice inherited with the Brynteg business.

TGR 347/22: Ammanford (Square) to Burry Port (Railway Station) via: Saron, Capel Hendre, Penygroes, Gorslas, Cross Hands Square, Drefach, Upper Tumble, Cwmmawr, Pontyberem, Pontyates, Trimsaran, Pinged and Pembrey.

Service of stage carriage to operate daily throughout the year including Sundays.

Special Conditions:

(1) No double decker vehicles shall be used on the portion of the authorised route between the Post Office and Workmens Hall at Tumble.

(2) The licensee shall not on the outward journey from Ammanford to Burry Port be entitled to take up any passengers after reaching the Butchers Arms, Pembrey and shall not on the inward journey from Burry Port be entitled to take up any passengers before reaching the Butchers Arms, except passengers bound for a destination beyond that point.

(3) Inter availability of return tickets at intermediate points of the journey between Ammanford and Tumble, between the Western Welsh O.C., West Wales Motors, and J. James & Sons Ltd

A journey time of 1 hour 50 minutes was given for this route, having a mileage of 24.7 miles.

The Ammanford to Burry Port route travelled the whole length of the Gwendraeth Valley, running virtually parallel with their only competitor on the route: a railway, formerly owned by the Burry Port and Gwendraeth Valley Railway Co., which was in the ownership of G.W.R. Co, at this time. The railway operated both passenger and freight services through the valley from Cwmmawr to Burry Port, serving the same villages. In fact the G.W.R. Co., was the only objector to James' application for this licence. James also applied for a modification to the restriction placed on this service, asking for permission to pick up passengers between Butchers Arms and Burry Port. The application however, was unsuccessful. The complexity of the timetable on this route, also required a vehicle to be outstationed overnight, this time at the Speedway Garage, Pembrey, manned by crews living in the Burry Port and Pembrey area.

With the inevitable absorption of 'Brynteg's' services taking place in June 1935, the remaining 'Brynteg' vehicles were taken into stock 6 months later, marking the end of the 'Brynteg' fleetname. The staff, however, transferred to James, and remained in their employ for several years afterwards, many of them were Jones 'Brynteg' family members i.e. William; David; Gomer; Trevor, Tom; Mary Ann; Hiram and Edgar Jones. Tom Jones received the position of Garage Foreman with James, David Jones became an Inspector and Mary Ann was a 'clippy' (conductress).

In 1935, a very interesting vehicle was taken into stock. Receiving fleet No. 45 (TF 7310), it was a former Leyland Motors demonstrator bodied in 1932. The chassis was one of the first TD2 type 'Titan's' built in 1931, and had originally been fitted with a 'Gearless' transmission unit during its 3 year spell as a demonstration vehicle. The 'Gearless Bus' as they were called, was an early form of automatic transmission, fitted with torque converter (fluid flywheel) and pre-select gearbox. This type of transmission was only in its infancy at the time, and some operators were rather sceptical of it. The torque converter transmission gave impressions of being sluggish, due to hydraulic slip of the fluid flywheel. Additionally, fuel consumption of vehicles fitted with this type of transmission was noticeably worse, at a time when operators were becoming increasingly keen on fuel economy. The bus, however, had been converted to normal clutch and 4 speed constant mesh (manual) gearbox before delivery to James in April, 1935, and undoubtedly converted to James' requirements.

This all Leyland 'Titan' registered TF 7310 was built in late 1931 and entered service in May 1932 as a demonstrator for Leyland Motors Ltd., fitted with 'gearless' transmission. It operated as a demonstrator with Birmingham C.T., as their No. 94 before returning to Leyland Motors in 1935. After return to Leyland it was converted to a manual gearbox, refurbished and sold to J. James & Sons Ltd., as their No45.
In 1949, when owned by Eynon of Trimsaran, the bodywork was extensively rebuilt by Jeffreys Motors, Swansea, completely altering its piano fronted upper deck. (R. Marshall Collection.)

As mentioned earlier in the story, the James family's generosity was very good, sponsoring several charity events in the community, free staff outings and a Christmas gift of 50 cigarettes to each employee with 'cordial seasons greetings'. In May 1935 they decided to give each member of staff, some 120 in all, a gift of 10 shillings on the occasion of H.M. King George V's silver jubilee. A sceptical point of view is that the money was given to pacify a discontented workforce who had failed to gain trade union recognition.

Continuous efforts by James' staff to secure trade union recognition had been ignored since 1929. Virtually all the staff were members of the Transport & General Workers Union, yet management refused to negotiate with representatives.

'The Ammanford Bus Strike'

The discontented busmen employed by J. James & Sons Ltd., together with employees of Rees & Williams Ltd., and West Wales Motors Ltd., collaborated and finally held a combined meeting organised by the Pontardawe branch of the T&GWU., at Gwaun-Cae-Gurwen on 30th July, 1935. At the meeting which lasted from midnight until 5.00.a.m., they decided to inform the companies concerned that work would be suspended from midnight on 2nd August, unless an agreement was attained over their request for higher wages and better working conditions, i.e. parity with employees of The South Wales Transport Co. This was refused and the strike went ahead on 3rd August.

The National Executive of the T&GWU however, decided that the strike action taken would not be officially recognised and instructed the men to return to work immediately to allow negotiations to take place with the employers. Staff employed at West Wales Motors Ltd., and Rees & Williams Ltd., returned to work, but the majority of James' employees stayed out with overwhelming support from 20,000 men employed by Amalgamated Collieries; The Trades & Labour Councils of the Amman and Gwendraeth Valleys; The Miners Federation in the areas of this dispute, and the inhabitants of Gwaun-Cae-Gurwen and District.

On 16th August, 20 'black leg' drivers were brought in by James' in order to restore their services. This inflamed a large crowd of non-busmen that had congregated in Ammanford Square that evening. The crowd clashed with the police and caused a 'riot' with bricks and stones being thrown, resulting in 6 windows being smashed on 4 of James' buses and considerable damage to the glass roof and decorative neon sign at the entrance to James' new bus station. The police made no less than 18 arrests during the disturbance that night.

By Sunday, 18th August, with no prospects of a settlement to the dispute, the action rapidly spread to involve 21 companies in the area. The companies affected were South Wales Transport; Wilmore Motors; Neath Omnibus Co.; Abbey Services; Osborne Bus

Service; N&C Luxury Coaches; Blue Bird Services; Windsor Bus Service; Richmond Services; Eclipse Saloon Services; Bassett & Sons; Enterprise Motor Services; John Bros (Grovesend); Bevan & Davies; West Wales Motors; Rees & Williams, J. James & Sons; W. Jones (Brynteg); Gower Vanguard; L. C. Williams and Swansea Bus Services. Surprisingly, employees of The Swansea Tramway system joined the stoppage.. Western Welsh O.C. employees, still members of the railmens union, nevertheless joined the dispute a week later, resulting in a 100% withdrawal of public transport in the Neath, Swansea, Gower, Llanelly and Amman Valley areas.

The strike, which lasted 6 weeks, came to an abrupt end on the 12th September, with services resuming after 4.00.p.m. that day. The strikers returned to work with an understanding that negotiations regarding their wage claim would only begin after their return to work. The talks took place and ten months later an amicable agreement was achieved; parity of wages and conditions with the South Wales Transport staff, which amounted to 1 penny an hour increase for drivers and conductors and 8 days holiday a year with pay – previously no holidays. This increase gave drivers one shilling and four pence per hour, and one shilling and two pence per hour for conductors, additionally overtime rates would be paid on over 48 hours per week, time-and-a-quarter for Sunday work and time-and-three-quarters for Bank Holidays. Needless to say the majority of other companies involved in this dispute eventually introduced similar agreements with their staff.

After the strike ended, J. James & Sons Ltd., sent a bill to Carmarthenshire County Council for damages sustained to their buses and garage buildings during the disturbances of August 16th. The bill amounting to £49-13s-0d, was surprisingly paid out by the council in February 1936, much to the astonishment of local ratepayers. Meanwhile, the 18 men arrested during the disturbances of August 16th appeared at Ammanford court on 25th November, 1935, to answer charges of alleged unlawful and riotous assembly in Ammanford Square. After the hearing they were committed for trial at Carmarthen Crown Court, resulting in 15 men being convicted for public order offences on 6th January, 1936.

Meanwhile, 2nd January, 1936, saw the final stage of 'Brynteg' takeover when the last 4 Brynteg vehicles were licenced to J. James & Sons Ltd. With the associate company fully integrated, James decided to introduce connections from other areas with their Aberystwyth service. By re-timing their existing services from Burry Port, Llanelly, Neath, Pontardawe and Swansea, connections could be made at Ammanford bus station on outward and inward journeys to and from Aberystwyth. Further connections were made at Ammanford, Llandebie and Cross Hands, with the services of West Wales Motors, Rees & Williams Ltd., and Bassett-Enterprise of Gorseinon respectively, offering travellers from South Wales a service to Aberystwyth, as competitors South Wales Transport; Jones Bros., Aberystwyth; J. D. Evans; L.C. Williams (L.C.W. Motors) and Goughs of Mountain Ash had all abandoned this service.

A year later in1937 a disagreement arose between the joint Swansea Valley route operators James, Eclipse and S.W.T., regarding the varying fares charged between them. At the request of the operators the Traffic Commissioners introduced a new standard fare table for all services operating between Swansea and the upper Swansea Valley in December 1937. However, when James' renewed their Swansea Valley licences a month later the 'Special Condition' regarding picking up and setting down of passengers within the Borough of Swansea had changed from Chemical Road, Ynysforgan, to Grove Place Chapel, Ynysforgan. This location however, was simply the same boarding stage, redesignated.

Continuing with their fleet modernisation scheme the company carried on re-bodying 5-year-old vehicles in 1937/8, with no less than 6 more receiving new Beadle bodies and diesel engines. However, the last stage of modernising the fleet was the introduction of a new vehicle livery and fleet renumbering in 1937. The vehicle renumbering was quite straightforward – simply to add a third digit to the existing fleet number, i.e., 1xx; for vehicles fitted with diesel engines only.

The new livery; flame red with maroon relief, cream roof and black wings, was introduced in February 1937 with the delivery of 3 new Leyland TS7 "Tigers' 146 – 148 (TH 8102 – 4). This pleasant livery was widely accepted by everyone and soon became the company's standard livery after the company's coach painter Phillip Wydenbach (who was an artist by profession), meticulously hand painted each vehicle to a very high standard.

Surprisingly, the new bus station built just 2 years earlier was getting too congested and extra space was desperately needed. Expansion was still the order of the day and the company directors realised the huge potential in acquiring a neighbouring property, the disused Pooles Cinema in nearby Margaret Street. Pooles cinema, as mentioned earlier had originally been built and owned by John James in a partnership with David Evans (1910 – 1912), passing to J. R. Pooles shortly afterwards. After purchasing the cinema in 1937, plans were drawn up to demolish the building in order to extend the bus station through into adjacent Margaret Street. The plan to build a 680 sq.yd. extension to the bus station, to create an entrance in Margaret Street and exit in College Street, was submitted to the Ammanford council in November 1937. Planning consent was duly given and when completed in 1938 became the largest undercover bus station in South Wales. With a floor area of some 2,416 square yards (half an acre) the bus station had a one-way-traffic system, which allowed buses to enter from Margaret Street only, and to exit through the original entrance in College Street. After completion of this new extension in 1938 the company's long established wedding car hire and funeral business was sold off, allowing the company to concentrate 100% on their bus activities.

For several years the company had considered the possibility of building a depot in the Ystalyfera area to house the vehicles outstationed there maintaining the Swansea Valley services. Since 1926, a vehicle had been parked overnight at Ystalyfera, (later at Gurnos

Cross) manned by crews living in that area. In 1930, this had increased to 3 vehicles and by 1939 with the prospect of war looming, secure premises with cleaning, fueling and office facilities was urgently needed in the Swansea Valley, to reduce unnecessary dead mileages. However, in September 1939, a suitable plot of land at Gurnos Cross near Ystalyfera was acquired on a 99-year lease, upon which a garage large enough to house 4 double deckers was built, and a parking area for approximately ten buses. The depot ideally sited at Gurnos Cross was situated at the junction of Gorof Road and Cwmphil Road (A4067 Swansea to Ystradgynlais road and A4068 Brynamman to Ystalyfera Road), alongside their well-established bus route from Ammanford to Swansea. The office was an adjacent house in Cwmphil Road, where crews booked on and off, paid in their takings and obtained all necessary schedules, tickets and instructions.

An annual ground rent was paid for the land with the arrangement of a free travel pass for the landowner to travel on James buses.

Meanwhile, in May 1939, the local press suggested that the Ammanford busmen were preparing for another strike. The local bus crews immediately denied these rumours stating that they had merely changed union membership from the T. & G.W.U., to a new breakaway organisation called The National Passenger Workers Union, and pointed out that their difficulties had been recognition of this new union by their employers.

With war now imminent, the Ammanford council asked Messrs. James about the possibility of converting a bus at short notice, for use as an ambulance in the event of an air raid. Angus James responded, giving the council assurance of 100% support in the event of any such emergency.

War was finally declared with Germany on 3rd September, 1939.

The last single decker purchased before the outbreak of World War II was this 1938 Leyland bodied 'Tiger' TS8; 149 (TH 9902). It narrowly missed being requisitioned by the War Department in 1940 as it had departed for Swansea when the government officials arrived at the depot to commandeer vehicles for military use. (R. Marshall Collection)

150 (TH 9901) was the only Leyland TD5 'Titan' owned by the company and happened to be the first metal framed double decker bus purchased. In this official Leyland view, clearly visible in the photograph is the 'special' green lamp fitted to the nearside of driver's cab – for passengers to distinguish JAMES' buses approaching in the dark. (R. Marshall Collection.)

This Leyland 'Tiger' was rebodied in 1937.

Leyland 'Tiger' TH8104 is pictured here at Western Welsh's Ely works, awaiting disposal in 1952. It ended its days as a tar spraying lorry.

THE DARK DAYS OF WAR

Just days after World War II began on 3rd September, 1939, the company introduced emergency timetables on all their services. This decision was carried out in order to conserve fuel when rationing commenced on 16th September. Some services were reduced to a very basic frequency, yet services that operated via collieries had extra journeys added to provide regular transport for the colliers, who were regarded as essential war workers.

As previously mentioned the Amman Valley had suffered high unemployment for more than a decade, caused by the depression. However, after war was declared large numbers of the community's male population enlisted and joined the armed forces. Most of the collieries re-opened, taking on large numbers of the unemployed, and coal was produced again to maximum capacity. The Ministry of Labour on the other hand, opened temporary offices at a local church vestry in Ammanford to recruit female labour for the munitions factories in South Wales.

Messrs. James & Sons, in the meantime aided the war effort in every possible way without financial gain to the company. Firstly they allowed a dog show to be held at the bus station in aid of the local "War Comforts Fund" and later allowed the depot to be used as a collection point for articles of aluminium and other scrap metals, assisting the war effort at a time of material shortages. Angus James even launched an appeal in 1940 and collected subscriptions towards an 'Ammanford Spitfire Fund'. A total of £20,712 -2s -2d was collected in a period of 3 months and paid to the Ministry of Aircraft Production in February 1941, to purchase more fighter planes. The bus station was also once used as an auction room for valuable household furniture. Additionally, staff dances were regularly held at the Drill Hall, the proceeds of which were donated to the J. James & Sons 'Staff Troop Comforts Fund'; Amman Valley Cottage Hospital; Swansea Hospital and the Red Cross.

As war progressed, the company became exceptionally busy transporting personnel to several munitions factories, military establishments and steel works situated across South Wales. To provide these extra services during the war, additional licences had to be applied for as usual, but were now only authorised by the Ministry of Defence (Ministry of War Transport), as were all other operational licences issued during the hostilities. Licences to operate Excursions & Tours were suspended in order to conserve fuel and rubber, as were the licences for Express Carriage services 3 years later. Nevertheless, the first Road Service Licences issued to the company under the new Ministry of Defence regulations came soon after war broke out in September 1939. They were:

TGR 347/23 — Ammanford (Square) to Pontardawe Steel Works,
via: Glanamman, Garnant, Gwaun-Cae-Gurwen, Cwmgorse and Rhydyfro.
Workmens service of stage carriage to run on a 3 shift pattern, on working days only Monday to Saturday throughout the year.

TGR 347/24: — Brynamman (New Road) to Pembrey Royal Ordinance Factory (R.O.F.)
via: Gwaun-Cae-Gurwen, Garnant, Glanamman, Ammanford, Llandebie, Saron, Capel Hendre, Penygroes Sq., Gorslas Sq., Cross Hands Sq., Drefach Sq., Lower Tumble, Upper Tumble (Tumble Hotel), Pontyberem Sq., Ponthenry, Pontyates (Station), Trimsaran (Bird-in-Hand), Pinged and Pembrey.
Workmens service of contract carriage to operate daily throughout the year.

TGR 347/25: — Llandebie (Square) to Briton Ferry, Wern Works (Baldwins Steelworks).
via: Ammanford, Glanamman, Garnant, Gwaun-Cae-Gurwen, Pontardawe, Neath and Briton Ferry.
Workmens service of contract carriage to operate daily Monday to Saturday throughout the year.

At the beginning of the war the supply of new Leyland buses was hardly affected and in January 1940 the company took delivery of another new double decker. This was 151(BBX 500) a Leyland TD7 'Titan', a new model that had superseded the TD5 'Titan' a month earlier. This again was fitted with a 48 seater lowbridge body built by Leyland Motors.

However, in July 1940 War Department officials toured all bus and coach operators in the U.K., requisitioning buses and coaches for military use, usually taking the operators' best buses and coaches. On the morning that the officials were due to arrive at Ammanford, Angus James, the company's general manager, had the foresight to send one of the newest vehicles out on service to Swansea. Angus' quick thinking paid off and the officials left without seeing the bus, 149, as it was away for some considerable time. Nevertheless, 7 single decker buses were requisitioned by the Ministry of Defence and taken away for 'troop transport', leaving the company short of vehicles to maintain their services.

Shortly afterwards, the government imposed a complete stoppage on all bus chassis production which took full effect in February 1941 when the stock of buses already built were 'frozen'.

This had a detrimental effect upon the company soon after loosing 25% of their fleet through M.O.D. requisitioning, coupled with an increased workload of contract services to several M.O.D. and Admiralty establishments throughout South Wales.

The M.O.D. contract services awarded in early 1940 were:-

TGR 347/26:	Penygroes to Bridgend (R.O.F.), via: Tycroes and Ammanford.
TGR 347/27:	Brynamman to Bridgend (R.O.F.), via: Cwmllynfell and Ystalyfera.
TGR 347/28:	Varteg to Bridgend (R.O.F.), via: Ystalyfera and Pontardawe.
TGR 347/29:	Hirwaun to Bridgend (R.O.F.), via: Glynneath and Neath.

Workers services of contract carriage to operate daily throughout the year.

In 1941 the company were requested to increase these workings to 3 journeys daily in order to accommodate workers on a three shift pattern of working. At the same time the service from Hirwaun to Bridgend was withdrawn.

In April 1942 the R.O.F. officials paid a very high tribute to the women workers of the Amman Valley, and were very sympathetic about the distance they travelled to work. To improve their travelling facilities the officials altered their travel arrangements, terminating the buses at Neath railway station, and transferring the workers to a special train for the factory at Tremains, Bridgend.

Whilst researching the company's history, a former employee recalled an incident that happened when he conducted on this contract service. Apparently there were 3 to 4 buses employed on this contract each shift, together with buses from other companies. These buses and crews had to wait three hours at Neath railway station for the train's return, bringing back workers from the previous shift. On the day in question the train had been excessively delayed, returning to Neath very late. The crews lay over time had been spent in a pub, having a 'liquid lunch', obviously long before the breathalyser had been introduced. As a result, one driver got himself rather inebriated and was incapable of driving his bus back to Ammanford. A hurried discussion held between the bus crews resulted in an impetuous decision to allow a conductor to drive the bus back to Ammanford fully loaded, without holding a P.S.V. driving licence. Having not even driven a bus before, he safely delivered everyone back to their destination!

Further military contracts awarded to the company in 1940/1 were:-

TGR 347/30: Ammanford to Templeton (R.A.F. base) via: Cefneithin, Carmarthen and Whitland.
Workmens service of contract carriage to operate daily throughout the year.

TGR 347/31: Ammanford to Llangennech (R.N.A.D.) via Llandebie, Penygroes, Gorslas (Square), Cross Hands (Square), Drefach, Upper Tumble (P.O.), Llannon (Greyhound Inn), Hendy (Square), Llangennech (R.N. Site).
Workmens service of contract carriage to operate daily (one shift) Monday to Saturday throughout the year.

Transport to convey the war workers was absolutely crucial at this time and a supply of new vehicles was desperately needed to maintain services. The stock of 'frozen' buses under the control of the Ministry of War Transport (M.O.W.T.), were eventually released in 1941 and 1942, two of which were supplied to James. This pair of 'unfrozen' Leyland TD7 deckers, originally intended for Scottish operator W. Alexander & Son's, Falkirk, arrived at Ammanford in October 1941 as 164/165 (BTH 174/5). Their Leyland bodies, however, did not comply with the M.O.W.T. wartime austerity specifications, as they were built before the regulations were imposed. The regulations specified that bodywork had to be constructed to save as much valuable raw material for the war effort as possible – hence the wooden slatted 'park bench type' seats fitted to buses built during the war. Additionally, all wartime purchases of buses, new and second-hand had to be sanctioned by the M.O.W.T., and granted in special circumstances only. The company were granted numerous extra vehicles by the M.O.W.T. to cover their increased workload, allowing the fleet to expand rapidly, reaching its maximum size before war ended in 1945. A motley collection of some 42 vehicles were acquired during the hostilities – 19 second-hand and 23 new, all authorised by the M.O.W.T. Livery of the wartime acquisitions differed slightly from the standard livery introduced in 1937. In retrospect, the cream roof and window surrounds were discontinued in favour of an all-over flame red livery with maroon waistband, which became the new fleet livery. Wings (or mudguards as they were sometimes called) were painted white – another wartime regulation, reverting to black wings after war ended.

A noteworthy purchase of second-hand double deckers in 1940, were three highbridge bodied Leyland 'Titan's' from Southdown Motor Services, Brighton. Numbered 156 – 158 (UF6469, 7408, 7426) they were the only 'Hybridge' deckers ever owned and were unable to operate any of James stage carriage routes due to their height. Alternatively, they were restricted to operating a military contract to Templeton R.A.F. base in Pembrokeshire. Besides this, extreme care had to be taken manoeuvring these deckers inside the bus station as the headroom of the area built in 1935 was too low to accommodate them. As a result the highbridge buses had to enter and leave the depot via Margaret Street, and to maintain them an inspection pit was built in that area of the bus station.

Ironically 156 – 8 were the only James vehicles to operate in a 'wartime grey' austere livery, the remainder of the fleet retained their normal livery.

Wartime photographs of James' buses are extremely rare, but I am indebted to Chris Taylor for this splendid view of James' Leyland 'Titan' 124 (TH800) pictured here at Llanwrda Square in 1940/1, working the Ammanford - Lampeter service. New to James in 1930, it originally carried fleet number 24 and a Leyland 48 seat lowbridge body. Rebodied by J. C. Beadle of Dartford in 1937, it was retro fitted with a Leyland diesel engine and renumbered 124. Additionally, it was the first decker to carry James' smart new livery of flame red and cream with maroon relief. Actually, this photograph answers a longstanding argument - whether James' buses carried the wartime all over grey livery. Furthermore, clearly visible in this view are the hooded headlamps and blacked out side lamps - a strict requirement during the war. However, it requires a little imagination, nowadays, to consider the hazards of driving in a wartime blackout, with only the glimmer of hooded headlamps to assist the driver. (Chris Taylor collection.)

Another wartime view supplied by Chris Taylor depicts Leyland 'Tiger' 149 (TH9902) at Lampeter about to depart for Ammanford in 1940. This view of 149 clearly shows the layout of the company's 1937 livery, cream roof and window surrounds, maroon waistband and flame red panelling. The wings and lifeguard rail - normally black were painted white during the war years - another wartime regulation.
(Chris Taylor collection.)

To assist the Company with their enormous workload during the war, James acquired no less than 20 'utility' type vehicles. The vehicles all sanctioned by the Ministry of War Transport, and built to strict wartime austerity specification including wooden slatted seats, were 10 Guy Arab's, 5 Daimler CWA6's and 5 Bedford OWB's. The Duple bodied Bedford OWB pictured here when new, is reputed to be the first Bedford acquired by James, which would be 166 (BTH652) delivered in September 1942.

The only photograph available of the 'Hybridge' deckers operated by James during W.W.II, is this one pictured here operating in Brighton with the original owners Southdown Motor Services. This 1931 Leyland TD1 with Short Bros., body was one of 3 acquired in 1939/40 to cover vehicle shortages. Registered UF7408 it received fleet No. 157 with James and operated in wartime grey livery.

Another wartime purchase was this 1930 Leyland 'Tiger' TS3, 159 (FV1649) which had been rebodied in 1937 by Beadle coachworks.

Looking somewhat battered, and fitted with an unmatched replacement headlamp to its off side, is one of the 'unfrozen' Leyland TD7 'Titans'; 165 (BTH175) acquired in 1941. Built to the order of Walter Alexander & Sons of Falkirk, it is pictured here at Wind Street, Ammanford in 1950, still fitted with the unique Alexander style destination box. It was sold in 1955 to Samuel Eynon & Sons, Trimsaran, where it saw a further 3 years service. (A.B. Cross collection)

From late 1942, however, new bus chassis began to appear again, built on government approval to M.O.W.T. specification. These chassis:- Guy Arab, Daimler CWG5 and CWA6's, Karrier W4 (Trolleybuses) and Bedford OWB were the only P.S.V. chassis built in Britain during the war. Reluctantly breaking their long association with Leyland Motors the pressurised company took delivery of 20 new buses between 1942 and 1945; 10 Guy Arab double deckers (169 – 173, 179, 183 – 186); 5 Daimler CWA6 double deckers with A.E.C. 7.7 litre engines (180 – 182, 187, 188), and 5 Bedford OWB (wartime Bedford OB) single deckers (166 – 168, 174, 175) all constructed to the austere specification laid down by the Government. Leyland vehicles, being James' preference, were not produced after 1942 when the factory switched production building tanks for the war effort, but the company returned faithfully again to Leyland in 1946 for all their subsequent vehicle purchases.

This was one of the 10 'utility' bodied Guy Arab's acquired during W.W.II. The Strachan 'Utility' body of this 1943 Guy Arab II (CBX 7) was refurbished by Jeffreys Commercial Motors Ltd., of Swansea in 1950.

Seen here, parked up at Church Street, Ammanford, minus the 'Indians Head' is 172 (CBX 54) another Strachans bodied Guy Arab II. This one had its body overhauled by Bruce Coachworks at Cardiff in 1950 with rubber mounted front upper deck windows and a redesigned destination box. (R. Marshall collection.)

The company's operational difficulties during the war however were not confined to vehicle and fuel shortages, there was also a staff shortage, an item previously unknown to the company. Office and road staff vacancies were often advertised in order to maintain the manning levels required. Despite this, the dismissal of an employee in October 1944 triggered off another strike within the company. The strike which only lasted a few days caused utter chaos to the M.O.D. contract services operated. As a result the Government establishments affected, brought in Military Transport to convey their personnel to and from work until the dispute ended.

In addition to their heavy workload, the company still continued to expand, even through the war years, by acquiring two more local competitors. Firstly in November 1943 they agreed to purchase the business of Bevan & Davies at Garnswllt for £3,000. After M.O.W.T. approval, their takeover took place on 17th December, 1943, with James acquiring their 3 elderly A.E.C. Regal saloon buses (UH 8624, 8626, 8629) together with the following Road Service Licences:-

TGR 347/32:	Pantyffynnon (Railway Station) to Tairgwaith, via:- Ammanford (Iscennen Road), Glanamman, Garnant, Gwaun-Cae Gurwen, and Tairgwaith. Service of stage carriage to operate daily throughout the year, Sundays to Saturdays.
TGR 347/33:	Ammanford (Wind Street) to Tycroes (Square) via: Penybank. Service of stage carriage to operate daily throughout the year, Monday to Saturday.
TGR 347/34:	Ammanford (Iscennen Road) to Pontardulais (Dulais Square, Water Street), via: Bettws, Garnswllt, Troedyrhiw, Tycerrig, Pentrebach and Glynhir Road. Service of stage carriage to operate daily throughout the year, Sundays to Saturdays.
TGR 347/35:	Twyn (Garnant) to Ammanford (Iscennen Road) via: Tircoed, Glanamman, Mount Pleasant and Pontamman. Service of stage carriage to operate daily throughout the year, Mondays to Saturdays.
TGR 347/36	Ammanford (Square) to Port Tennant (Steelworks). Workmen's service of contract carriage to operate daily.

The above services TGR 347/32, 34 and 35 were then modified to operate via. James' Bus Station, previously Iscennen Road.

Only one driver transferred to James with the take over, D. J. Davies continued farming and running his haulage business.

Thirteen months later an agreement was made to purchase the small business owned by R. & W. J. Jones, T/A; Jones Bros. (Brynawel) Ltd, at Penygroes for £4,500. With this take over which took place in February 1945 came four Tilling Stevens 32 seater buses and one Road Service Licence:-

TGR 347/37: Ammanford (Square) to Cwmmawr (Railway Station) via: Tirydail, Saron, Capel Hendre, Penygroes, Gorslas, Cross Hands and Drefach.
Service of stage carriage to operate daily throughout the year, Mondays to Saturdays.

Rhys Jones, a partner of 'Brynawel' and one other driver transferred with the business. This inevitable take over resulted in Carmarthenshire's premier operator J. James & Sons. Ltd., reaching its largest size, operating 21 services with 54 vehicles.

This Strachan bodied Tilling Stevens of 1932 vintage was one of four T.S.M.'s acquired with the Jones Bros., 'Brynawel' business in 1945. Registered TH 2385 it was allocated fleet number 190 during its short stay with J. James & Sons. Ltd.

180 (CBX 299) was the first of 5 Daimler 'utilities' that arrived in 1944. Bodied by Brush Coachworks this Daimler CWA6 (Commercial Wartime A.E.C. 6 cylinder engine) also had its body refurbished in 1951 by Bruce Coachworks, Cardiff.

Taking on passengers for the Amman Valley, outside James' Bus Station in College Street, Ammanford, is another 'utility' Daimler CWA6. 181 (CBX 311) also bodied by Brush Coachworks is seen in its original form before its refurbishment by Bruce Coachworks. (D.A. Jones collection)

Showing signs of its age in 1956 was this Roe bodied Guy Arab II, 184(CBX 406) seen parked in Trinity Place, Swansea. Note the redesigned destination box and front upper deck windows, which had been rubber mounted during its refurbishment by Bruce coachworks in 1951.

Roe bodied Guy Arab II, 185(CBX476) is captured here at College Street, Ammanford on route to Tairgwaith in the Amman Valley. The village of Tairgwaith (translated means three works), received this unusual name after the siting of three collieries at that location. The service to Tairgwaith was inherited with the business of Bevan & Davies, Garnswllt in 1943. The building visible to the right hand side of this view was the Company's workshops, with the entrance gate into Ammanford Primary School in the foreground. (J.F. Higham collection.)

186 was numerically the last Guy Arab 'Utility' acquired by the company in 1944. It is seen here parked between two Strachan bodied Leyland 'Tigers' in Church Street, Ammanford shortly before withdrawal in 1956. (R. Marshall collection.)

THE POST WAR YEARS

After the wartime hostilities were over in 1945, Angus James decided to try his hand at farming. Buying a farm at Glanamman, known as Ystradamman Farm, he appropriately renamed it "Brynderwen". The farm, which was run by a manager, was soon stocked with the finest herd of prize winning Ayrshire cattle seen in the area, bought at auction in Ayr at 200 guineas each (£210).

"On the other side of the fence", most of the company's vehicles requisitioned by the M.O.D. returned in full camouflage livery (green and brown), replacing several elderly pre-war buses that were showing signs of their age. Simultaneously the company were in a position to dispose of surplus vehicles, as most of the wartime contract services had finished.

Industries in the community soon returned to normal working with full employment for everyone and a new factory owned by Pullman Springfilled Co. Ltd., moved into the area taking on large numbers of people.

James immediately extended certain services beyond their terminus at Ammanford Bus Station to provide transport to the new factory situated ¾ miles away on the Pantyffynnon Road. Several other modifications were made to their services at this time, mainly to provide workers with adequate travelling facilities. The Ammanford to Tairgwaith service was extended to reach Steer Pit, and the Ammanford to Brynamman service was extended from Brynamman Railway Station to The Derlwyn Arms. Return and period tickets became interchangeable between the relevant joint operators of common services and in 1950 road/rail tickets became interchangeable between the points of Lampeter and Aberystwyth.

The first new Road Service Licences applied for immediately after war ended was a local school journey:-

TGR 347/38: Ammanford (Bus Station) to Heol-ddu, via: College Street, High Street,. and Wernddu Road.
Service of stage carriage to operate on school days only.

Licence application numbers TGR 347/39 and TGR 347/40 were not used.

In September 1946 another new licence was applied for:-

TGR 347/41: Ystalyfera (New Swan) to Neath (Railway Station), via: Ystalyfera (Smiths Arms), Panteg School, Godre'rgraig, Ynysymeudw, Pontardawe Cross, Rhos, Fforestgoch and Bryncoch.

Service of stage carriage to operate Sundays to Saturdays throughout the year on a frequency of every 120 minutes. Connections at Ystalyfera (New Swan) with buses operating on the Ammanford – Brynamman – Swansea service, and connections at Neath Railway Station for the London Trains.

This application received two public hearings due to objections from Western Welsh Omnibus Co., South Wales Transport Co., and United Welsh Services Ltd. The licence was finally granted in February 1947 with a condition that no passengers be taken up and set down between Pontardawe (Police Station) and Neath on certain timed journeys. This restriction was lifted in August 1949 and in 1953 tickets became interchangeable.

The immediate post war period however, suffered an acute shortage of new buses, as most of those built were for the export market. Nevertheless, renewing their association with Leyland Motors, the company replaced more ageing stock with new Leylands in late 1946, acquiring two PS1 'Tigers' 193/194 (CTH 490/615), and four PD1 'Titans', 195 – 198 (CTH 823/5 – 7), all fitted with the new 7.4 litre diesel engine. These engines fitted to the 'Titan's' proved to be underpowered on the Welsh hills.

In 1947 another four new PS1 'Tigers' arrived followed in 1948 by three more identical 'Tigers' all fitted with Strachan 32 seat front entrance saloon bodies. These Leylands replaced the last Bedford OWB 'utilities' that were uneconomical with their thirsty 28 h.p. petrol engines. They arrived soon after the company had restored their 'Excursions & Tours' licences, which had been suspended due to war. After an eight-year interval, the demand for excursions was very high, requiring several extra vehicles. The new 'Tigers' with their comfortable moquette seating were a regular feature on private hire and excursions in addition to their normal service duties.

The first post war vehicle acquired in 1946 was this Burlingham bodied Leyland PS1 'Tiger' 193 (CTH 490). It is pictured here at Ystalyfera about to leave for Rhiwfawr. Rhiwfawr (translated means Big Hill), was situated on top of a mountain, 1000 ft. above sea level, and was only accessible by single deckers due to a very low bridge at Lower Cwmtwrch. (R. Marshall collection.)

Numerically, the first post war double decker acquired, was this Leyland PD1 'Titan' 195 (CTH 823) with Leyland body. It is seen here leaving James' Bus Station in College Street, Ammanford, for Pontardulais via. Garnswllt in 1958.

Leyland bodied 'Titan' 197 (CTH 826) is pictured here outside Ammanford Police Station on its return journey from Burry Port in 1957.

One of the seven Strachan bodied 32 seater Leyland 'Tigers' delivered in 1947/8 was 200 (DBX 260) pictured here in this official view when new. A more suitable description for these 'saloon buses' that were frequently used on tours, would have been 'dual purpose' as they were fitted with sloping floors for panoramic viewing and moquette seating for comfort. It must have been the destination box design and bus livery that gave them this unfair description. Nevertheless, they must have been 'super luxury coaches' compared to the wooden seated 'utility' Bedfords they replaced. Note the logo 'British Buses' above James' name. This logo was applied to most of the fleet at the time. (R. Marshall Collection)

This logo 'British Buses' was created by The British Omnibus Company's Public Relations Committee. It appeared on all the company's time tables and official documentation from 1943 to 1949. It also appeared on notices published by the local press during 1946/7 condemning the labour government's proposal to Nationalise buses. The company however, strongly supported this committee, fitting transfers of the logo to the sides of their buses; as seen on the photograph of bus No. 200 above.

In the daytime James' depot at Ammanford would be used as a bus station. Buses that were 'off service' at the time would normally be parked here at Church Street, around the corner from the depot. Seen here at Church Street in June 1956 are 202 (DBX 638), Strachans bodied 'Tiger' PS1; 186 (CBX 477) a Roe bodied Guy Arab utility; 199 (DBX 259) another Strachans bodied 'Tiger' and 172 (CBX 54) a Strachans bodied Guy Arab utility. (R. Marshall collection.)

Pictured outside Ammanford Central Police Station in June 1962, this James' Leyland double decker, 205 (EBX 663) had amazingly begun its working life 14 years earlier as a single decker! Its single decker type chassis, a Leyland 'Tiger' PS1 built in 1948 was originally fitted with a front entrance 32 seat saloon body built by Strachan Coachworks, and worked as such until 1954, when it became 'redundant' along with sister vehicle 204 (EBX 662). Leylands being the General Manager's preference, it was decided to retain and rebody the 'Tigers' into double deckers, which in turn would replace older non-standard stock – the wartime ultility Daimiers. Western Welsh Omnibus Co., carried out the extensive work of removing the old bodies and rebuilding their chassis frames to PD1 (double decker) specification at their Central works in Cardiff. The rebuilt ' Tiger' chassis were then fitted with new 55 seat lowbridge type bodies by Longwell Green Coachworks at Bristol in April 1954, giving them an extended life. This particular vehicle, 205 had a sliding cab window fitted immediately behind the driver, giving it a second role as a driver training vehicle, and was the only 'PS1 rebuild' to pass into S.W.T ownership in 1962. (Roy Marshall collection)

The penultimate Strachan bodied 'Tiger' PSI, 204 (EBX 662) is captured outside James' depot in College St. Ammanford, en route to Brynamman c. 1950. In 1954, at just 6-years old, it was re-bodied with a 55 seat lowbridge type double decker body by Longwell Green Coachworks pictured later in the book. (D.S. Giles collection)

On the 7th June 1949, Mrs. Elizabeth Ann James, widow of the company's founder, John James, sadly passed away at the age of 87. Succeeding her husband by 17 years, Mrs. James a senior director of the company was described as being a kind hearted, homely, inoffensive, dear old lady. Living at Porthcawl since the death of her husband she had intended returning to her native Ammanford a week later, but passed away before her earnest wish was realised.

After Mrs. James' death, the company directors were given as the late John James' three sons and their wives; J. Percy James; Edith M. James; R. Lindsay James; Lilian V. James; Angus R. James; Eira W. James.

This era of the company's operation 1947 – 1951 is reputed to have been the heyday of bus travel in West Wales; a time when passenger levels reached its peak, yet passengers regularly complained of infrequent services and of buses passing them fully loaded.

In October 1948, the Rhiwfawr to Ystalyfera; Friday & Saturday only service, was modified to operate daily. This improvement had been long awaited by local residents, especially workers employed at the Anglo-Celtic Watch Factory in Ystalyfera. Simultaneously, Ystradgynlais council asked the company to consider extending their Neath to Ystalyfera service to reach Upper Cwmtwrch. The company, however, rejected the council's request in 1950 stating that they did not have sufficient buses, and thanked them for their continued support! Conversely, residents of Hopkinstown, a small district of the Amman Valley were plaguing the Ammanford Council for public transport, especially transport for school children attending Bettws primary school. Their request was ignored for 3 years until April 1949 when Edgar Jones, a driver previously employed by James, applied for a licence to operate a new daily service between Ammanford (Y.M.C.A., Iscennen Road) and Hopkinstown (Pontamman) via Bettws Square, accommodating the Hopkinstown school children. Edgar, (son of David Jones from the erstwhile Jones Bros. 'Brynteg' partnership) created quite a stir when he applied for this licence. An objection to the application was immediately lodged by his former employers, J. James & Sons. Ltd., which led to a public hearing. A licence was granted in July 1949.

Ably assisted by his brother Hiram, Edgar commenced his new service with a new Bedford OB bus, operating from Brynteg Garage, Upper Tumble. Ironically, this was the operating base used by his predecessors, the Jones brothers 'Brynteg' some 20 years earlier.

A short while later, Edgar applied for a licence to extend his service beyond Ammanford to Llanelly, on Llanelly market days – Thursdays and Saturdays only. This was refused in November 1949 after objections were received from the five stage carriage operators in Ammanford, yet three weeks later, Messrs. J. James & Sons. Ltd., made an application for a similar Llanelly market days service from Ammanford. Objections to their application were also received but the licence was granted to them in March 1950:-

TGR 347/42: Ammanford (James Bus Station) to Llanelly (Railway Station) via: Saron, Capel Hendre, Penygroes, Gorsddu, Gorslas, Cross Hands, Upper Tumble, Llannon, Felinfoel and Llanelly.

Special conditions:

(1) Subject in all respects to the proviso of the Llanelly & District Traction Act 1930, regarding no picking up of passengers between Felinfoel vicarage and Llanelly Railway Station.

(2) To operate on a 'more direct' route from Ammanford to Llanelly.

(3) The service of stage carriage to operate on Thursdays and Saturdays only.

(4) Return tickets interchangeable over common sections with West Wales Motors Ltd., and Western Welsh Omnibus Co. Ltd.

In February 1950, the Minister of Transport announced that all new 4 wheeler buses and coaches registered after 1st June that year would be permitted to have an increased overall length of up to 30 feet long. The company however didn't take advantage of this new legislation, as their 1950 vehicle purchases, all 27 feet 6 inches long consisted of 4 Leyland bodied PD2/1 'Titans', 206 – 209 (FTH 680 – 683), and 2 newly developed Leyland HR40 'Olympic' saloons 210/211 (FTH 717/8). These ultra modern 40-seater saloons were somewhat different to any other vehicle owned by the company. They were of integral construction (chassis-less) built by Metropolitan-Cammell-Weymann Motor Bodies Ltd., incorporating Leyland running units, powered by the new 9.8 litre Leyland 0.600 diesel engine, mounted horizontally under the mid-floor of the vehicle. This pair of rare 'Olympic's' were very early examples, having body numbers 17 and 18.

Victoria Gardens Neath is the backdrop for this splendid view of Leyland bodied PD2/1, 207 (FTH 681) in 1954. The car speeding past to the left of the picture is a rare FORD "C" type convertible, fitted with 10 hp side valve engine and 3 speed gearbox.

Integrally built Leyland 'Olympic' 210 (FTH 717) was one of a pair operated by the company. New in September 1950, they were constructed by M-C-W Motor Bodies Ltd., using Leyland running units, featuring a Leyland 0.600 engine. In this view, 210 is about to leave Ammanford Bus Station bound for Swansea via Ystalyfera, a route operated only by single deckers, due to the extremely low bridge situated at Lower Cwmtwrch. (R.F. Mack collection.)

Captured here at College St. Ammanford, directly opposite Ammanford Bus Station, is the second and last Leyland Olympic in the fleet 211 (FTH 718), outside Dunns shoe-shop. (Photobus)

1950 all Leyland PD2/1 'Titan' 209 (FTH 683) is seen here leaving James' bus station at Ammanford through the College Street exit in 1960, bound for Brynamman. The low headroom at the depot exit is clearly visible in this view.

Parked outside James' Gurnos depot in the mid 1950's, are Leyland 'Titan' 206 (FTH 680) and Strachan bodied Leyland 'Tiger' 202 (DBX 638). The garage built in 1939 still exists today, virtually unchanged, as a heavy construction plant workshop. Note the low headroom inside this garage also.

By 1950, the 7 year old wartime Guy and Daimler 'utility bodied' deckers required extensive body repairs and modernisation to bring them in line with the remainder of the fleet. Due to the ruggedness and reliability of these Guy Arab and Daimler CWA6 chassis, the company decided to have the bodies refurbished over a period of 2 years; 1950/1. One of the Guy Arabs 171 (CBX 7) had its body overhauled locally by Jeffreys Coachworks, Neath Road, Plasmarl, Swansea. The oldest pair of Guy Arab's (169/170 (BTH 813/910 were sent to Chas. Roe Coachworks, Leeds, in 1951 and rebodied with new 53 seater lowbridge bodies, extending their life by another 9 years. The remaining Guy's together with all the Daimlers were refurbished by Bruce Coachworks (an associate company of East Lancs., Coachbuilders) at the old Cardiff Airport, Pengam, Cardiff. Extending their working life by several more years, their refurbishment included rubber mounted windows, to eliminate window rattles, modern headlamps, re-panelling and new 'dunlopillo' upholstered seating replaced the wooden slatted utility seats. In some cases the Guy's were retro-fitted with larger 6 cylinder Gardner 6LW engines, in exchange for their 5 cylinder 5LW units.

This 1943 Guy Arab MkI, number 169 (BTH 813) was one of a pair that were rebodied in 1951 by Chas H. Roe. In this view taken at Llanelly Railway Station in 1952, can be seen one of the Llanelly & District Traction Co.'s Leyland trolley buses shortly before their demise in 1952. (Roy Marshall collection.)

Guy Arab Mk1, 170 (BTH 910) was also rebodied by Chas. H. Roe in 1951. It is seen here parked up inside James' bus station in 1958 accompanied by PD1 and PD2 Leyland 'Titans' and the company's 'Canadian' Ford breakdown truck. Both Mk1 Arab's 169/170 were retrofitted with 6LW engines.

NATIONALISATION

After the General Election of 1945, a Labour government came to power, obtaining a mandate from the electorate to Nationalise all transport services. This inevitably resulted in the Transport Act of 1947, which empowered the government to make the necessary acquisitions of railways, road passenger services and road haulage services.

Nationalisation however was the next major episode in the company's history, as negotiations for James' business were completed on 19th September, 1950 - ending a great story of private enterprise and achievement. On the 1st October, 1950, this well established family business, J. James & Sons, Ltd., fell victim of the 1947 Transport Act and sadly became Nationalised. The whole undertaking with a fleet of 43 vehicles was purchased for £1/4 million, by the British Electric Traction Company Ltd., (B.E.T.) who already owned Western Welsh Omnibus Co. Ltd., and The South Wales Transport Co. Ltd.

Nevertheless the company retained its separate entity: J. James & Sons Ltd., Central Garages, Ammanford, along with the livery, as the policy of B.E.T. was to retain the identity of any medium sized fleets taken over by Nationalisation. The take-over inevitably gave the company a new registered office address at 'Piccadilly, London, W.1'. All James' employees were retained by the new owners, including Angus James the General Manager, who retained his position until retirement in 1962. His elder brothers, Percy and Lindsay, were retained in a non-supervisory capacity. Lindsay however, moved on in August 1951 purchasing a Hotel at Monmouth known as 'THE WHITE SWAN', which he ran with his wife, Lilian. Percy on the other hand retired in 1953 and sadly passed away 5 years later aged 67.

On 5th October, 1950, the local newspaper, Amman Valley Chronicle, reported the company's take-over:-

'J. JAMES & SONS LTD., ACQUIRED BY B.E.T.'

The whole share capital of J. James & Sons Ltd., Ammanford, operators of omnibus services in the counties of Carmarthen, Glamorgan and Cardigan has been acquired by British Electric Traction Company Ltd. The former directors have all retired from the board, and have been replaced by representatives of the B.E.T. company. Mr. W. T. James, O.B.E., a director of the B.E.T. is the new chairman. For the time being the company will continue to operate under the name of J. James & Sons Ltd., and Mr. Angus James, one of the former directors, remains as general manager.

The firm was founded over 50 years ago by the late Mr. John James; father of Angus James, who until the acquisition was the managing director, and of Lindsay and Percy James also directors. From a small beginning it became one of the leading omnibus companies in South Wales. The garage in College Street was extended from time to time and part of it occupies the site of the old Poole's Pictorium. The firm originally ran a service along the Amman Valley route, and to Neath, and gradually the few buses were increased in numbers to become one of the biggest fleets of buses operating in West Wales. Truly it can be said that John James was the pioneer of road passenger transport in the area, and his name became a household word over a wide area.

With the company under B.E.T. ownership, closer links were formed with neighbouring B.E.T. companies, Western Welsh Omnibus Co., and The South Wales Transport Co. James soon began a pattern of joint operation with S.W.T., on the Swansea Valley services, with return tickets becoming inter-changeable on common sections of the route from March 1951. Additionally, in keeping with other Ammanford area operators, James withdrew their workers special fares and introduced a revised scale of weekly and season tickets. Other changes were also evident after the take-over, including a noticeable major change to vehicle maintenance schedules. Western Welsh, having excellent workshop facilities at their 'Ely Works' (Central workshops) in Cardiff, undertook extensive overhaul and maintenance work on James' vehicles. They also took delivery of all James' new vehicles, carrying out a pre-delivery inspection on them before collection by James' staff. Surplus James vehicles were also stored at Ely Works pending disposal.

Strangely, the close association between the three companies still did not allow them to use James' bus station at Ammanford.

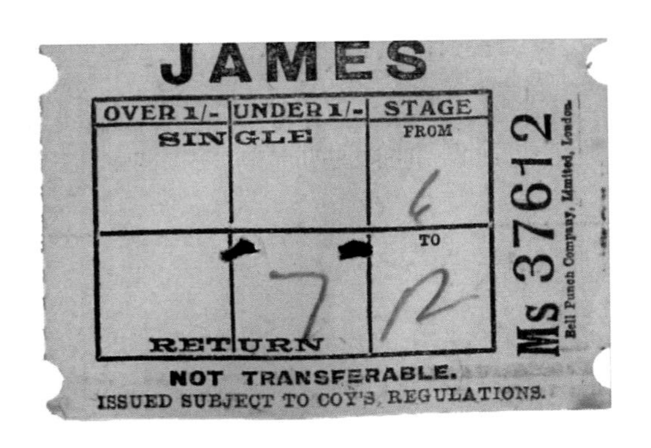

Colour photographs of vehicles operated by J. James & Sons Ltd. are extremely scarce. And have been difficult to track down. Nevertheless, I am indebted to Chris Carter of London, who had the foresight to capture on colour transparency, the view of James' 1946 Leyland PD1 'Titan', 198 (CTH 827) outside Llanelly Railway Station in June 1952 – when he visited Llanelly to photograph the Llanelly Trolleybus system. Unfortunately, this bus came to a very sad end in January 1959, when it overturned on an icy road at Glanamman, injuring several schoolchildren.

The first vehicle taken into stock after B.E.T. take over arrived a year later in September 1951. Numbered 212 (GTH 297) it was the company's first Leyland 'Royal Tiger'. This particular new type of passenger chassis from the Leyland factory had a 17 feet 6 inch wheel base, fitted with the 9.8 litre Leyland 0.600 power unit mounted horizontally under mid-floor. The body was built by Duple Coachworks to the new permitted length of 30 feet, and was followed 8 months later by another identical pair of 'Royal Tigers' 213/214 (HBX 60/1).

JAMES

DAY TOURS

FROM

CROSS HANDS

DURING MINERS' HOLIDAY WEEK—AUGUST 5–12, 1951

Day	Date	Tour to	Departure Time	Arrive Back about	Fare s. d.
Sunday	5th August ...	SAUNDERSFOOT ...	10.50 a.m. ...	9.40 p.m. ...	5 3
Monday	6th August ...	WYE VALLEY ...	10.00 a.m. ...	10.20 p.m. ...	11 6
Tuesday	7th August ...	RHAYADER ...	10.30 a.m. ...	9.30 p.m. ...	8 9
Wednesday	8th August ...	ABERYSTWYTH ...	9.15 a.m. ...	10.15 p.m. ...	8 6
Thursday	9th August ...	NEWQUAY ...	10.00 a.m. ...	10.00 p.m. ...	7 6
Friday	10th August ...	RHOSSILLY ...	11.30 a.m. ...	10.00 p.m. ...	4 6
Sunday	12th August ...	PORTHCAWL ...	1.40 p.m. ...	11.00 p.m. ...	5 6

All Tours start from **CROSS HANDS SQUARE.**

Picking up at Gorslas, Penygroes and Tumble.

Seats must be Booked in advance at **CENTRAL GARAGE, AMMANFORD** (Tele. 35)

or Booking Agents:

At Cross Hands: Howells & Jones, The Haven Fish and Chip Saloon, Cross Hands.
At Gorslas: Frank Jones, Regent Hairdressing Saloon (Tele: Cross Hands 28).
At Penygroes: Charles Thomas, Rhoslan, Norton Road, Penygroes.

The Company reserve the right to cancel the running of any vehicle in connection with an advertised journey should there be insufficient passengers or for any other reason, and they do not accept liability for loss or delay to passengers in connection with any journey.

Issued subject to the Regulations and Conditions published in the Company's Time-Tables, Bills and Notices. Such Regulations and Conditions may be inspected free of charge at any of the Company's Offices.

ANGUS JAMES, General Manager. **J. JAMES & SONS LTD., AMMANFORD.** Tele. Ammanford 35.

"Amman Valley Chronicle," Ammanford.

212(GTH 297) was the first 'Royal Tiger' to enter James' fleet. Bodied by Duple Coachworks at their Hendon works, it is pictured here about to leave the factory before delivery to South Wales. (R. Marshall collection.)

Two more Duple bodied 'Royal Tigers' were purchased by the company in 1952. The pair 213/214 (HBX 60/1) were almost identical in appearance to the first 'Royal Tiger' delivered 7 months earlier, except for an increased seating capacity of 44. 213 (HBX 60) is pictured here at the 'new' Swansea terminus, St. Mary's Square in 1958. (R. Marshall collection.)

This splendid rear off-side view of 'Royal Tiger' 213 (HBX 60) shows the unusual positioning of the emergency exit; in the centre of the vehicle's back end.

Captured here on colour film, is Duple bodied ' Royal Tiger' 212 (GTH 297) on a lay over at St. Mary's Square, Swansea, shortly before departure to Ammanford in 1960. The 'Royal Tigers' were regular performers of the Ammanford – Ystalyfera – Swansea service, as were the newer Weymann bodied 'Tiger Cubs'. The reason for their regular sightings on this route was due to a very low bridge at Lower Cwmtwrch in the upper Swansea Valley which was only negotiable by single decker buses.

Comparing this with an official view taken at the Duple factory before delivery in 1951, there is evidence of a major front end rebuild incorporating modified windscreens; the type fitted to Weymann bodied 'Tiger Cubs' (Photobus)

212 (GTH 297) is seen here at Ammanford Square negotiating the right hand turn from High Street into College Street on its return from Swansea.

In the meantime, the pattern of joint operation arranged between the three B.E.T. companies in the Amman Valley, seriously affected Rees & Williams' service; Brynamman to Ammanford and Carmarthen, resulting in their complete withdrawal of the route in November 1951. This meant that the Amman Valley route, once plied for by nine operators, was for the first time in 40 years reduced to three - all B.E.T. owned.

At the same time there were a number of small local coach operators applying to the Traffic Commissioners for licences to operate a variety of workers services, excursions and tours. After several objections from the established operators, including James, most applications were refused. However, when James themselves applied for extra licences in 1951 to provide 3 workmen's services of stage carriage, they were all granted as follows:

TGR 347/43: Ammanford (James' Bus Station) to Brynamman (Derlwyn Arms) via:- Glanamman, Garnant, Gwaun-Cae-Gurwen, Cwmgorse and Steer Pit. Granted September 1951 with condition (1) *The service of stage carriage (workmen's) to operate Monday to Friday, with Saturday journeys operated only on request from the National Coal Board.*

TGR 347/44: Ammanford (Pullman's Factory) to Brynamman (New Road) via:- Ammanford (James' Bus Station), Glanamman, Garnant, and Gwaun-Cae-Gurwen.
Granted September 1951 with condition (1) *The service of stage carriage (workmen's) to operate only when Pullman's Factory is working.*

TGR 347/45: Ammanford (James' Ammanford (Bus Station) to Pontyberem (Pentremawr Colliery)
via:- Saron, Capel Hendre (and/or via: Llandebie and Blaenau), Penygroes, Cross Hands, Drefach, Cwmmawr, Lower Tumble and Pontyberem. (2 separate routes). Granted February 1952 with condition (1) *The service of stage carriage (workmen's) to operate only when Pentremawr, Pontyberem, Blaenhirwaun, Cross Hands, Great Mountain and Tumble collieries are working.*

Eighteen months later the Ammanford to Pontyberem route TGR 347/45 was extended 2 miles beyond Pontyberem to reach Ponthenry (Post Office), after the Gwendraeth valley's passenger railway closed.

Furthermore, a short period 'special occasions' licence was granted to the company in March 1952 to operate special late night buses from the Regal Ballroom, Ammanford, after normal service hours at 11.50.p.m. on Saturdays or any other special occasion days, to any point on their main service routes outward from Ammanford.

On the other hand, the local stage carriage service TGR 347/38, from Ammanford (James' Bus Station) to Heol-ddu, (school days only) was withdrawn in April 1952, as it became unremunerative.

Meanwhile, on 30th April, 1952, competitor Edgar Jones trading as 'Brynteg Bus Company' abandoned his Ammanford to Hopkinstown service due to financial problems. Following Jones' failure the Ammanford Council persuaded Messrs. J. James & Sons, Ltd., to operate the Hopkinstown service on a trial basis. On 12th May, 1952, James applied for the licence previously held by Edgar Jones for the Hopkinstown service. They were immediately issued with temporary 'short period; licences: TGR 347/sp/8, 9, 10, 11 and 12 to continue Jones' service between Hopkinstown and Ammanford (Pullmans Factory). On 9th July, 1952 the licence was officially granted:-

TGR 347/47: Ammanford (Pullmans Factory) to Hopkinstown.
via:- Ammanford (James' Bus Station), Bettws Square, Waungron Road, and Maesyquarre Road.
Service of stage carriage to operate Mondays to Saturdays throughout the year.

At the same time, an application was made for a road service licence to operate a local school service:-

TGR 347/46: Penygroes (Waterloo Square) to Llandebie (Secondary Modern School)
via: Capel Hendre Square, Saron School, Blaenau Square and Llandebie Square.
Service of stage carriage to operate on school days only.

This service had previously been operated by Edgar Jones without a licence. The company were again issued with temporary 'short period' licences:- TGR 347/sp/4, 5, 6, and 7, to operate the service on a trial basis from 5th May to 30th May, 1952 inclusive. However, the full term application TGR 347/46 above was withdrawn by 30th May after the company decided they did not want the service.

As mentioned earlier, Edgar Jones, previously a driver employed by James didn't return to bus driving after his business venture collapsed, instead he made a complete change and drove coal lorries.

In August 1953, four express carriage licences were applied for to provide special services for pantomime performances held at Swansea and Llanelly. All four licences granted in October 1953 were:

TGR 347/48: Gwaun-Cae-Gurwen to Swansea (Grand and Empire Theatres),
via:- Brynamman, Cwmllynfell, Ystalyfera, Pontardawe, Clydach and Morriston.

TGR 347/49: Ammanford (James' Bus Station) to Swansea (Grand and Empire Theatres),
via: Glanamman, Garnant, Gwaun-Cae-Gurwen, Cwmgorse, Pontardawe, Clydach and Morriston.

TGR 347/50: Ammanford (James' Bus Station) to Llanelly (Astoria Theatre),
via: Saron, Capel Hendre, Brynawel, Penygroes, Gorslas, Cross Hands Square, Upper Tumble, Llannon and Ystradfai.

TGR 347/51: Ammanford (James' Bus Station) to Swansea (Grand and Empire Theatres),
via:- Bettws, Cathan Terrace, Garnswllt, Troedyrhiw, Ynys, Pontardulais and Penllergaer.

Special conditions attached to the above licences were:

(1) The service to be operated as required on the occasions of matinee and evening performances of pantomimes at The Grand and Empire Theatres, Swansea, and/or Astoria Theatre, Llanelly.

(2) *To leave 2 hours prior to the commencement of, and to return from the Theatres as soon as possible after the performance.*

(3) *Return fares only to be issued, and these are to be as already authorised for the stage carriage service except that the minimum fare will be 1/- (one shilling).*

(4) *Double decker vehicles to be used on each service (except TGR 347/48, where double deckers will only be used from Cwmtwrch to Swansea).*

Bus 216 (JBX941) is captured here at Gurnos depot.

JAMES

TOURS & EXCURSIONS

FROM

AMMANFORD

CORONATION WEEK

	Leave	Arrive back	Fare
Sunday (31st May, 1953)			
Porthcawl	‡12.00 noon	10.30 p.m.	4/9
Caswell Bay	x 2.00 p.m.	8.30 p.m.	3/6
Monday (1st June, 1953)			
St. David's and Fishguard	*10.00 a.m.	10.00 p.m.	9/9
Aberystwyth	† 9.15 a.m.	10.15 p.m.	8/6
Tuesday (2nd June, 1953)			
Cader Idris, Dolgelly, Aberdovey	† 9.30 a.m.	10.00 p.m.	13/6
Caswell Bay	x 2.00 p.m.	9.00 p.m.	3/6
Wednesday (3rd June, 1953)			
Tenby	*10.00 a.m.	9.30 p.m.	6/6
Mystery Tour	5.00 p.m.	10.00 p.m.	5/9
Thursday (4th June, 1953)			
Aberystwyth	† 9.15 a.m.	10.15 p.m.	8/6
Caswell Bay	x 2.00 p.m.	9.00 p.m.	3/6
Friday (5th June, 1953)			
Barry	‡10.00 a.m.	10.00 p.m.	7/9
Mystery Tour	5.30 p.m.	10.00 p.m.	4/9

* Picks up en route to Capel Hendre. † Picks up en route to Llandebie.
‡ Picks up en route to Gwaun-cae-gurwen. || Picks up en route to Brynamman.
x Picks up en route to Tycroes.

ALL TOURS START FROM CENTRAL GARAGES, AMMANFORD.

Seats must be booked in advance from Central Garages, Ammanford (Tel. 35).

The Company Reserve the Right to Cancel the running of any vehicle in connection with an Advertised Journey should there be insufficient passengers or for any other reason, and they do not accept liability for loss or delay to passengers in connection with any journey.

Issued subject to the Regulations and Conditions published in the Company's Time-Tables, Bills and Notices. Such Regulations and Conditions may be inspected, free of charge, at any of the Company's Offices.

J. JAMES & SONS, LTD. AMMANFORD

(Tel. Ammanford 35). ANGUS JAMES, General Manager.

JAMES

TOURS & EXCURSIONS

FROM

AMMANFORD

WHITSUN WEEK

	Leave	Arrive back	Fare
Whit-Sunday, (24th May, 1953)			
Tenby	*10.40 a.m.v	10.00 p.m.	6/6
Whit-Monday (25th May, 1953)			
Rhayader, Elan Valley, Devil's Bridge . .	†10.15 a.m.	10.00 p.m.	10/9
Porthcawl	‡12.00 noon	10.30 p.m.	4/9
Whit-Tuesday (26th May, 1953)			
Aberdovey	† 9.30 a.m.	9.30 p.m.	12/0
Barry	‡10.00 a.m.	10.00 p.m.	7/9
Wednesday, 27th May, 1953			
Wye Valley	†10.00 a.m.	10.00 p.m.	11/6
Tenby	* 9.45 a.m.	9.15 p.m.	6/6
Thursday, 28th May, 1953			
Hereford	9.15 a.m.	10.00 p.m.	11/0
Mystery Tour	2.00 p.m.	9.15 p.m.	7/0
Friday, 29th May, 1953			
Cardigan Bay	† 9.00 a.m.	10.00 p.m.	9/9
Caswell Bay	x 2.00 p.m.	9.00 p.m.	3/6
Saturday, 30th May, 1953			
Aberystwyth	† 9.15 a.m.	10.15 p.m.	8/6

v Connects with Western Welsh arriving from Neath 10.35 a.m.
* Picks up en route to Capel Hendre. † Picks up en route to Llandebie.
‡ Picks up en route to Gwaun-cae-gurwen. ‖ Picks up en route to Brynamman
x Picks up en route to Tycroes.

ALL TOURS START FROM CENTRAL GARAGES, AMMANFORD.

Seats must be booked in advance from Central Garages, Ammanford (Tel. 35).

The Company Reserve the Right to Cancel the running of any vehicle in connection with an Advertised Journey should there be insufficient passengers or for any other reason, and they do not accept liability for loss or delay to passengers in connection with any journey.

Issued subject to the Regulations and Conditions published in the Company's Time-Tables, Bills and Notices. Such Regulations and Conditions may be inspected, free of charge, at any of the Company's Offices.

J. JAMES & SONS, LTD. AMMANFORD

(Tel. Ammanford 35). ANGUS JAMES, General Manager.

J. JAMES & SONS, LTD.

BLACKPOOL ILLUMINATIONS

11th SEPTEMBER TO 25th OCTOBER, 1953

Commencing Friday, Sept. 18th

Trips to Blackpool will operate each Friday, departing Ammanford 8 p.m., returning from Blackpool 12 noon on Sundays, during period of Illuminations

FARE - 30/-

Accommodation for Saturday nights can be booked in advance if required

ALL TOURS START FROM CENTRAL GARAGES, AMMANFORD

(Passengers picked up en route to Llandebie)

Seats must be booked in advance at Central Garages, Ammanford (Tel.: 35)

The Company Reserve the Right to Cancel the running of any vehicle [illegible] connection with an Advertised Joruney should there be insufficient passengers or for any other reason, and they do not accept liability for loss or delay to passengers in connection with any [illegible]ourney

Issued subject to the Regulations and Conditions published in the Company's Time-Tables, Bills and Notices. Such Regulations and Conditions may be inspected, free of charge, at any of the Company's Offices.

J. JAMES & SONS, LTD., AMMANFORD

(Tel:. Ammanford 35) ANGUS JAMES, General Manager.

J. JAMES & SONS, LTD.

PANTOMIME SEASON
SWANSEA - 1953/54

EMPIRE THEATRE

ALADDIN AND HIS WONDERFUL LAMP

Commencing 24th December, 1953

GRAND THEATRE

GOLDILOCKS AND THE THREE BEARS

Commencing 26th December, 1953

TO ORGANISERS OF PRIVATE PARTIES

WE ARE LICENSED TO CARRY PRIVATE PARTIES TO EITHER OF THE ABOVE PANTOMIMES DURING THE SEASON, AND CAN ALSO BOOK YOUR THEATRE TICKETS IN ADVANCE

LET US ARRANGE ALL DETAILS FOR YOU

For further information enquire at the Company's Offices

Central Garages, AMMANFORD

J. JAMES & SONS, LTD.

Telephone: Ammanford 25

In September 1953, five and a half years after nationalisation of the railways, the new railway executive 'British Railways' withdrew passenger services on the Gwendraeth Valley branch line (Cwmmawr to Burry Port). The railway with its antiquated rolling stock had been James' last competitor on the Ammanford to Burry Port route. After the railways closure on 21st September, 1953, James modified their two Gwendraeth Valley services, diverting them into the centre of Ponthenry village, as buses were now the only transport link between the Gwendraeth Valley villages and Burry Port town.

Two months later the company were the subject of a lengthy inquiry, held at Swansea's Guildhall in November and December 1953. Eleven local authorities from the area appealed to the Ministry of Transport against the fare increases granted to J. James & Sons Ltd., in March 1953. The increases had been granted specifically to bring the company's fares in line with the fares charged by other companies operating the same routes in the Swansea Valley - a case of coming into line and charging uniform fares. The company claimed they needed additional finances in order to pay for extra operational expenses and income tax liabilities. It was allegedly said that James were a very prosperous company showing surpluses, and revenue of such extent, making it clear that no increases were justified. It was also stated that revenue per mile was higher than that of any other company in the area, and profit per bus was not only the highest in South Wales but the highest within the B.E.T. group, allowing the company to pay a dividend of 10% to their shareholders.

After the inquiry ended in July 1954, the Transport Minister decided not to make any order on the South Wales Traffic Area Licencing Authority, in respect of the appeal made by the local authorities. He also decided to exercise his powers under section 47 of the Road & Rail Act 1933; that all costs incurred by him in conjunction with the inquiry shall be divided equally between the appellants. However, when the company applied for another fares increase 17 months later, calculated on scales involving mileages, they were refused.

During the early part of 1954, four more Road Service Licences were applied for:

TGR 347/52: Excursions & Tours starting from Ammanford (James' Bus Station), with pick up points at Tycroes, Saron, Capel Hendre and Llandebie.
Granted in April 1954, this licence superseded the 'Excursions & Tours' licence TGR 347/6, three months later.

TGR 347/53: Ammanford (James' Bus Station) to Saron (Square).
via:- Wind Street, Penybank (Golden Lion), Ammanford Road (Tycroes) and Cwmfferws Road.
Service of stage carriage to operate Mondays to Saturdays. Granted in May 1954, it superseded application TGR 347/33; Ammanford (Wind Street) to Tycroes (Square), which in turn was surrendered two months later.

TGR 347/54: Ammanford (James' Bus Station) to Garnswllt (Square),
via:- Bettws and Cathan Terrace.
Service of stage carriage to operate daily, Sundays to Saturdays, was also granted in May 1954. This service was originally authorised under application TGR 347/34; Ammanford to Pontardulais (which continued), but the journeys operating between Ammanford (James' Bus Station) and Garnswllt Square only, became authorised separately on TGR 347/54.

TGR 347/55: Was an application made in August 1954 for stage carriage service between any two points specified on existing stage carriage licences held by the company. The services were to operate after cessation of normal services, as required, to cater for late dances, special events, etc. Fares:- before midnight, ordinary single fares, after midnight, double ordinary single fares. Return tickets were not available. The licence was granted in November 1954.

Furthermore, in August 1954 modifications were granted to licence applications TGR 347/2 and TGR 347/41, permitting inward journeys to Neath Railway Station, to deviate and set down passengers at Victoria Gardens (Neath).

J. JAMES & SONS, LTD.

CENTRAL GARAGES, AMMANFORD

ROYAL WELSH SHOW MACHYNLLETH

WEDNESDAY, THURSDAY and FRIDAY, JULY 21st, 22nd and 23rd, 1954

COACH TRIPS

will be operated to the above Show as follows:

Depart Ammanford 8 a.m.* Depart Machynlleth 7.15 p.m.
Arrive back about 10.30 p.m.

Fare - 10/6

*** Departs from Central Garages and picks up en route to Llandebie**

All Seats must be booked in advance from Central Garages, Ammanford (Tel.: 35)

The Company Reserve the Right to Cancel the running of any vehicles in connection with an Advertised Journey should there be insufficient passengers or for any other reason, and they do not accept liability for loss or delay to passengers in connection with any journey

Issued subject to the Regulations and Conditions published in the Company's Time Tables, Bills and Notices. Such Regulations and Conditions may be inspected, free of charge, at any of the Company's Offices.

ANGUS JAMES, General Manager.

J. JAMES & SONS, LTD.

CENTRAL GARAGES - AMMANFORD

PORTHCAWL FIREWORKS DISPLAYS

A Coach will leave Central Garages, Ammanford, every Thursday, Friday and Saturday (except Thursday, 30th September), until 2nd October, 1954, as follows:

THURSDAYS & FRIDAYS

Depart Central Garages, Ammanford ... 5 p.m.

SATURDAYS

Depart Central Garages, Ammanford ... 5.45 p.m.

The Return Journey will be made within 15 minutes after Termination of Display

FARE: Adults, 4/9; Children, 3/3

Seats must be booked in advance at Central Garages, Ammanford (Tel. 35)

The Company Reserve the Right to Cancel the running of any vehicle in connection with an Advertised Journey should there be insufficient passengers or for any other reason, and they do not accept liability for loss or delay to passengers in connection with any journey

Issued subject to the Regulations and Conditions published in the Company's Time-Tables, Bills and Notices. Such Regulations and Conditions may be inspected, free of charge, at any of the Company's Offices.

J. JAMES & SONS, LTD., AMMANFORD

(Tel. Ammanford 35) ANGUS JAMES, General Manager.

On the other hand, new vehicle deliveries during 1954 only amounted to three. There were two Leyland 'Titan' PD2/12 deckers, 215/216 (JBX 940/1) with Leyland 53-seat lowbridge bodies, delivered in February that year, which were the last in a long line of Leyland bodied vehicles purchased by the company, as Leyland Motors closed their bodybuilding factory in late 1954 to concentrate solely on chassis manufacture. The other vehicle acquired in 1954 was the first luxury coach purchased for several years, 217 (JTH 291) a Leyland 'Royal Tiger' PSU1/16 with attractive but heavy Burlingham 'Seagull' 39 seat coach body, arriving in April that year ready for the summer season's tours.

For several years after W.W. II ended there were no luxury coaches in the fleet. Saloon buses were used for private hire and coach travel, with deckers supplementing saloons on Sunday-school outings to the seaside. Twenty years had lapsed before this stylish 'Seagull' coach, 217 (JTH 291) arrived in April 1954. Bodied by H. V. Burlingham of Blackpool, the 'Seagull' 39 seat body with centre entrance was fitted to a Leyland 'Royal Tiger' PSU1/16 chassis, and was used mainly for the advertised tours operated by the company.

215 (JBX 940) was one of a pair of Leyland 'Titan' PD2's purchased in 1954. The Leyland 53 seat body was regarded by many as a '*classic design*' and was the ultimate Leyland double decker body style. Production of Leyland bodies ceased altogether in late 1954. 215 is seen here at Wind Street, Ammanford in 1962, on route to nearby Pantyffynnon. (P. Yeoman collection)

Photographed outside Aberystwyth Railway Station in 1958 is Leyland 'Titan' PD2, 216 (JBX 941) about to depart on its lengthy 3 hour; 61 mile return journey to Ammanford. (C. Carter collection.)

However, the company's advertised day tours proved to be very popular in the community, with new destinations further a field explored each season, i.e. North Wales, Shrewsbury, Birmingham, Bourton-on-the Water, Stratford-upon-Avon, Bristol Zoo and Blackpool for the illuminations. Extra booking agents were recruited to cope with the demand, one of these being L.C.W. Motors, the omnibus proprietors at Llandilo. Simultaneously they extended the tour season by nine weeks, to start third week of May and finish at the end of August, (previously only 4 weeks during August). In fact, one very satisfied passenger wrote to the local newspaper giving a detailed account of his exhilarating day tour of the Elan Valley, and his verdict: 'CARRY ON JAMES AND DON'T SPARE THE HORSEPOWER.'

A new addition to the day tours itinerary in 1955 was the introduction of combined coach and boat cruises, sailing from Swansea Docks across the Bristol Channel to Ilfracome, Bideford, Clovelly and Western-Super-Mare.

The paddle steamer "Lady Moyra" is pictured here leaving Swansea Docks for an evening cruise in Swansea Bay and the Bristol Channel.

WHITE FUNNEL FLEET

DAY TOURS

FROM

AMMANFORD

in conjunction with

J. JAMES & SONS LTD.

DURING MINERS' HOLIDAY, JULY 3rd to 16th, 1955

Day	Date	Tour	Depart James Garage	Depart Swansea Docks	Return Journey Depart	Arrive Ammanford Approx.	Fare
Sun.	3rd ...	†ILFRACOMBE ... ... Approx. 8 hours ashore.	8.50 a.m. ...	10.00 a.m. ...	8.00 p.m. ...	11.00 p.m. ...	16 6
Mon.	4th ...	*ILFRACOMBE ... ... & BIDEFORD (Afternoon)	7.45 a.m. ...	9.00 a.m. ...	8.20 p.m. ... 6.35 p.m.	11.20 p.m. ...	16 6 20 6
Tues.	5th ...	†Evening Cruise SCARWEATHER LIGHT SHIP	6.30 p.m. ...	7.40 p.m. ...	— ...	10.40 p.m. ...	6 6
Wed.	6th ...	*ILFRACOMBE ... ... & CLOVELLY	8.35 a.m. ...	9.45 a.m. ...	7.15 p.m. ... 5.20 p.m.	10.15 p.m. ...	16 6 20 6
Thurs.	7th ...	†Evening Cruise PORTHCAWL (not to land)	6.40 p.m. ...	7.50 p.m.	—	11.00 p.m. ...	6 6
Sat.	9th ...	*ILFRACOMBE ... ... Approx. 7½ hours ashore.	8.00 a.m. ...	9.15 a.m. ...	7.15 p.m. ...	10.15 p.m. ...	16 6
Sun.	10th ...	†WESTON-SUPER-MARE ... Calling PORT TALBOT, PORTHCAWL and BARRY	8.20 a.m. ...	9.30 a.m. ...	7.00 p.m. ...	12.15 a.m. ...	16 6
Tues.	12th ...	*Evening Cruise PORTHCAWL (not to land)	7.20 p.m. ...	8.30 p.m.	—	11.45 p.m. ...	6 6
Wed.	13th ...	†ILFRACOMBE ... ... & LUNDY ISLAND	7.50 a.m. ...	9.00 a.m. ...	6.15 p.m. ... 4.30 p.m.	9.15 p.m. ...	16 6 21 6
Thurs.	14th ...	*ILFRACOMBE ... ... & CLOVELLY	7.50 a.m. ...	9.00 a.m. ...	5.15 p.m. ... 3.30 p.m.	8.15 p.m. ...	16 6 20 6
Fri.	15th ...	†ILFRACOMBE ... ... CLOVELLY & LUNDY ISLAND	7.20 a.m. ...	8.30 a.m. ...	7.00 p.m. ... 4.40 p.m. 3.30 p.m.	10.00 p.m. ...	16 6 20 6 21 6
Sat.	16th ...	*ILFRACOMBE ... ... 8 hours ashore.	8.15 a.m. ...	9.30 a.m. ...	6.15 p.m. ...	9.15 p.m. ...	16 6

† Picks up en-route to GWAUN-CAE-GURWEN * Picks up en-route to TYCROES

SEATS MUST BE BOOKED IN ADVANCE AT CENTRAL GARAGE, AMMANFORD (Tel 35).

The Companies reserve the right to cancel the running of any vehicle or vessel in connection with an advertised journey should there be insufficient passengers or for any other reason, and they do not accept liability for loss or delay to passengers in connection with any journey.

Issued subject to the Regulations and Conditions published in the Companies' Time-Tables, Bills and Notices. Such Regulations and Conditions may be inspected free of charge at any of the Companies' Offices and on their steamers.

Jones & Mainwaring (Printers) Ltd., Ammanford

In August 1955, an application was made for another Road Service Licence to provide a workmens service of stage carriage. The licence granted in October that year was:-

TGR 347/56: Ystalyfera (Pwllbach Yard) to Pwllbach Colliery,
via: Tirbach Road.
Service of stage carriage to operate daily including Sundays, only when Pwllbach Colliery is working, jointly operated between J. James & Sons Ltd., South Wales Transport Co. Ltd., and United Welsh Services Ltd., with interchangeable return tickets.

New vehicle purchases for 1955 were a pair of Leyland 'Tiger Cub' 44 seater saloons, 218/219 (KBX 997/8) bodied by Weymann. The 'Tiger Cubs' were regarded as being remarkably economical, having a fuel consumption of 13.6 M.P.G. from their 5.7 litre Leyland 0.350 'underslung' engines. They were followed by two more identical 'Tiger Cubs', in September 1956. Registered (NBX 77/78), these were given fleet numbers 220/221 respectively.

The first Leyland Tiger Cub in James' fleet was 218 (KBX 997) in February 1955.
Fitted with a Weymann 44 seat bus body it is pictured here in 1958 passing Ammanford Police Station in College Street, heading North for Lampeter via Llandilo.

Weymann bodied 'Tiger Cub' 219 (KBX 998) is seen here in 1961 outside the Margaret Street entrance of James' Bus Station in Ammanford.

Delivery of the new 'Tiger Cubs' and 'Royal Tigers' mentioned earlier, between 1952 and 1955 not only updated and modernised the fleet, but ousted most of the old fashioned looking halfcab 'Tigers'. Surprisingly, two redundant 'Tigers' 204/205 (EBX 662/3) were taken to Western Welsh Omnibus Co.'s Ely Works at Cardiff in early 1954 where their 5½-year-old Strachan saloon bodies were removed and scrapped. Their chassis were overhauled by Western Welsh and rebuilt from PS1 to PD1 (double decker) specification by incorporating new chassis members. The rebuilt chassis were then despatched to Longwell Green Coachworks at Bristol, where they received new 55 seat Longwell Green lowbridge double decker bodies in April 1954.

The following year three more surplus 'Tigers', 194/201/203 (CTH 615, DBX 637, DTH 722) were similarly treated; stripped of their saloon bodies and rebuilt to PD1 specification also at Ely Works. Their rebuilt chassis however, were dispatched to Metropolitan-Cammell-Weymann's Coachworks (M.C.W.), where they were fitted with attractive new M.C.W. 'Orion' 55 seat lowbridge double decker bodies.

Numerous people questioned the company's decision to re-body five redundant Leyland 'Tigers' into double deckers. It was simply a cost cutting exercise - the cheapest option of replacing older non-standard wartime utility vehicles with Leylands - the General Manager's preference. The five rebodied 'Tigers' replaced the five utility Daimler CWA6's.

After delivery of more new 'Tiger Cubs' in late 1956, two of the remaining three 'Tigers' had to be disposed of. This, again, was a difficult choice as the oldest 'Tiger' 193 had the best body. It was then decided to remove the Burlingham saloon body from 193, scrap its chassis and donate the body to a newer PS1 'Tiger' chassis, that of 200 (DBX 260), giving it an extended life. The extensive work was again carried out by Western Welsh at Ely Works, and the original Strachan body removed from 200 was afterwards fitted to the chasis of 193 for disposal, along with the other surplus 'Tiger' 199.

Seen here at Church Street, Ammanford during its daytime layover in 1960 is 194 (CTH 615), one of the Leyland 'Tiger' PS1 rebuilds. This one received a new M.C.W. 'Orion' lowbridge body in 1955. After its withdrawal in 1961, the body was transferred to Leyland 'Titan', 208 (FTH 682).

Leyland 'Tiger' PS1 201 (DBX 637) is seen here at College Street, Ammanford with its original Strachan body, before receiving its new double decker body - seen in the next photograph.

201(DBX 637) seen above as a single decker was another Leyland 'Tiger' PS1 rebuild. It is pictured here at Neath, soon after receiving its new M.C.W. 'Orion' body in 1955. After withdrawal from service in early 1961, the body was removed and fitted to Leyland 'Titan' 207 (FTH 681) in April, 1961, and its chassis subsequently scrapped.

Pictured here at Margaret Street, Ammanford in 1960, about to negotiate the bus station entrance is 203 (DTH 722) another PS1 'Tiger' rebuild. This one was also fitted with a new M.C.W. 'Orion' 55 seat lowbridge body, and after withdrawal in 1961, the body was transferred to Leyland 'Titan' 206 (FTH 680) and its chassis scrapped. Close behind 203 can be seen 207 (FTH 681) an all Leyland PD2 of 1950 vintage.

204/205 were the first two Leyland 'Tigers' to be rebuilt into double deckers in early 1954, both receiving new Longwell Green 55 seat lowbridge bodies. During the rebuild, this vehicle, 204 (EBX 662) received a chrome radiator surround as shown in this photograph taken at Church Street, Ammanford in 1956. Parked behind 204 is another PS1 'Tiger', 202 (DBX 638) carrying a Strachan B32F saloon body, identical to the body originally carried by 204. When 204 was withdrawn in 1961, its body was removed and fitted to Leyland 'Titan' 209 (FTH 683) (R. Marshall collection.)

Pictured here at College Street, Ammanford, negotiating the right hand turn into Margaret Street is Leyland 'Tiger' rebuild 205 (EBX 663). This also received a new Longwell Green 55 seat lowbridge body in 1954. 205 was suitably adapted with a sliding window partition behind the drivers cab, which gave the vehicle a second role as a driver training vehicle.

Photographed after sale to Eynon's of Trimsaran, is Leyland PS1 ' Tiger', 200 (DBX 260) of 1947 vintage, carrying the second hand 1946 Burlingham 34 seat body removed from James' 193 (CTH 490), another PS1 'Tiger' during James' ownership in 1957. A picture of this vehicle carrying its original body can be seen earlier in this book.

During the 1950's Swansea town centre was extensively rebuilt following the wartime blitz. As a result of this redevelopment, the terminus for James' Swansea Valley services at Trinity Place was permanently moved to a new terminus, 450 yards away at St. Mary's Square in 1956.

On the other hand, fuel rationing was implemented by the government in December 1956, brought about by a severe shortage of crude oil due to troubles in the Middle East and Suez Canal. The company were then reluctantly compelled to revise all timetables, to reduce services and conserve fuel - the first time since W.W.II ended. The comparatively new local service: Ammanford to Saron via Penybank and Cwmfferws Road (TGR 347/53) was permanently withdrawn.

Coupled to the fuel shortage was a massive increase in fuel prices. With a surcharge of 20% imposed, the cost inevitably had to be passed on to the travelling public. Bearing this in mind, a fares increase of only 8.5% was granted to the company in January 1957, after objections from 12 local authorities at the public hearing. Four months later however, the surcharge was removed and fares reverted back to normal, with the company bearing an additional 4d per gallon cost of fuel over the pre-Suez crisis price..

At the same time, the company took part in a National campaign to abolish the tax (duty) of 250% on fuel oil used in buses and coaches, which attributed to fare increases nationally. The campaign supported by The Passenger Vehicle Operators Association, The Public Transport Association, and The Municipal Road Passenger Transport Association, was backed with leaflets distributed to passengers and posters displayed on all buses.

Nevertheless, new vehicles continued to arrive at Ammanford, with two more 'Tiger Cubs' 220/1 (NBX 77/8) arriving in September 1956. In 1957 the first 8 feet wide, 30 feet long double deckers arrived, seven years after government legislation permitted an increase in maximum overall length from 27 feet 6 inches. Fitted with Weymann 67 seat lowbridge bodies, the pair of Leyland 'Titan' PD3's, 223/224 (NTH 850/1) were joined by a solitary PD2/12 'Titan', fitted with M.C.W. 'Orion' body, 222 (NTH 33). All three entered service in June 1957, and were ironically the last traditional type front engined vehicles acquired. Two months later the last pair of 'Tiger Cubs' acquired, 225/226 (OBX 780/1) went into service.

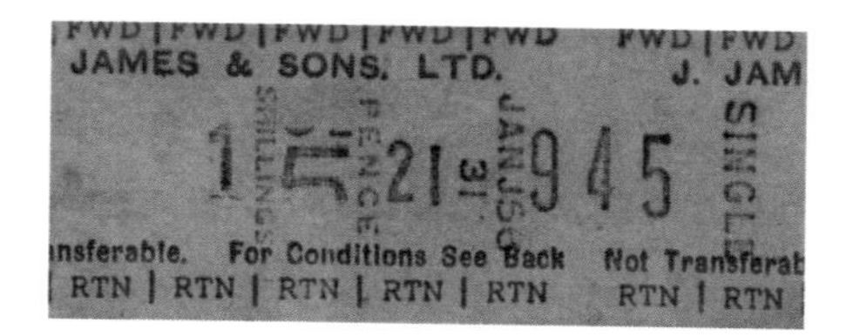

Another Weymann bodied 'Tiger Cub' 220 (NBX 77) was new in 1956. It is seen here in Ammanford, turning right from College Street into Margaret Street (outside the Co-operative Stores), on arrival from Swansea and the Amman Valley in 1961. Note the little green light clearly visible above the nearside windscreen - a prominent feature of James' buses, used to identify an approaching JAMES bus during the hours of darkness.

Weymann bodied Leyland PSUC1/1 'Tiger Cub' 221 (NBX 78) is pictured here at Castle Square, Swansea, passing the ruin of Swansea Castle and original office premises of the 'South Wales Evening Post' newspaper. R. F. Mack collection.

M.C.W. 'Orion' bodied PD2/12 'Titan' 222 (NTH 33) is seen here dropping off passengers at Broadway, Llanelly in 1959, on route from Ammanford to Llanelly Railway Station. Broadway, a street which ran parallel with lower Stepney Street disappeared in later years with the redevelopment of Llanelly town centre. (R.F. Mack collection)

223 (NTH 850) was numerically the first of only two Leyland PD3 (8 feet wide) 'Titan's acquired by the company in 1957. It is pictured here opposite Ammanford Police Station, College Street, in 1960 working the afternoon shift journey to Pentremawr Colliery, Pontyberem. Clearly visible behind 223 is an Ex War Department Austin lorry, once a common sight on the roads of South Wales, 'snapped up' usually 'by hauliers and coal merchants.

Photographed at College Street, Ammanford, on route to Burry Port in 1959 is 224 (NTH 851) the second and last Weymann bodied PD3 'Titan' acquired by the company. The 'Titans' 222 - 224 however were the only deckers fitted with rear platform doors. Was this a sign of the tough old colliers weakening?

The last vehicle fitted with the famous 'green lamp' was this Leyland PSUC1/1'Tiger Cub', 226 (OBX 781). It was also the last 'Tiger Cub' and the last single decker acquired by the company in 1957. 226 is pictured here at College Street, Ammanford, opposite James' Bus Station on its return journey from Swansea and the Amman Valley. Note the 'Regent' petrol pump on the pavement outside Shepherd's the Ironmongers shop (situated on the extreme right of the photograph). This method of selling petrol across the pavement became illegal many years ago.

Tiger Cub' 225 (OBX 780) is seen here at Garnant in the Amman Valley heading for Swansea with a full load of passengers in 1958.

J. James & Sons Ltd.

Easter Holiday - 1957

EXCURSIONS AND TOURS

FROM

AMMANFORD

Day	Date	Tour	Departure Time	Arrive Back About	Fare s. d.
Easter Sunday	21st April	*TENBY, via Saron, Capel Hendre, Gorslas, Cross Hands, Porthyrhyd, Carmarthen, St. Clears, Red Roses, Begelly, Hill, New Hedges.	v10.40 a.m.	10.00 p.m.	7/9
		‡PORTHCAWL, via Garnant, Neath, Port Talbot. (5½ hours at Porthcawl)	1.30 p.m.	10.30 p.m.	5/9
Easter Monday	22nd April	‡CHEPSTOW RACES, via Garnant, Gwmgors Pontardawe, Neath, Port Talbot, Pyle, Cowbridge Cardiff, Newport, Blakeney.	9.00 a.m.	10.00 p.m.	12/9
		†STRATFORD-ON-AVON, via Llandovery, Brecon, Bronllys, Glasbury, Witney, Willersley, Hereford, Bromyard, Worcester, Alcester, Stratford-on-Avon (1.00 p.m. — 5.30 p.m.) Alcester, Worcester, Bromyard, Hereford, Witney Brecon, Llandovery.	8.00 a.m.	10.30 p.m.	19/0
		‡PORTHCAWL, via Garnant, Neath, Port Talbot. (5½ hours at Porthcawl)	1.30 p.m.	10.30 p.m.	5/9
Easter Tuesday	23rd April	†RHAYADER, ELAN VALLEY, CLAERWEN DAM, via Llandeilo, Llandovery, Builth (11.45 a.m.—1.00 p.m.), Rhayader, Elan Valley, Claerwen Dam (2.00 p.m.—2.30 p.m.) Rhayader, Llangurig, Ponterwyd, Devil's Bridge, Aberystwyth (5.00 p.m.—7.15 p.m.). Aberayron, Lampeter, Llanwrda, Llandeilo.	9.45 a.m.	10.00 p.m.	12/9
		‡CHEPSTOW RACES, via Garnant, Cwmgors, Pontardawe, Neath, Port Talbot, Pyle, Cowbridge Cardiff, Newport, Blakeney.	9.00 a.m.	10.00 p.m.	12/9

† Picks up en route to Llandebie. ‡ Picks up en route to Gwaun-Cae-Gurwen

v Waits for Western Welsh bus from Neath * Picks up en route to Capel Hendre

ALL TOURS START FROM CENTRAL GARAGES, AMMANFORD.

Seats must be booked in advance from Central Garages, Ammanford (Tel. 35).

The Company Reserve the Right to Cancel the running of any vehicles in connection with an Advertised Journey should there be insufficient passengers or for any other reason, and they do not accept liability for loss or delay to passengers in connection with any journey.

Issued subject to the Regulations and Conditions published in the Company's Time-Tables, Bills and Notices. Such Regulations and Conditions may be inspected, free of charge, at any of the Company's Offices.

J. JAMES & SONS, LTD., AMMANFORD

(Tel.: Ammanford 35). ANGUS JAMES, General Manager

As the 1950's progressed, there was a slow decline in public transport nationally, caused mainly by public ownership of motor cars. By 1958 however, only 8 years after nationalisation, James' fleet had been reduced by 11%; from 43 to 38 vehicles. Railways were also in decline, losing revenue due to lack of passengers. This inevitably resulted in the British Transport Commission's decision to close the Brynamman to Pantyffynnon branch line to passenger traffic in August 1958, as the service had become unremunerative. The railways closure marked not only the end of an era in the Amman Valley, but the end of James' lengthy battle against the railway company previously known as the 'Great Western Railway' (G.W.R.); between Ammanford and Brynamman which had started 39 years earlier.

Closure of the railway inevitably caused problems to the valley's bus service at peak periods. Buses were seriously overloaded, with school children having to sit 3 to-a-seat, stand on open rear platforms or being left behind. This intolerable situation eventually forced the Education Department to provide special school buses for children attending the Valley schools of Amman Valley Grammar School and Ammanford, Llandebie, Pontardulais Secondary Modern Schools.

On the other hand, in November 1958 the National Coal Board asked the company to provide a workers service to Mount Colliery near Ammanford. The company promptly applied for a R.S.L., to operate the service:

TGR 347/57: Ammanford (James' Bus Station) to Mount Colliery, via:-
(a) College Street., Quay Street, Colonel Road, Waungron, Maesquarre Road, and unclassified road to Mount Colliery.
(b) College Street, High Street, Pontamman Bridge, Maesquarre Road, Pentwyn Road, Colonel Road, Waungron, Maesquarre Road and unclassified road to Mount Colliery.

Two special short-term licences were issued to run the daily service from 16th November to 15th March, 1959 inclusive, but for unknown reasons the licence application was withdrawn after three months.

At this point in time however, the whole emphasis was changing to larger capacity passenger vehicles. Consequently, after six years developing and experimenting with prototype chassis, Leyland Motors Ltd., introduced a completely new revolutionary double decker chassis in 1958. Designated PDR1/1 and named the 'Atlantean' it boasted a chassis of low floor design, fitted with a 125 b.h.p., Leyland 0.600 engine transversely mounted at the rear, coupled to a pneumo-cyclic (semi-automatic) gearbox. James were amongst the first customers ordering these 'Atlantean's, placing an initial order for five. First of the batch, 227 (RTH 637) was exhibited on the Leyland Motors' stand at the 1958 Commercial Motor Show, Earls Court, London, that October. The chassis of this vehicle was one of four pre-production prototypes built, and was fitted with 73 seat semi-lowbridge bodywork built by Metropolitan-Cammell-Weymann. This particular type of uncommon body design, with partial sunken upper deck gangway (as shown in drawing), was quite rare on the 'Atlantean' chassis, as only 344 were ever built. The complete vehicle with an overall height of 13 feet 4 inches had un unladen weight of 8 tons 11cwt.

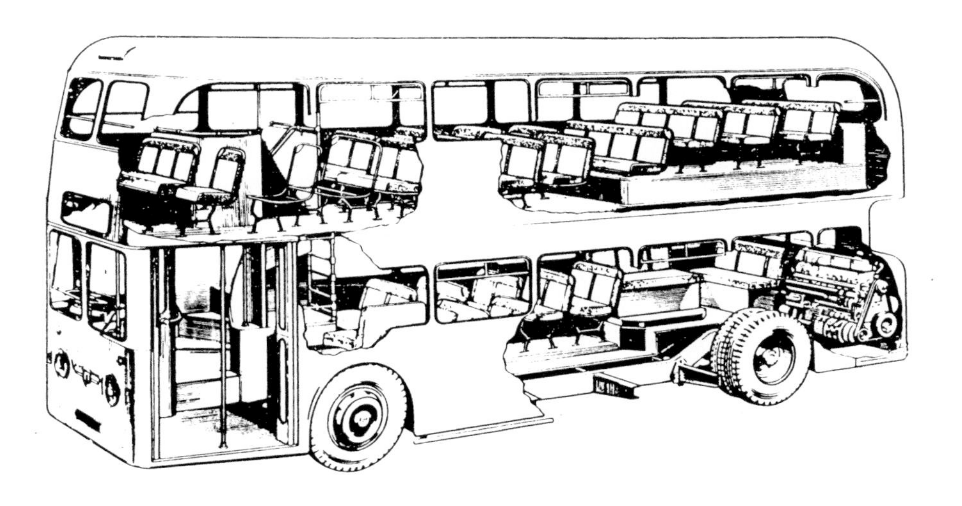

This cut-away drawing of the M.C.W. bodied low-height 'Atlantean' shows how the rear four rows of seats on the upper deck were raised to allow headroom in the lower deck. Note the partial sunken gangway on the near side of the upper deck.

After a brief spell demonstrating to Ribble Motor Services at Preston, it was delivered to Leyland's Cardiff depot, where it received a pre-delivery service before delivery to James' closely associated company, Western Welsh at Ely Works, Cardiff. After receiving a second inspection and pre-delivery service at Ely Works it was collected by Angus James the General manager himself on Wednesday, 3rd December, 1958. Without any driver familiarisation it was pressed into service the following day, Thursday, 4th December, on the Ammanford to Llanelly route, making it the first 'Atlantean' to enter passenger service in the world.

The remaining four 'Atlantean's' from the initial order, 228 - 231 (RTH 638 - 641) were not built until early 1959, and entered service in April that year. They were all favourably received by the travelling public.

The '*first*' pre-production prototype Leyland 'Atlantean' to enter passenger service in the world, was James' M.C.W. bodied low-height 73 seater; 227 (RTH 637) pictured here on a Sunday-School outing to Aberavon Beach in 1961. There were several minor differences in the build of this vehicle compared to later models, probably because it was a show exhibit. Notable differences were extra window vents and twin fog lights. The published price when announced in 1958 was £7,000. (Roy Marshall collection.)

Numerically the second Metropolitan-Cammell-Weymann bodied 'Atlantean' 228 (RTH 638) entered service in April 1959. It is viewed here inside the Margaret Street entrance of James' Bus Station about to depart for Pontardawe in 1962.

A rear off-side view of 'Atlantean' 228, at Castle Street, Swansea.

'Atlantean' 229 (RTH 639) is captured here outside James' Bus Station in College Street, Ammanford, picking up passengers for the journey to Neath. Clearly visible in the background (above the bus roof) is the company's famous 'Neon sign' depicting JAMES BUS STATION and the outline of a red double decker bus with spoked wheels that flashed in rotation, giving an impression of the wheels turning - representing perpetual motion. (Robert Mack collection)

The terminus of James' Ammanford to Neath service was the forecourt of Neath railway station, the setting for this 1960 view of M.C.W. bodied 'Atlantean' 230 (RTH 640), which is about to leave for Ammanford.

Numerically the last 'Atlantean' from the initial order of five was 231 (RTH 641) which entered service in April 1959. (P. Yeoman collection).

It was claimed that these early production 'Atlantean's' were plagued with a series of design faults which included engine overheating problems. Despite these problems, the company were not disillusioned by them as they ordered a further eight for delivery over the next two years.

The second batch of five 'Atlanteans' ordered in 1959 entered service in November that year as 232 - 236 (UBX 45 - 49). Fitted with Weymann 73 seat lowbridge bodies they were followed by a similar pair 13 months later in December 1960. The latter two, 237/238 (WTH 113/114) were also fitted with Weymann lowbridge bodies but differed slightly - they only seated 72 passengers and had vents fitted to their near side front windscreens.

A noteworthy and unusual private hire job was performed by one of these early 'Atlantean's' on 9th October, 1959. It was used to convey a party of civic dignitaries together with B.E.T. group officials to an opening ceremony, testing the clearance underneath a railway bridge at Port Tennant, Swansea, after lowering the road.

However, spasmodic delivery of these 'Atlantean's' ousted the last remaining Guy utilities, together with all four PD1 'Titans'; the last two PS1 'Tiger' saloons; and four of the five PS1 'Tiger rebuilds' with bodies just 6 years old. The PS1 rebuilds 194/201/203/204 were surplus to requirements and put into store at Western Welsh's Neath depot late in 1960 pending disposal. A few months later in early 1961, they were taken to Western Welsh's Ely Works, Cardiff, to have their bodies removed and fitted to newer Leyland PD2 'Titan' chassis of 1950 vintage. The PD2's involved; 206 - 209 (FTH 680 - 683) had their original 1950 Leyland bodies removed and scrapped, receiving the second hand bodies salvaged from the 'Tiger rebuilds' 203/201/194/204 respectively. After the re-bodying programme was completed, the surplus 'rebuilt Tiger' chassis were also scrapped.

Seen here leaving Ammanford Bus Station in 1962, on route to Tairgwaith in the Amman Valley, is a 1950 Leyland PD2/12 'Titan' 206 (FTH 680) rebodied with the second-hand 1955 M.C.W. 'Orion' body, removed from a withdrawn Leyland PS1 'Tiger' rebuild, 203 (DTH 722) in 1961. One wonders what sort of road holding it had when fitted with these 'Bald' front tyres.

In 1961, PD2/12 'Titan 207 (FTH 681) was also rebodied with a second-hand body. It is pictured here at Bird-in-Hand Square, Trimsaran, in 1961 soon after receiving its 1955 M.C.W. 'Orion' body, removed from another redundant Leyland PS1 'Tiger' rebuild, 201 (DBX 637) (P. Yeomans collection)

208 (FTH 682) was numerically the third PD2/12 'Titan' acquired by the company. Originally fitted with a Leyland lowbridge body, it was seen here parked up outside Amman Valley Grammar School at Church Street, Ammanford in 1961, soon after receiving this second hand 1955 M.C.W. 'Orion' body removed from withdrawn PS1 'Tiger' rebuild, 194 (CTH 615). (A. K. Harris collection).

1950 Leyland PD2/12 'Titan' 209 (FTH 683) also had its 11 year old Leyland lowbridge body replaced in 1961. This one was fitted with a second-hand 1954 Longwell Green body donated by redundant PS1 'Tiger' rebuild, 204 (EBX 662)

The second order for 'Atlantean's' 232 - 236 (UBX 45 - 49) arrived in November 1959. Their bodies were identical in appearance to the 5 Metropolitan-Cammell-Weymann bodied examples previously received, yet these were bodied by M.C.W.'s associate company, Weymann's of Addlestone, Surrey. 233 (UBX 46) numerically the second vehicle of the second order is pictured here when new.

Weymann bodied PDR1/1 'Atlantean' 234 (UBX 47) is pictured here outside James' Bus Station, loading up passengers on a Sunday evening journey to Neath. The 'Atlantean's with their high seating capacity were a regular feature on Sunday evening Amman Valley services, conveying thirsty colliers to their favourite watering holes across the border in Glamorganshire. Carmarthenshire's antiquated licencing law did not permit Sunday opening of public houses in those far gone days. R. F. Mack collection

Atlantean' 235 (UBX 48) is captured here inside the Margaret Street entrance to James' Bus Station at Ammanford in 1961. This particular area of the depot was previously the location of 'Pooles Cinema' acquired by the company in 1937. (P. Yeoman collection.

Pictured here at Pontyberem Square, on its return journey from Burry Port to Ammanford in early 1962 is Weymann bodied 'Atlantean' 236 (UBX 49). The building to the extreme left of the picture, Pontyberem Primary School has since been demolished to make way for a road improvement. (P. Yeoman collection.)

The late 1950's and early 1960's produced several more service changes. Some changes were brought about by colliery closures and new collieries opening, others were simply a cost cutting exercise.

The first major change came on New Year's Day 1959, when the Aberystwyth service - jointly operated with Western Welsh, changed from crew operated vehicles to one-man-operated (O.M.O.) single deckers - subject to vehicle availability. If a single decker was replaced by a double decker, this was crew operated as the law did not permit O.M.O. deckers at this time.

Nine months later return tickets became interchangeable with Crosville Motor Services between Aberystwyth and Lampeter.

In another attempt to reduce running costs, Western Welsh and James sought permission to relinquish joint operation of 2 services:- Ammanford to Aberystwyth and Ammanford to Llanelly. Permission for this was granted in June 1960, with James taking over Western Welsh's share of the Ammanford to Llanelly service; in exchange James gave their share of the Ammanford to Aberystwyth service to Western Welsh, transferring all their staff based at Cwmanne outstation. Furthermore, Western Welsh were then permitted to use James' bus station at Ammanford for arrival and departure of all Aberystwyth journeys.

On the other hand, no fewer than 6 new R.S.L.'s were applied for between 1960 - 62, to provide new services of stage carriage. They were:-

TGR 347/58: Burry Port (Railway Station) to Cynheidre Colliery (Shaft No.3), via: Pembrey Square, Butchers Arms, Pinged, Trimsaran (Bird-in-Hand), Carway, Pontyates Station, Ponthenry Square, Pontyberem Square, and Pontyberem (Llannon Road).
Service of stage carriage to operate Monday to Friday, only when Cynheidre Colliery is working.

TGR 347/59: Ammanford (James' Bus Station) to Cynheidre Colliery (Shaft No.3) *This service operated on 2 different routes*
(1) via: Bonllwyn, Llandebie Square, Blaenau Square, Penygroes Square, Gorslas Square, Cross Hands Square, Blaenhirwaun Colliery, Drefach Square, Cwmmawr, Lower Tumble, Upper Tumble, Bryndu Square (Llannon) and Cynheidre No.3.
(2) via: Tirydail Station, Saron, Capel Hendre Square, Cwmgwili (P.O.), Gorslas Square, Cross Hands Square, Blaenhirwaun Colliery, Drefach Square, Cwmmawr, Lower Tumble, Upper Tumble, Bryndu Square (Llannon) and Cynheidre No.3.
Service of stage carriage for National Coal Board employees only, to operate Monday to Saturday, only when Cynheidre colliery is working. Fares subsidised by the N.C.B.

TGR 347/60: Ystalyfera (Swan Hotel) to Cwmgorse (Abernant Colliery).
via: Gurnos (Cross), Lower Cwmtwrch, Ystradowen, Cwmllynfell, Brynamman and Gwaun-Cae-Gurwen.
Service of stage carriage jointly operated with United Welsh Services, Ltd., with interchangeable return tickets.

TGR 347/61: Ammanford (James' Bus Station) to Brynamman (Derlwyn Arms).
via: Glanamman, Garnant, Gwaun-Cae-Gurwen, Brynamman (Derlwyn Arms), Cwmgorse, Abernant, Steer Pit and East Pit (Collieries).
Service of stage carriage to operate Monday to Friday only when the collieries are working. Return tickets interchangeable with United Welsh Services between Abernant colliery and Brynamman, and on the buses of S.W.T. Co., and W.W.O.Co., between Ammanford and Gwaun-Cae-Gurwen.

TGR 347/62: Ammanford (James' Bus Station) to Cynheidre Colliery (Shafts 1 & 2).
This service operated on 3 different routes.
(1) via: Tirydail Station, Saron, Capel Hendre, Penygroes Square,
Gorslas Square, Cross Hands Square, Blaenhirwaun Colliery, Drefach Square, Cwmmawr, Lower Tumble (Tumble Hotel), Pontyberem Square, Pentremawr Colliery, Ponthenry Square, (P.O.), Pontyates (Gwendraeth Arms) and Cynheidre.
(2) via: Bonllwyn, Llandebie Square, Blaenau, Penygroes Square, Gorslas Square, Cross Hands Square, Upper Tumble, Lower Tumble, Cwmmawr, Pontyberem Square, Pentremawr Colliery, Ponthenry Square (P.O.) Pontyates (Gwendraeth Arms) and Cynheidre.
(3) Trimsaran (Bird-in-Hand) to Cynheidre Colliery (Shafts 1 & 2 via: Trimsaran, Carway, Pontyates Station and Cynheidre.
Service of stage carriage operated for employees of the National Coal Board only. The service will operate only when Cynheidre No. 1, 2 & 3, Pentremawr, Pontyberem, Great Mountain, Blaenhirwaun, and Cross Hands Collieries are working.

TGR 347/63: Ystalyfera (Swan Hotel) to Ystalyfera (Alltygrug).
via: Wern Road and Penywern Road.
Service of stage carriage to operate jointly with South Wales Transport Co. Ltd., and United Welsh Services Ltd., Monday to Saturday only.

The services TGR 347/58 to 62 mentioned above all operated under special licences, from the dates of their application; February 1960, August 1960, and January 1961 (TGR 347/60,61,62) respectively, until full term licences were granted.

Application TGR 347/63 had its licence refused in July 1961, but was re-applied for by all three companies in January 1962. James soon withdrew their application and the licence was eventually granted jointly between S.W.T. Co., and U.W.S. Ltd., in April 1962.

Applications TGR 347/61 and TGR 347/62 were merely services that superseded TGR 347/43 and TGR 347/45 respectively.

Furthermore, in June 1961 the company were granted permission to use double decker buses with driver operated doors on certain day and half-day excursions - a feature that became commonplace on Sunday-School outings.

Another Weymann bodied 'Atlantean', 237(WTH 113) was one of a pair delivered in December 1960. It is pictured here at Ammanford bus station in 1961 about to depart for Llanelly on the company's 'direct' route via Saron, Cross Hands and Upper Tumble, a service that operated on Llanelly market days, Thursday and Saturday only.

Pictured here at Glynmoch Flats in the Amman Valley is Weymann bodied 'Atlantean' 238(WTH 114) on route to Neath in 1961. Note the non-existence of service route numbers - a practice never adopted by the company.

During this period, Ammanford councillors were complaining about James' buses being parked up all day outside the Grammar School, and houses at Church Street and Margaret Street. With a harsh reply, the company threatened to close their bus station and move out of town if their parking facilities were removed

Shortly afterwards the company took delivery of their 13th Leyland 'Atlantean', 239 (YTH 805). Entering service in January 1962, it was fitted with a Weymann 72 seat lowbridge body identical to the 1960 deliveries, 237/8. Bearing in mind that the James family were constantly superstitious about the number '13' it was incredible that the 13th Atlantean became 'unlucky 13th' - it turned out to be the last Atlantean and the very last vehicle acquired by the James concern. On 23rd July, 1962 the sad news of the company's demise was announced.

Unfortunately, there had been a slow decline in passenger numbers since nationalisation 12 years earlier, due to an ever-increasing number of private motorcars, coupled with rising operating costs and an overlap of routes operated by the three B.E.T. companies. This together with the General Manager Angus James' wish to retire from the bus industry, having already reached retirement age, all contributed to the company's demise. A report published in the local newspaper, The South Wales Guardian, briefly read:-

AMMANFORD BUS FIRM REACHES END OF LINE

> *Before long, the familiar green light which told night travellers that the bus approaching was one of James' buses will disappear. For, on September 1st, the old Ammanford bus company J. James & Sons Ltd., will merge with Swansea based South Wales Transport Co., Ltd.*
>
> *The reason for the merger is that costs are so high, the companies decided it was better for them to merge on economic grounds. General Manager, Mr. Angus James gave an assurance that there would be no redundancies and the jobs of almost 200 employees were assured. The Ammanford depot would remain open, and thatservices would remain virtually unchanged, but the fleetname* ***'JAMES'*** *would disappear forever along with the livery. He also said that he had been due to retire at the end of the past year (1961), but was asked to continue in this capacity until the merger had been completed.*

Everyone was astonished with the news, as James' association with locally based Western Welsh had been far greater than their association with South Wales Transport.

However, in August 1962, the South Wales Transport Co., applied to the Traffic Commissioners for all 30 Road Service Licences held by J. James & Sons Ltd., and auditors J. Wallace Williams & Co., Cardiff were called in to liquidate the company.

Neath Railway Station is the backdrop for this view of Weymann bodied 'Atlantean' 239 (YTH 805). New in January 1962, its external appearance differed slightly from its stable mates, having window vents fitted to the upper and lower deck windscreens and an offside illuminated advertisement panel - a popular feature of the 1960's. 239 was the thirteenth 'Atlantean' and unfortunately the last vehicle acquired by the company before its demise.

This view of James' last 'Atlantean', 239 (YTH 805) was taken in July 1962 shortly before the company merged with South Wales Transport. The location, St. Mary's Square, Swansea, was the company's 'new' terminus, having moved here from Trinity Place in 1956 when the town was redeveloped after the wartime blitz.

This Canadian Ford F30 four-wheel drive lorry fitted with V8 petrol engine was purchased for the engineering department. Registered as DBX 22 in January 1947, it was used for towing and recovery work and remained in use until the company's demise in 1962, by this time running on garage trade plates.

As a tribute, and fond farewell to the much loved company, an unknown photographer had the foresight to capture James' 'Atlantean', 230 (RTH 640) leaving Ammanford bus station for Llanelly shortly before the company's demise on Friday, 31st August, 1962 In this historical view of College Street, the premises from left to right are: (33) Co-operative Stores; (31 Rainford, radio and cycle dealer; (29) James the Sadler; (27) Fletcher, newsagent, with 'Evening Post' Morris 1000 van; (25) J. James & Sons Ltd., office, former residence of John James; (23) James' Bus Station vehicle exit; (21) the former Army & Navy Stores, by this time occupied by J. James & Sons Ltd., as their staff canteen. The advertisement in the canteen window reads: Regal Ballroom annual August Bank Holiday Ball. (Chris Taylor collection.)

EPILOGUE

On Saturday, 1st September 1962, South Wales Transport officially took control of the James undertaking, swiftly discarding the name and livery. All members of staff transferred to the new company, except Angus James, the company's General Manager, who retired to his farm at Glanamman.

With this merger, 35 Leylands passed into South Wales Transport's 100% A.E.C. fleet, after an absence of 7 years. The three 36 feet long Leyland PSU3/3R ' Leopards' on order at the time of merger (2 dual purpose and 1 bus bodied) were delivered to S.W.T. in 1963 fitted with 53 seat Marshall bus bodies - a change of order. Bearing full S.W.T. livery they were registered consecutively, amidst a batch of S.W.T., A.E.C. Reliances as 893 - 895 DCY.

Pictured here when new is Marshall bodied Leyland 'Leopard' 952 (895 DCY), one of 3 Leopards ordered by J. James & Sons. Ltd., before their merger with South Wales Transport in 1962. All 3 delivered to S.W.T. in 1963 were fitted with off side illuminated advertisements, this one advertising S.W.T. tours.

James' Swansea Valley depot at Gurnos Cross also passed into S.W.T. ownership, remaining operational for just 15 months. Its early closure was brought about by rationalisation, with vehicles and staff transferring to S.W.T.'s Swansea Valley depot at Pontardawe.

On the other hand, S.W.T. were issued with 30 special short-term Road Service Licences in September 1962, permitting them to operate James' services on a temporary basis until full term licences were granted.

The full term licences were granted on 25th October 1962, and consequently the accountant J. Wallace Williams & Co., liquidated the James business the very same day.

Listed below are some interesting figures extracted from the auditors balance sheet for the period 1st January to 25th October 1962 (liquidation date)

J. James & Sons Ltd:- valued at £143,332

Fixed assets:		
Rolling stock,	35 buses	£ 90,762
	3 service vehicles	£ 392
Freehold land and buildings		£ 9,169
Leasehold land and buildings		£ 155

Revenue for the period 1/1/1962 to 25/10/1962	£ 148,179
Fuel consumed for the period 1/1/1962 to 25/10/1962	112,341 galls
Fuel cost (less tax) @ 2/9d per gall.	£ 15,446
Road vehicle duty	£ 884-6-2d

After the S.W.T./James merger it was so strange to see A.E.C. buses working out of Ammanford bus station, especially operating James' services. In this view, South Wales' 1963 A..E.C. Reliance, 963 (732 FCY) is seen leaving Ammanford bus station for Swansea via: Cwmllynfell, a service previously operated by James. Furthermore, S.W.T. wasted no time removing the neon sign 'JAMES BUS STATION' from the bus station roof, replacing it with a plain South Wales Transport Co. Ltd., sign as seen in this view of the depot entrance/ exit in College Street. The building to the left hand side of the depot entrance was formerly John James' residence, Brynderwen Mews, No.25 College Street, latterly used as the depot office, and the building to the right hand side of entrance, No.21 College Street, originally a shop 'The Famous Army & Navy Stores', was latterly the company's staff canteen.

Another A.E.C. pictured leaving Ammanford depot in 1963 was this low height A.E.C. Bridgemaster, 1211 (WCY 891) working S.W.T's *original* Swansea route via:- Cwmgorse and Pontardawe. The warning sign barely visible inside the depot reads:- Warning - low bridge type buses only beyond this point. A sign on the entrance wall is for Western Welsh's Aberystwyth service (previously operated jointly with James), which now also departs from the bus station. (A. K. Harris collection).

Repainting of James' buses into S.W.T. livery soon commenced with 'Atlantean' 234, now 1234 (UBX 47) emerging from the paintshop in full S.W.T. livery in October 1962.

A few weeks later however, on 13th December 1962, 'Atlantean' 1236 (UBX 49) came to grief on an icy hill at Ponthenry, crashing into the parapet of a stone river bridge. The fully laden bus taking morning shift colliers to Cynheidre colliery sustained extensive damage. Several passengers were badly injured but miraculously no-one was killed. The extensive rebuild of 1236, which followed in 1963, included a new chassis frame.

The extensive damage to 1236 (UBX 49) is clearly visible in this photograph taken at the scene of the accident, with the parapet of the bridge embedded 12 feet down the lower deck gangway - almost halfway down the bus' length. Note: this accident happened on the 13th to a vehicle with a registration number that added up to '13' - Superstition?

Unfortunately, the downturn in public transport continued, resulting in premature closure of Western Welsh Omnibus Co.'s Ammanford depot in January 1966. On the other hand, S.W.T., drew up plans to modernise their facilities at Ammanford. The old staff canteen (No. 21 College Street) was demolished in 1967, and replaced with a S.W.T. Travel Agent's booking office and first floor staff canteen. The extensive work included a wider depot exit into College Street for the bigger buses. This was achieved by removing half of the glass roof, complete with structure, covering the exit. The old office block, No. 25 College Street (Brynderwen Mews) was eventually sold off in 1971, and converted into a 'Chinese Takeaway'.

When most of the low bridges in Llanelly's 'New Dock' district were demolished in 1970, S.W.T.'s unique A.E.C. Regent V low height single deckers were surplus to requirement at Llanelly and found new homes at other depots. This particular Roe bodied 37 seater; 37(281 DWN) found refuge here at Ammanford, as it was ideally suited for the 127 route. It is seen here in 1970 leaving the modernised Ammanford bus station on the notorious 127 service to Garnswllt shortly before the company discontinued the service. Also visible in this view is the 'modified' glass roof at the depot exit and part of the new Travel Agent's shop.

However, retaining their separate entity, South Wales Transport was absorbed by the 'National Bus Company' (N.B.C.) upon its formation in January 1969, Rationalisation of services soon followed, almost closing Ammanford depot (Central Garage) in January 1977, as extensive service reductions in the area reduced Ammanford's vehicle allocation from 27 to 7, a substantial reduction since James' heyday. The depot was only saved from closure after help from the local authority, Dyfed County Council, who purchased Central Garage in January 1977 for continued use as a bus station, allowing S.W.T. continued access to the premises.

On 7th January, 1980, however, Central Garage finally closed to the public as a bus station, with local services alternatively terminating at nearby streets. The 7 buses allocated to Ammanford nevertheless remained garaged there until a suitable outstation was found at the yard of local omnibus proprietors, West Wales Motor Services Ltd., Tycroes.

After Central Garage was vacated in 1980, the local authority went ahead with redevelopment of the site. Within months, all buildings were demolished, including the late John James' house. 'Brynderwen Mews' (latterly a Chinese Takeaway) to create a new 'open-air' bus station and access roadway to a new car park situated behind

Margaret Street. This work was completed in July 1981, when the present Ammanford bus station opened.

Ironically, three walls of the former Central Garage building still remain intact (although reduced in height) forming part of the new bus station and access roadway.

A recent view of Ammanford bus station shows the exact location of John James' former residence Brynderwen Mews (25 College Street), and former site of Central Garage. To the left of the picture: Antique shop ' Aladdin's Cave' (No. 27 College Street), was previously a newsagent shop owned by John James' brother in law J. Fletcher. The Grey wall in the centre of the view is one of the three remaining walls of James' bus station (although reduced in height). The access roadway into the current bus station, (in background) was also part of James' bus station, and former site of Pooles Pictorium.

Compare this recent view of Ammanford bus station against the 1962 historical view of College Street on page 142

SUMMARY OF ROAD SERVICE LICENCES

TGR 347/1	Ammanford (James Bus Station)	- Swansea (Trinity Place)
TGR 347/2	Ammanford (James Bus Station)	- Neath (Railway Station)
TGR 347/3	Varteg (Johnsons Stores)	- Swansea (Trinity Place)
TGR 347/4	Rhiwfawr	- Ystalyfera (New Swan)
TGR 347/5	Ammanford (James Bus Station)	- Brynamman (Derlwyn Arms)
TGR 347/6	Excursions & Tours starting from	- Ammanford & District
TGR 347/7	Excursions & Tours starting from	- Brynamman
TGR 347/8	Excursions & Tours starting from	- Cross Hands & District
TGR 347/9	Excursions & Tours starting from	- Ystalyfera & District
TGR 347/10	Excursions & Tours starting from	- Llandilo & Ffairfach
TGR 347/11	Excursions & Tours starting from	- Neath
TGR 347/12	Excursions & Tours starting from	- Llanelly
TGR 347/13	Excursions & Tours starting from	- Pontardulais
TGR/347/14	Excursions & Tours starting from	- Cwmllynfell
TGR/347/15	Excursions & Tours starting from	- Pontyberem & Ponthenry
TGR 347/16	Excursions & Tours starting from	- Swansea
TGR 347/17	Excursions & Tours starting from	- Clydach
TGR 347/18	Excursions & Tours starting from	- Cwmtwrch
TGR 347/19	Excursions & Tours starting from	- Pontardawe & District
TGR 247/20	Ammanford (James Bus Station)	- Llanelly (Railway Station)
TGR 347/21	Ammanford (James Bus Station)	- Aberystwyth (Railway Station)
TGR 347/22	Ammanford (James Bus Station)	- Burry Port (Railway Station)
TGR 347/23	Ammanford (Square)	- Pontardawe (Steel Works)
TGR 347/24	Brynamman (New Road)	- Pembrey (Royal Ord'nance Factory)
TGR 347/25	Llandebie	- Briton Ferry (Wern Works)
TGR 348/26	Penygroes	- Bridgend (R.O.F.)
TGR 347/27	Brynamman	- Bridgend (R.O.F.)
TGR 347/28	Varteg	- Bridgend (R.O.F.)
TGR 347/29	Hirwaun	- Bridgend (R.O.F.)
TGR 347/30	Ammanford	- Templeton (R.A.F. Base)
TGR 347/31	Ammanford	- Llangennech (R.N.A.D.) Royal Navy Armaments Depot
TGR 347/32	Pantyffynnon (Railway Station)	- Tairgwaith
TGR 347/33	Ammanford (Church Room Wind Street)	- Tycroes (Square)

TGR 347/34	Ammanford (James Bus Station)	-	Pontardulais (Dulais Glen Hotel)
TGR 347/35	Twyn (Garnant)	-	Ammanford (Iscennen Road)
TGR 347/36	Ammanford (Square)	-	Port Tennant (Steel Works)
TGR 347/37	Ammanford (James Bus Station)	-	Cwmmawr (Railway Station)
TGR 347/38	Ammanford (James Bus Station)	-	Heol Ddu (Ammanford)
TGR 347/39	Not applied for	-	
TGR 347/40	Not applied for	-	
TGR 347/41	Ystalyfera (New Swan)	-	Neath (Railway Station)
TGR 347/42	Ammanford (James Bus Station)	-	Llanelly (Railway Station)
TGR 347/43	Ammanford (James Bus Station)	-	Bryanamman (Derlwyn Arms)
TGR 347/44	Ammanford (Pullman Factory)	-	Brynamman (New Road)
TGR 347/45	Ammanford (James Bus Station)	-	Pontyberem (Pentremawr Colliery)
TGR 347/46	Penygroes (Waterloo Square)	-	Llandebie (Sec. Mod. School)
TGR 347/47	Ammanford (James Bus Station)	-	Hopkinstown
TGR 347/48	Gwaun-Cae-Gurwen	-	Swansea (Grand & Empire Theatres)
TGR 347/49	Ammanford (James Bus Station)	-	Swansea (Grand & Empire Theatres)
TGR 347/50	Ammanford (James Bus Station)	-	Llanelly (Astoria Theatre)
TGR 347/51	Ammanford (James Bus Station)	-	Swansea (Grand & Empire Theatres)
TGR 347/52	Excursions & Tours starting from	-	Ammanford (James Bus Station)
TGR 347/53	Ammanford (James Bus Station)	-	Saron (Square)
TGR 347/54	Ammanford (James Bus Station)	-	Garnswllt (Square)
TGR 347/55	Special service of stage carriage to operate after the cessation of normal services to cater for the late dances, special events, etc.		
TGR 347/56	Ystalyfera (Pwllbach Yard)	-	Pwllbach Colliery
TGR 347/57	Ammanford (James Bus Station)	-	Mount Colliery
TGR 347/58	Burry Port (Railway Station)	-	Cynheidre Colliery (Shaft No. 3)
TGR 347/59	Ammanford (James Bus Station)	-	Cynheidre Colliery (Shaft No. 3)
TGR 347/60	Ystalyfera (Swan Hotel)	-	Abernant Colliery & Cwmgorse Colliery
TGR 347/61	Ammanford (James Bus Station)	-	Abernant Colliery
TGR 347/62	Ammanford (James Bus Station)	-	Cynheidre Colliery (Shafts No. 1 & 2) & Trimsaran
TGR 347/63	Ystalyfera (Swan Hotel)	-	Ystalyfera (Alltygrug)

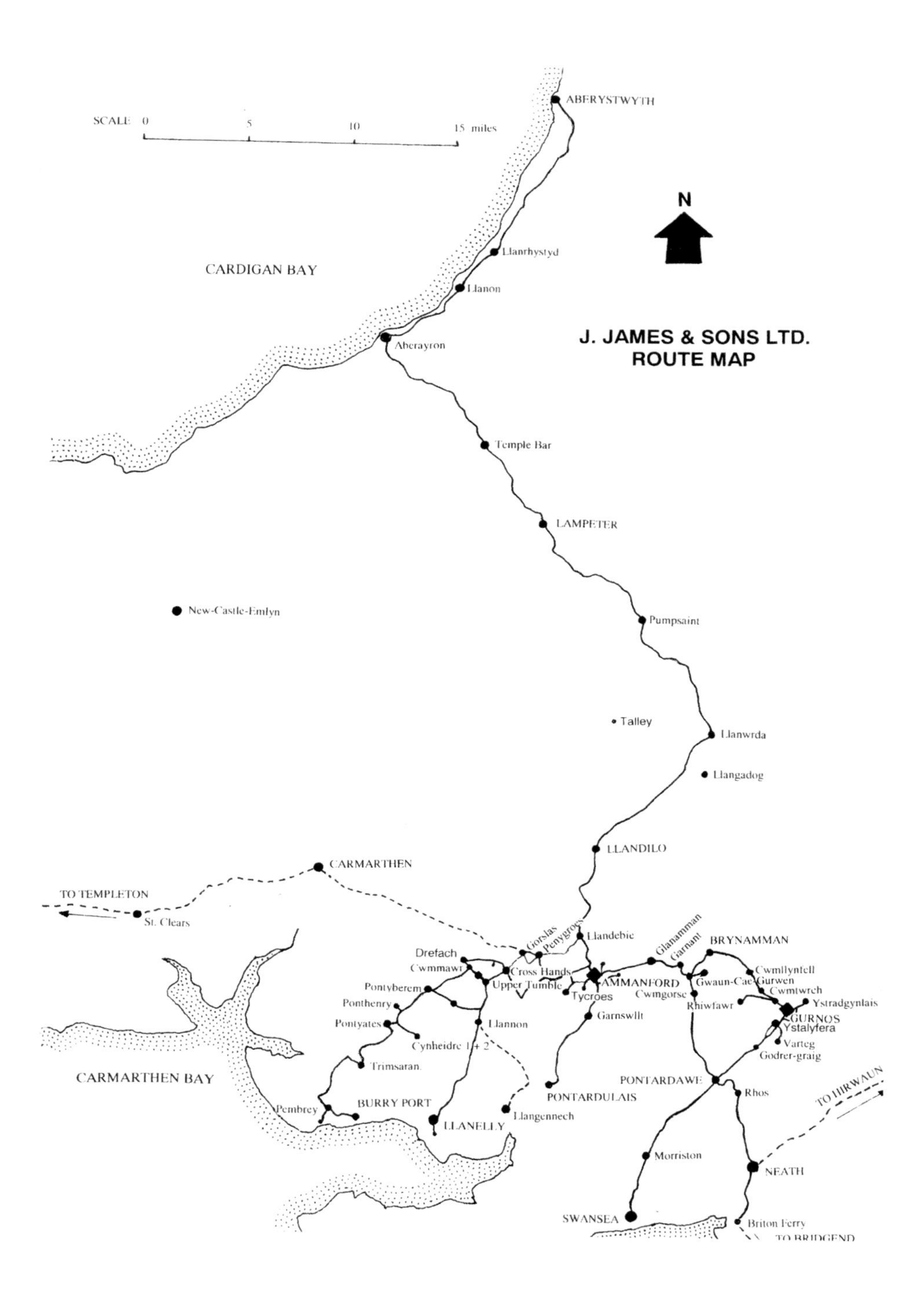
ABERYSTWYTH
SCALE 0 5 10 15 miles
N
Llanrhystyd
CARDIGAN BAY
Llanon
J. JAMES & SONS LTD.
ROUTE MAP
Aberayron
Temple Bar
LAMPETER
New-Castle-Emlyn
Pumpsaint
Talley
Llanwrda
Llangadog
LLANDILO
CARMARTHEN
TO TEMPLETON
St. Clears
Gorslas
Penygroes
Llandebie
Glanamman
Garnant
BRYNAMMAN
Drefach
Cwmmawr
Cross Hands
AMMANFORD
Upper Tumble
Tycroes
Gwaun-Cae-Gurwen
Cwmllynfell
Cwmtwrch
Pontyberem
Cwmgorse
Rhiwfawr
Ystradgynlais
GURNOS
Ystalyfera
Ponthenry
Pontyates
Llannon
Garnswllt
Varteg
Godrer-graig
Cynheidre 1 + 2
CARMARTHEN BAY
Trimsaran
PONTARDAWE
Rhos
PONTARDULAIS
TO HIRWAUN
Pembrey
BURRY PORT
LLANELLY
Llangennech
Morriston
NEATH
SWANSEA
Briton Ferry
TO BRIDGEND

TICKETS USED

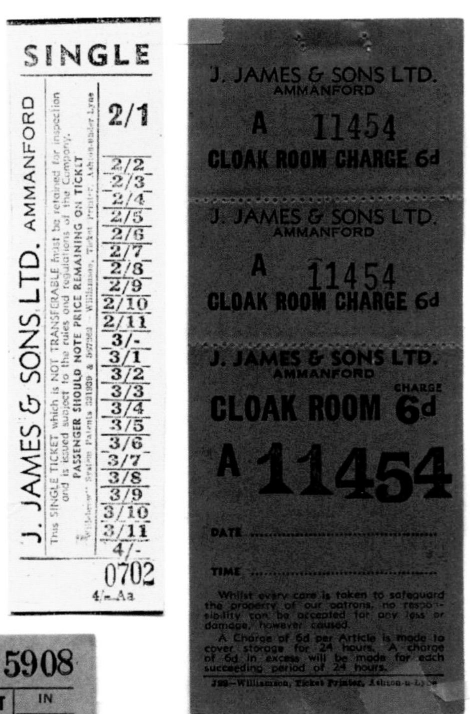

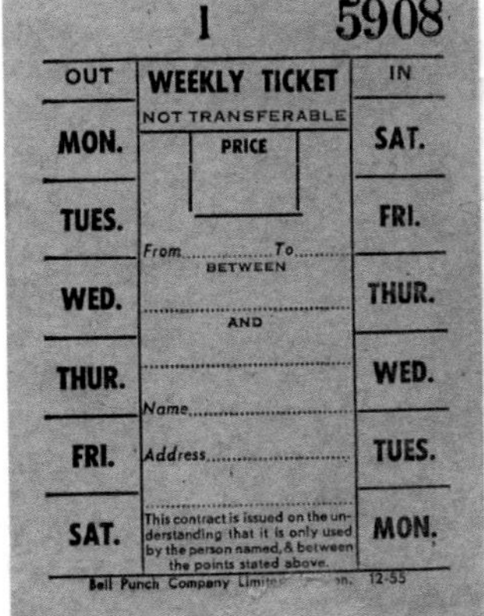

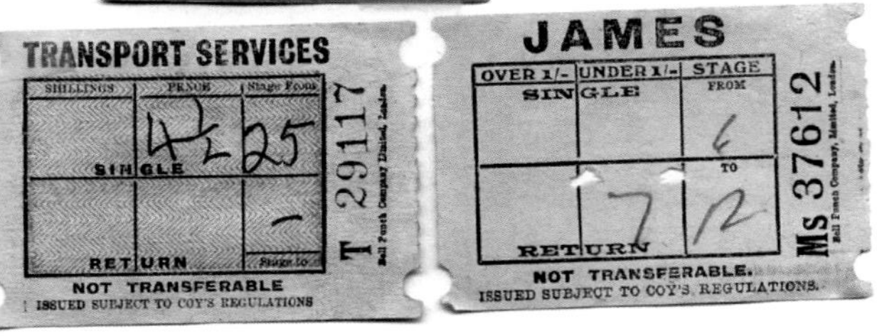

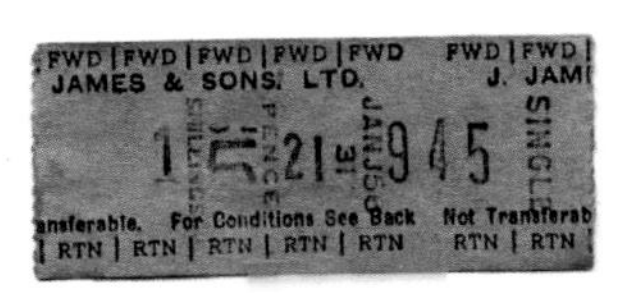

A selection of tickets used by J. James & Sons Ltd.:-
Top: Williamson "Willebrew" used up to 1939
Intermediate: Bell Punch Company, used 1939 to 1957
Bottom: Setright, used 1957 to 1962

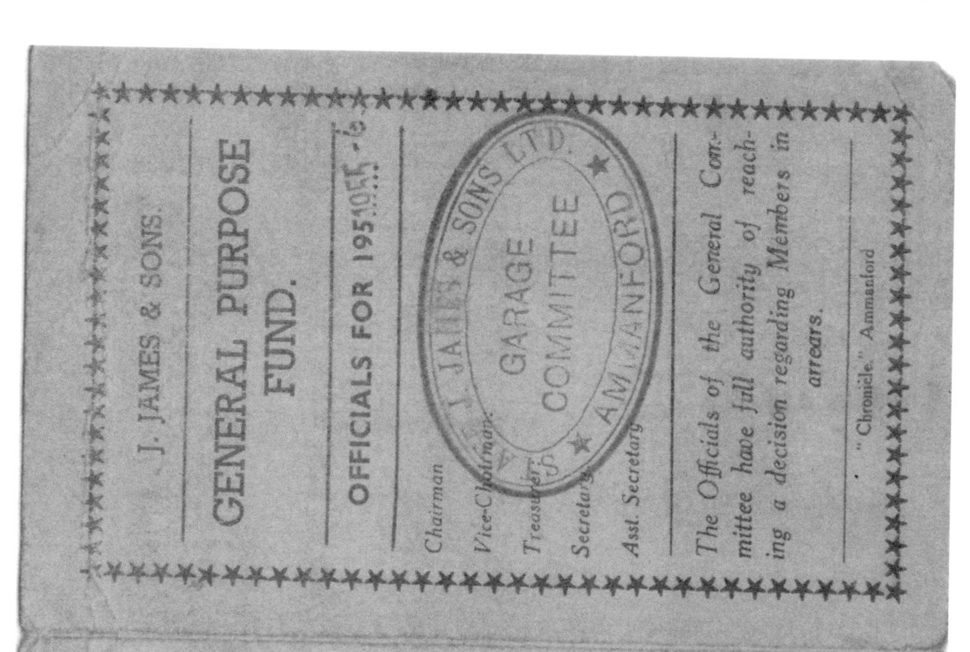

J. JAMES & SONS.

GENERAL PURPOSE FUND.

OFFICIALS FOR 1955-56

Chairman

Vice-Chairman

Treasurer

Secretary

Asst. Secretary

The Officials of the General Committee have full authority of reaching a decision regarding Members in arrears.

"Chronicle." Ammanford

J. JAMES & SONS LTD. GARAGE COMMITTEE AMMANFORD

STANDING ORDERS.

1.—Any Member who is six weeks in arrears shall not be entitled to Benefit for anything that occurs after that time.

2.—The Member should carry this Card with him always, and produce it to a Committee-man when required.

3.—If you dispute Arrears as shown, please return this Card for investigation.

4.—Remember this is for your benefit, and a Record of your payment.

5.—Should this Card be lost, the Register counts.

6.—PLEASE KEEP CARDS CLEAR.

If the tasks before our country are to be accomplished, we must

Keep on Saving

The South West Wales

SAVINGS BANK

Temporary Head Office:
32 Cradock Street, Swansea.

Offices:

Swansea - -	81 Brynymor Road
Morriston -	108 Woodfield Street
Llanelly - -	12 Market Street
Neath - -	127 Windsor Road
Port Talbot -	35 Station Road
Gorseinon -	2 Temple Buildings
Glyn Neath -	Leicester House
Ammanford -	12 High Street
Cardigan -	Kensington House

provides

A Complete Service for Saving

combined with

ABSOLUTE SECURITY.

STAFF J. JAMES & SONS LTD.
GARAGE
COMMITTEE
AMMANFORD

Savings Bank

1951-52

RULES.

Deposits will be received Weekly

Withdrawals cannot be made before December, unless under exceptional circumstances, in which case a week's notice will be required.

This Card must be presented when money is paid in or withdrawn.

PLEASE KEEP THIS CARD CLEAN.

T. C. Frame & Co., Printers, Swansea

J. James & Sons Ltd.; employees savings bank cards

DEPOT LAYOUTS

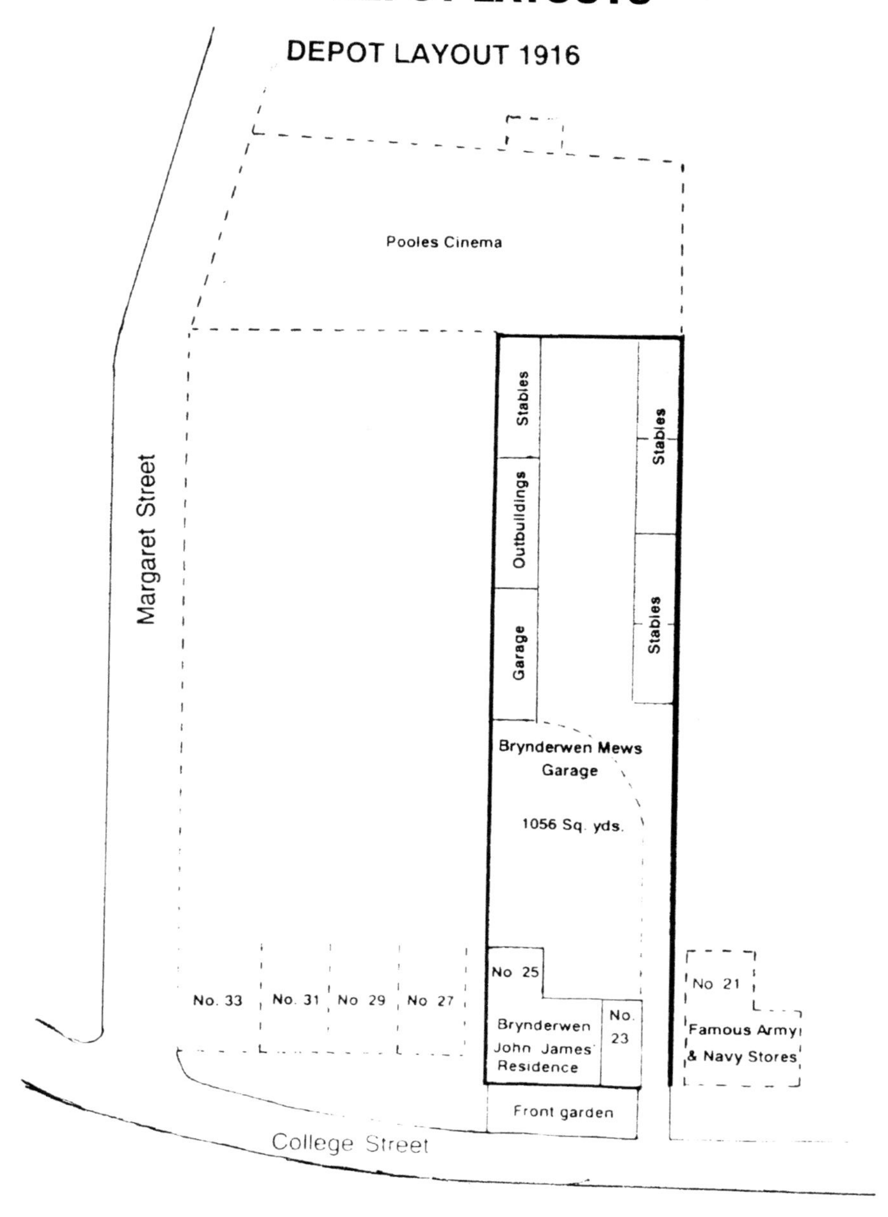

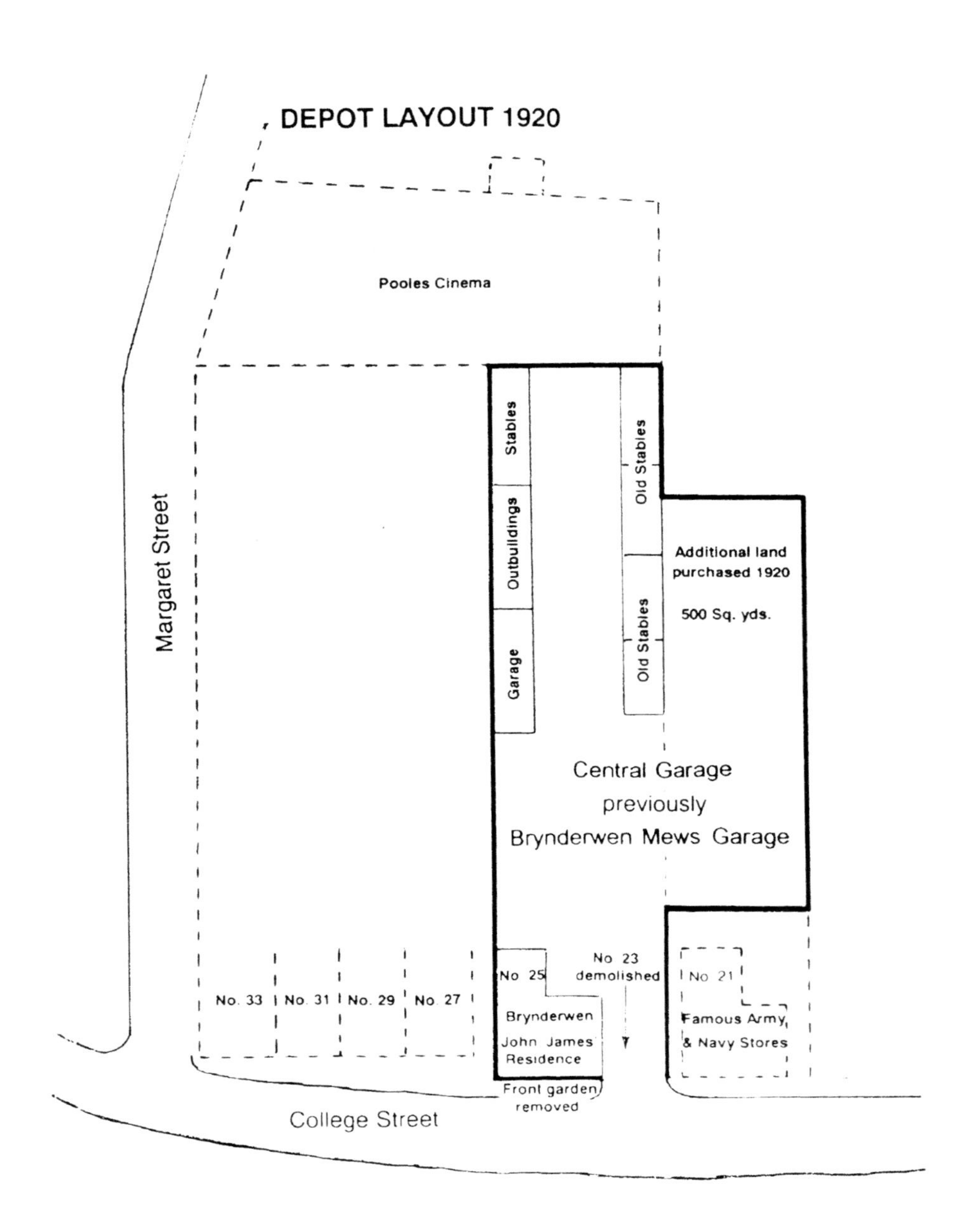
DEPOT LAYOUT 1920
Pooles Cinema
Margaret Street
Stables
Outbuildings
Garage
Old Stables
Old Stables
Additional land purchased 1920
500 Sq. yds.
Central Garage
previously
Brynderwen Mews Garage
No. 33
No. 31
No. 29
No. 27
No 25
Brynderwen
John James
Residence
No 23
demolished
No 21
Famous Army
& Navy Stores
Front garden
removed
College Street

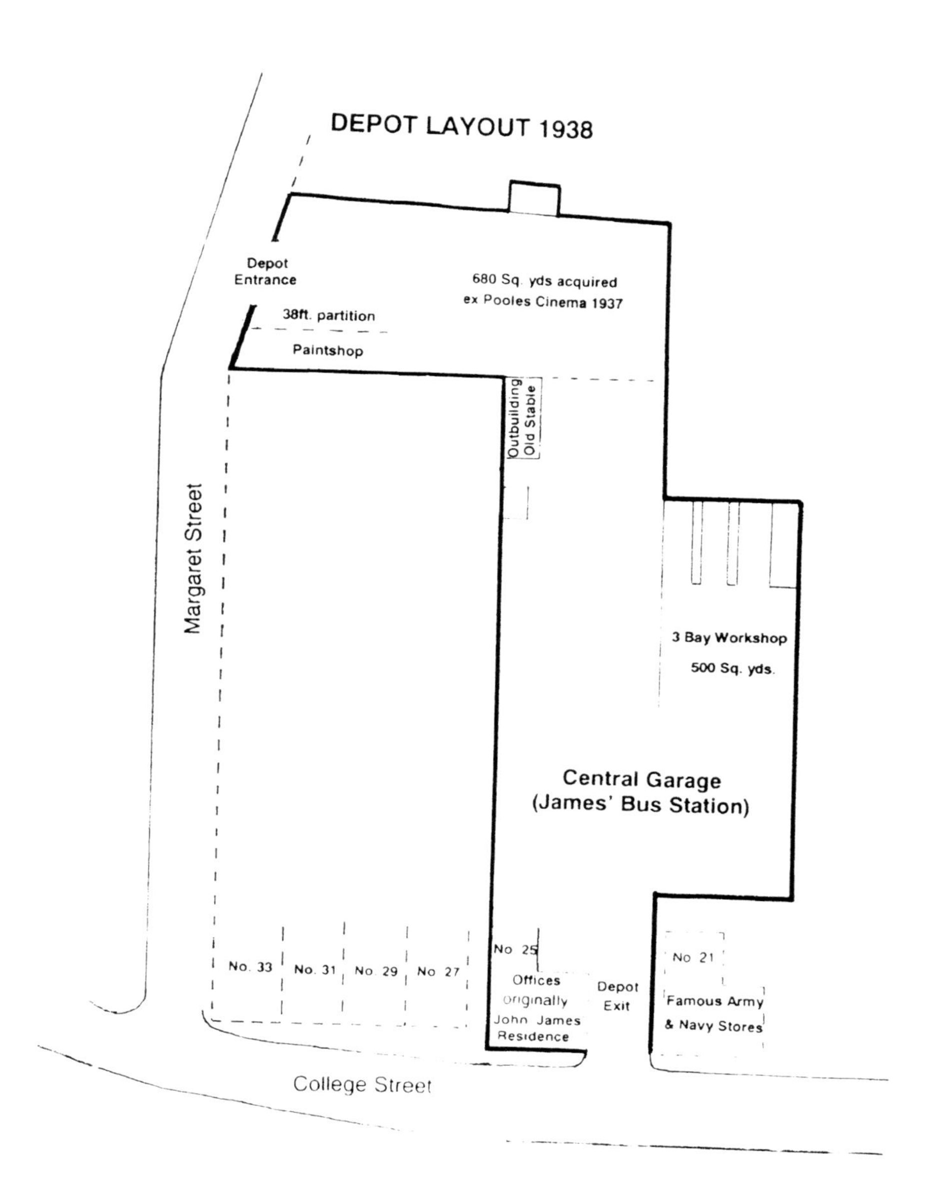
DEPOT LAYOUT 1938
Depot
Entrance
680 Sq. yds acquired
ex Pooles Cinema 1937
38ft. partition
Paintshop
Outbuilding
Old Stable
Margaret Street
3 Bay Workshop
500 Sq. yds.
Central Garage
(James' Bus Station)
No. 33
No. 31
No. 29
No. 27
No. 25
Offices
originally
John James
Residence
Depot
Exit
No. 21
Famous Army
& Navy Stores
College Street

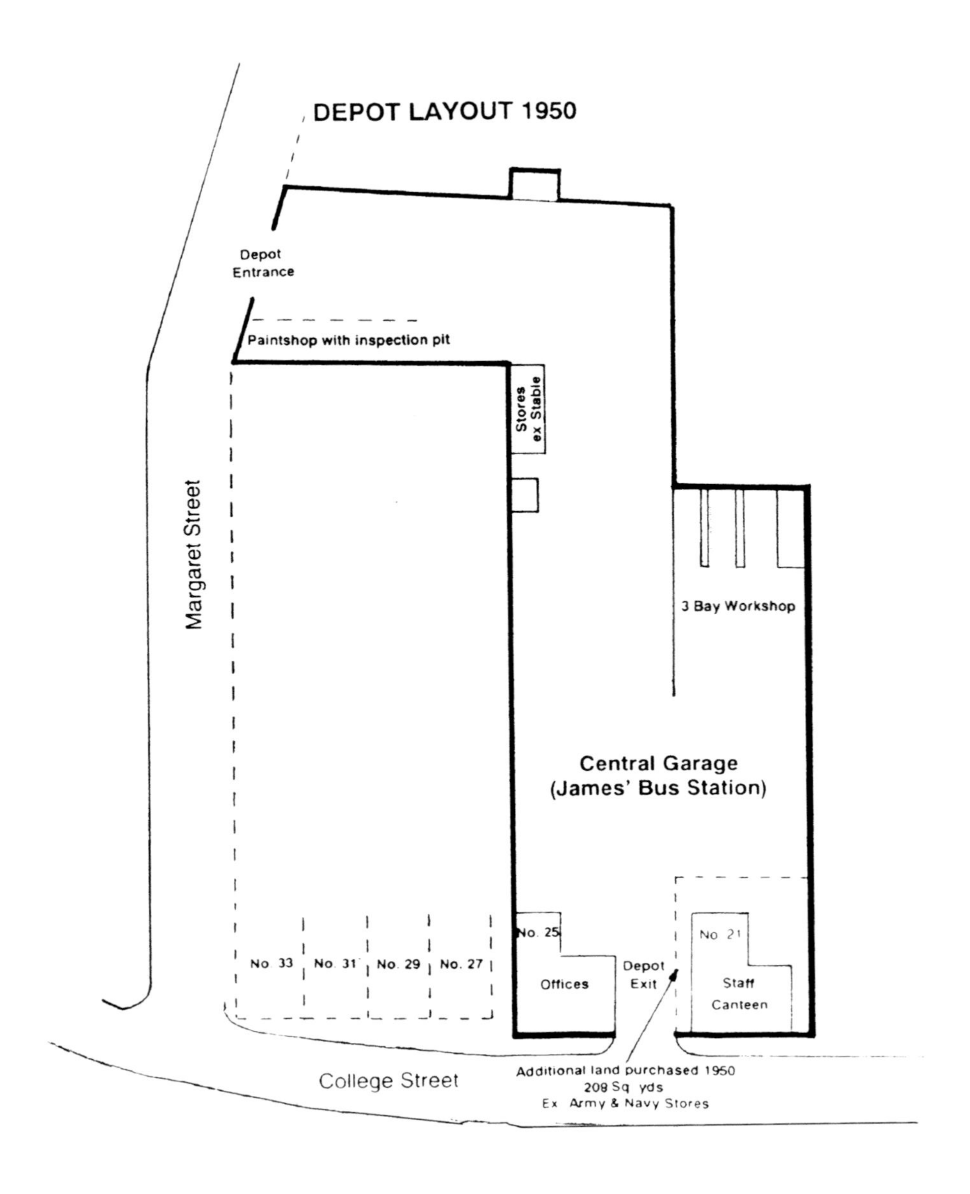
DEPOT LAYOUT 1950
Depot Entrance
Paintshop with inspection pit
Stores ex Stable
Margaret Street
3 Bay Workshop
Central Garage
(James' Bus Station)
No. 33
No. 31
No. 29
No. 27
No. 25
Offices
Depot Exit
No. 21
Staff Canteen
College Street
Additional land purchased 1950
208 Sq. yds
Ex Army & Navy Stores

VEHICLE DETAILS

All vehicles acquired new – unless otherwise stated

Fleet No.	Reg. No.	Chassis		Body		Date New	Remarks / Additional Information	Date Withdrawn
		Make & Type	Number	Make	Type			
	BX234	Ford 'T' 20hp		Charabanc	Ch8	9/1912	(Colour – Black)	6/1920
	BX463	Royal Enfield 18hp	(30 cwt)	Charabanc	Ch	9/1914	(Colour – Grey)	
	BX477	Maxwell 18hp	(16½ cwt)			12/1914		
	BX795	Royal Enfield 24hp	(2 Ton)	Charabanc	Ch20	1/1917	Named – 'The Whippet' (Colour Champagne)	8/1924
	BX1565	Daimler 20hp	(32 cwt)	Landaulette		10/1920	(Colour – Dark Blue)	
1	BX1735	Leyland G7	12235	Leyland	B32R	2/1921	4 Ton chassis range	1928
2	BX2237	Leyland G7	12381	Leyland	B32R	5/1921	4 Ton chassis range	
3	BX2725	Leyland RAF	22578	Leyland	B32R	5/1922	Rebuilt 4 Ton RAF type chassis	1928
4	BX3280	Leyland SG7	12581	Leyland	FB40D	3/1923	4 Ton chassis range	
5		Leyland SG6	12632	Leyland	FB40D	7/1923	4 Ton chassis range	
6	BX4914	Lancia Pentaiota		Northern Counties	B20R	8/1924		1/1925
6	BX5196	S.P.A.			B--	1/1925	Replacement for Lancia No.6 above	7/1926
7	BX5197	Leyland SG9(f/c)	13211	Leyland	B38D	1/1925	4 Ton chassis range	
8	BX5198	Leyland SG9(f/c)	13214	Leyland	B38D	3/1925	4 Ton chassis range	12/1926
9	BX5204	Leyland C9(36hp)	35133	Leyland	B26R	3/1925	2/3 Ton chassis range	
10	BX5205	Leyland C9(36hp)	35134	Leyland	B26R	2/1925		9/1930
11		Thorneycroft A1			B20	7/1926	Ex. Thorneycroft demonstrator	
	BX7332	Registration reserved by James – not taken up – Passed to T. Daniels, Pontyberem & District Transport.						
12	BX7333	Leyland Lion PLSC1	45314	Leyland	B29D	11/1926	Later converted to B31D	by 3/1932
13	Fleet number not used (James were supersticious).							
14	BX8220	Leyland Lion PLSC3	46045	Leyland	B32R	9/1927		7/1932
15	BX8221	Leyland Lion PLSC3	46046	Leyland	B32R	9/1927		

16	BX8222	Leyland Lion PLSC3	46144	Leyland	B32R	9/1927		
17	BX8400	Leyland Tiger TS1	60013	Leyland	B32R	1/1928	Renumbered 40 } See note - A	
18	BX8530	Leyland Tiger TS1	60012	Leyland	B32R	4/1928	Renumbered 42 } See note - A	
19	BX9119	Leyland Lion PLSC3	47525	Leyland	B32R	10/1928		
20	BX9850	Leyland Tiger TS2	60449	Leyland	B32R	7/1929	Renumbered 120, See note – B	
21	TH120	Leyland Tiger TS2	60615	Leyland	B32R	10/1929	See note – C	By 6/1947
22	TH260	Leyland Tiger TS2	60855	Leyland	B32R	12/1929	See note – C	By 6/1947
23	TX5630	Tilling Stevens T.S.M. B10A2	5756	Vickers	B32R	6/1928	Acquired with the business of W.L. Davies (Cambrian Express) Clydach – 5/1930	11/1930
24	TH800	Leyland Titan TD1	71419	Leyland	L24/24R	5/1930	Renumbered 124, See note – D	By 7/1947
25	TH801	Leyland Titan TD1	71484	Leyland	L24/24R	6/1930	Renumbered 125, See Note – D	3/1947
26	TH1070	Leyland Tiger TS3	60977	Leyland	B32R	8/1930		
27	TH1280	Leyland Tiger TS3	61281	Leyland	B32R	12/1930	Renumbered 127 in 1937, See note - E	-/1947
28	TH1850	Leyland Tiger TS1	61844	Leyland	B32R	7/1931	Renumbered 128 in 1937, See note – E	
29	TH2300	Leyland Titan TD2	2583	Leyland	L24/24R	2/1932		8/1945
30	TH2727	Leyland Tiger TS4	192	Leyland	B32R	7/1932	Requisitioned by War Department 18/7/1940	5/1947
31	TH3060	Leyland Tiger TS4	2211	Leyland	B32R	1/1933		1/1947
	BX8638	Thorneycroft A1	16240		20	4/1928	Acquired with the business of A. Morgan (Morgan Bros) Ammanford in 12/1932	9/1933
	TH396	Thorneycroft A6	18338		20	2/1930		5/1933
32	TH2515	Commer Invader 6TK	27999		20	4/1932		7/1934
33	TH3580	Leyland Tiger TS6	2903	Beadle	C32R	7/1933	Requisitioned by War Department 18/7/1940	7/1940
34	TH3581	Leyland Tiger TS6	2904	Beadle	C32R	7/1933	Renumbered 134 in 1937	10/1948
35	TH3636	Leyland Tiger TS6	3021	Beadle	C32R	8/1933	Renumbered 135 in 1937 Requisitioned by War Department 18/7/1940	10/1951
36	TH3637	Leyland Tiger TS6	3022	Beadle	C32R	8/1933	Renumbered 136 in 1937 Requisitioned by War Department 18/7/1940	-/1951

	BX6711					3/1926		
	BX9954				20	7/1929		
37	TH256	G.M.C. T60		Duple	B26D	11/1929	James acquired control of these vehicles with the business of Wm. Jones & Sons, (Brynteg) Ltd., Upper Tumble, Carms., in 1932. 38/39/41 were licenced to James 1/1936	
38	TH2844	Tilling Stevens Express	9030	Beadle	C32R	10/1932		9/1938
39	TH2845	Tilling Stevens Express	9026	Beadle	C32R	10/1932		7/1940
41	TH3030	Tilling Stevens C60A7	9031	Beadle	C32R	12/1932		7/1938
40	BX8400	Leyland Tiger TS1	60013	Beadle (1933)	C31C	1/1928	Previously No.17 with J. James. See additional note – A	4/1943
42	BX8530	Leyland Tiger TS1	60012	Beadle (1934)	C31C	4/1928	Previously No.18 with J. James. See additional note – A	By 7/1946
43	TH4501	Leyland Lion LT5A	3972	Beadle	B32R	6/1934	Renumbered 143 in 1937	1945
44	TH4502	Leyland Lion LT5A	3973	Beadle	B32R	6/1934	Renumbered 144 in 1937	1945
45	TF7310	Leyland Titan TD2	130	Leyland	L24/24R	12/1931	Ex. Leyland Motors Ltd (Demonstrator) built in 1932 as TD2c, & operated by Birmingham C.T. as No.94 until 1934. Refurbished by Leyland Motors Ltd., before delivery to James in 4/1935. Renumbered 145 in 1937	1945
146	TH8102	Leyland Tiger TS7	12237	Leyland	B32R	2/1937	Requisitioned by War Department 18/7/1940 and operated for U.S. Air Force.	7/1940
147	TH8103	Leyland Tiger TS7	12238	Leyland	B32R	2/1937	Requisitioned by War Department 18/7/1940	-/1952
148	TH8104	Leyland Tiger TS7	12239	Leyland	B32R	2/1937		
149	TH9902	Leyland Tiger TS8	17343	Leyland	B32R	3/1938		11/1951
150	TH9901	Leyland Titan TD5	17342	Leyland	L24/24R	3/1938		11/1951
151	BBX500	Leyland Titan TD7	304114	Leyland	L24/24R	1/1940		11/1951
152	WN2785	Leyland Titan TD1	71090	Leyland	L27/24R	3/1930	Ex. Swan Motor Services, Bishopston, Swansea, No.11, -/1940	12/1944
153	WN2786	Leyland Titan TD1	71091	Leyland	L27/24R	4/1930	Ex. Swan Motor Services, Bishopston, Swansea, No.12, -/1940	-/1943

154	RB4885	Leyland Titan	TD1	72299	Leyland	L24/24R	9/1931	Originally – Chesterfield Corporation Transport, No.42 Ex. Swan Motor Services, Bishopston, Swansea, -/1940	11/1944
155	TF3183	Leyland Tiger	TS3	60906	Leyland	B32R	11/1930	Ex.Yarrow Motor Coaches, Eccleston, Lancs, No.9 -/1940 - See Note F	7/1945
156	UF6469	Leyland Titan	TD1	71410	Leyland	H24/24R	7/1930	Ex. Southdown Motor Services Ltd., Brighton (869) - -/1940 Via: W.R. Wintour (Dealer), London SE17 See note – G	
157	UF7408	Leyland Titan	TD1	71827	Short	H26/24R	-/1931	Ex. Southdown Motor Services Ltd., Brighton (908) c9/1939. Licenced -/1940 See note G	
158	UF7426	Leyland Titan	TD1	71979	Short	H26/24R	-/1931	Ex. Southdown Motor Services Ltd., Brighton (926). 9/1939. Licenced -/1940 See note – G	
159	FV1649	Leyland Tiger	TS3	61434	Beadle (1937)	C32F	11/1930	Ex. J.Jones & Sons, Ystradgynlais, Brecs. See note – H	2/1946
160	TH1418	Leyland Lion	LT2	51345	Thomas & Thomas	B32F	3/1931	Ex. Dan Jones, Abergwili, Carmarthen. 7/1941	1945
161	AWN753	Leyland Cheetah	LZ2A	13115	Duple	C32	4/1937	Ex. Swan Motor Services, Bishopston, Swansea. No.1 -/1940	
162	AWN766	Leyland Tiger	TS7	13426	Burlingham	C31F	3/1937	Ex. Swan Motor Services, Bishopston, Swansea, -/1941	By 1946
163	DLT20	Leyland Tiger	TS7	12675	Duple	C33F	3/1937	Ex.L.Adnams,Wimbledon,London,SW19 By 6/1941	3/1946
164	BTH174	Leyland Titan	TD7	307105	Leyland	L27/26R	10/1941	See note - I	-/1953
165	BTH175	Leyland Titan	TD7	307106	Leyland	L27/26R	10/1941	See note - I	1955
166	BTH652	Bedford	OWB	9291	Duple	UB32F	9/1942		1947
167	BTH854	Bedford	OWB	12198	Duple	UB32F	2/1943		
168	CBX85	Bedford	OWB	16093	Duple	UB32F	10/1943		3/1946
169	BTH813	Guy Arab MkI	5LW	FD25741	Brush	UL27/28R	3/1943	See note – J	12/1959

170	BTH910	Guy Arab MkI 5LW	FD25880	Brush	UL27/28R	5/1943	See note – J	12/1959
171	CBX7	Guy Arab MkII 5LW	FD26005	Strachan	UL27/28R	8/1943	See note – K	4/1957
172	CBX54	Guy Arab MkII 5LW	FD26074	Strachan	UL27/28R	9/1943	See note – L	11/1959
173	CBX141	Guy Arab MkII 6LW	FD26414	Strachan	UL27/28R	2/1944	See note – L	6/1957
174	CBX86	Bedford OWB	16098	Duple	UB32F	10/1943		5/1947
175	CBX87	Bedford OWB	16113	Duple	UB32F	10/1943		1/1947
176	UH8624	A.E.C. Regal	0662465	Hall Lewis	B30R	9/1930	Acquired with the business of Bevan & Davies, Garnswllt, Glam., 12/1943 See note – M	6/1946
177	UH8626	A.E.C. Regal	0662467	Hall Lewis	B30R	9/1930		4/1945
178	UH8629	A.E.C. Regal	0662470	Hall Lewis	B30R	10/1930		6/1946
179	CBX298	Guy Arab MkII 5LW	FD26698	Roe	UL27/28R	5/1944	See note – N	1959
180	CBX299	Daimler CWA6	11692	Brush	UL27/28R	5/1944	See note – N	1955
181	CBX311	Daimler CWA6	11685	Brush	UL27/28R	5/1944	See note – N	1954
182	CBX312	Daimler CWA6	11686	Brush	UL27/28R	5/1944	See note – N	1955
183	CBX341	Guy Arab MkII 6LW	FD26758	Roe	UL27/28R	6/1944	See note – N	1956
184	CBX406	Guy Arab MkII 6LW	FD26760	Roe	UL27/28R	7/1944	See note – N	1958
185	CBX476	Guy Arab MkII 6LW	FD27041	Roe	UL27/28R	11/1944	See note – N	l/1959
186	CBX477	Guy Arab MkII 6LW	FD27042	Roe	UL27/28R	10/1944	See note – N	6/1957
187	CBX488	Daimler CWA6	11874	Duple	UL27/28R	11/1944	See note – N	1954
188	CBX494	Daimler CWA6	11875	Duple	UL27/28R	11/1944	See note – N	1954
189	AKE884	Tillilng Stevens T.S.M. B49A7	8526		32	1/1933	Acquired with the business of Jones Bros. (Brynawel) Penygroes, Carms. 2/1945	1945
190	TH2385	Tilling Stevens Express	9018	Strachan	B32R	5/1932		1946
191	TH2845	Tilling Stevens Express	9026	Beadle	C35R	10/1932		1946
192	WN5629	Tillilng Stevens T.S.M. B49A7	8650	Beadle	B32R	6/1933		1945

193	CTH490	Leyland Tiger PS1	461063	Burlingham	B34F	9/1946		1957
194	CTH615	Leyland Tiger PS1	461185	Burlingham	B34F	10/1946	See note – O	1961
195	CTH823	Leyland Tiger PD1	462244	Leyland	L27/26R	12/1946		4/1959
196	CTH825	Leyland Titan PD1	462245	Leyland	L27/26R	12/1946		4/1959
197	CTH826	Leyland Titan PD1	462493	Leyland	L27/26R	12/1946		4/1959
198	CTH827	Leyland Titan PD1	462494	Leyland	L27/26R	12/1946		1/1959
199	DBX259	Leyland Tiger PS1	462100	Strachan	B34F	4/1947		12/1956
200	DBX260	Leyland Tiger PS1	462767	Strachan	B34F	5/1947	See note – P	12/1959
201	DBX637	Leyland Tiger PS1	462768	Strachan	B32F	7/1947	See note – R	12/1960
202	DBX638	Leyland Tiger PS1	462826	Strachan	B32F	8/1947	See note – S	1959
203	DTH722	Leyland Tiger PS1	470660	Strachan	B32F	2/1948	See note – R	12/1960
204	EBX662	Leyland Tiger PS1	470661	Strachan	B32F	8/1948	See note – T	1/1961
205	EBX663	Leyland Tiger PS1	471099	Strachan	B32F	8/1948	See note – T	9/1962
206	FTH680	Leyland Titan PD2/1	502649	Leyland	L27/26R	8/1950	See note – U	9/1962
207	FTH681	Leyland Titan PD2/1	502650	Leyland	L27/26R	8/1950	See note – U	9/1962
208	FTH682	Leyland Titan PD2/1	502651	Leyland	L27/26R	8/1950	See note – U	9/1962
209	FTH683	Leyland Titan PD2/1	502652	Leyland	L27/26R	8/1950	See note – U	9/1962
210	FTH717	Leyland-MCW Olympic HR40	496361	M.C.W.	B40F	8/1950		9/1962
211	FTH718	Leyland-MCW Olympic HR40	496362	M.C.W.	B40F	9/1950		7/1962
212	GTH297	Leyland Royal Tiger PSU1/13	511324	Duple	B40F	11/1951		9/1962
213	HBX60	Leyland Royal Tiger PSU1/13	515011	Duple	B44F	7/1952	Re-seated to B40F later	9/1962
214	HBX61	Leyland Royal Tiger PSU1/13	515012	Duple	B44F	7/1952	Re-seated to B40F later	9/1962

215	JBX940	Leyland Titan PD2/12	532588	Leyland	L27/26R	2/1954		9/1962
216	JBX941	Leyland Titan PD2/12	532587	Leyland	L27/26R	2/1954		9/1962
217	JTH291	Leyland Royal Tiger PSU1/16	540001	Burlingham Seagull	C39C	4/1954		9/1962
218	KBX997	Leyland Tiger Cub PSUC1/1	544957	Weymann	B44F	2/1955		9/1962
219	KBX998	Leyland Tiger Cub PSUC1/1	544958	Weymann	B44F	2/1955		9/1962
220	NBX77	Leyland Tiger Cub PSUC1/1	565671	Weymann	B44F	9/1956		9/1962
221	NBX78	Leyland Tiger Cub PSUC1/1	565672	Weymann	B44F	9/1956		9/1962
222	NTH33	Leyland Titan PD2/12	562803	M.C.W. Orion	L31/28RD	6/1957		9/1962
223	NTH850	Leyland Titan PD3/4	570873	Weymann	L35/32RD	6/1957		9/1962
224	NTH851	Leyland Titan PD3/4	570874	Weymann	L35/32RD	6/1957		9/1962
225	OBX780	Leyland Tiger Cub PSUC1/1	576299	Weymann	B44F	9/1957		9/1962
226	OBX781	Leyland Tiger Cub PSUC1/1	576300	Weymann	B44F	9/1957		9/1962
227	RTH637	Leyland Atlantean PDR1/1	582375	M.C.W.	L39/34F	12/1958	See note – V	9/1962
228	RTH638	Leyland Atlantean PDR1/1	590060	M.C.W.	L39/34F	4/1959		9/1962
229	RTH639	Leyland Atlantean PDR1/1	590061	M.C.W.	L39/34F	4/1959		9/1962
230	RTH640	Leyland Atlantean PDR1/1	590062	M.C.W.	L39/34F	4/1959		9/1962
231	RTH641	Leyland Atlantean PDR1/1	590063	M.C.W.	L39/34F	4/1959		9/1962
232	UBX45	Leyland Atlantean PDR1/1	591469	Weymann	L39/34F	11/1959		9/1962
233	UBX46	Leyland Atlantean PDR1/1	591485	Weymann	L39/34F	11/1959		9/1962

234	UBX47	Leyland Atlantean PDR1/1	591486	Weymann	L39/34F	11/1959		9/1962
235	UBX48	Leyland Atlantean PDR1/1	591470	Weymann	L39/34F	11/1959		9/1962
236	UBX49	Leyland Atlantean PDR1/1	591468	Weymann	L39/34F	11/1959		9/1962
237	WTH113	Leyland Atlantean PDR1/1	602290	Weymann	L39/33F	12/1960		9/1962
238	WTH114	Leyland Atlantean PDR1/1	602289	Weymann	L39/33F	12/1960		9/1962
239	YTH805	Leyland Atlantean PDR1/1	611130	Weymann	L39/33F	1/1962		9/1962

SERVICE VEHICLES

Reg. No.	Make & Type	Remarks	Date New	Remarks / Additional Information
BTH471	Fordson Tractor	30cwt. Industrial Tractor	27/3/1942	Same unladen weight as a Fordson Agricultural Tractor
DBX 22	Ford F30 Lorry	3ton 15cwt V8 engined 4x4 lorry	1/1/1947	DBX22, the Canadian Ford towing/recovery vehicle ran on trade plates 023BX
JBX971	Austin A40 Saloon Car	1200cc	21/12/1953	
OBX245	Morris 5cwt Van	948cc	28/2/1957	Supplied by Castle Garages, Ammanford.
UBX977	Austin A40 Saloon Car	948cc	25/11/1959	DBX22, OBX245, UBX977 all passed to S.W.T. on 1/9/1962.

ADDITIONAL VEHICLE NOTES:

	Vehicle renumbering: 20, 24, 25, 27, 28, 34, 35, 36, 40, 42, 43, 44, 45 were renumbered 120, 124, 125, 127, 128, 134, 135, 136, 140, 142, 143, 144, and 145 respectively in 1937.
Note A:	17/18 (BX8400/BX8530) were new to James in 1928. They were rebodied as one-and-a-half decker observation coaches by J.C. Beadle in 1933/4 respectively, retrofitted with 8.6 litre oil engines and renumbered 40/42 respectively. After re-bodying they were licenced to associate company Wm. Jones & Sons (Brynteg) Ltd., c/o J. James & Sons Ltd., Ammanford, and carried the 'Brynteg' fleet name, operating the Aberystwyth route. Both were re-licenced to J. James & Sons Ltd., from 1/1936, and renumbered 140/142 respectively in1937.
Note B:	20 (BX9850) was re-bodied by J. C. Beadle in 1937 as B32R; retrofitted with 8.6 litre oil engine and renumbered 120.
Note C:	21/22 (TH120/260) were both re-bodied by J. C. Beadle in 1937, as B32R.
Note D:	24/25 (TH800/801) were both re-bodied by J. C. Beadle in 1937 as L24/24R, retrofitted with 8.6 litre oil engines, and re-numbered 124/125 respectively.
Note E:	27/28 (TH1280/1850) were both re-bodied by J. C. Beadle in 1937 as B32R, retrofitted with 8.6 oil engines and renumbered 127/128 respectively.
Note F:	155(TF3183) was re-seated to B30F.
Note G:	156-8 (UF6469/7408/7426) were re-seated to H28/24R, H30/24R and H30/24R respectively by James.
Note H:	159 (FV1649) was new to S. & J. Woods (Seagull Coaches) Blackpool, Lancs., and was re-bodied by J. C. Beadle in 1937.
Note I:	164/165 (BTH174/5) were wartime 'unfrozen' vehicles, originally built to the order of W. Alexander & Sons Ltd., Falkirk. Scotland.
Note J:	169/170 (BTH813/910) were both re-bodied by C.H. Roe Coachworks, to L27/28R in 12/1951, and retrofitted with Gardner 6LW engines.
Note K:	171 (CBX 7) Body refurbished by Jeffreys Commercial Motors, Swansea, in 1950 and retrofitted with Gardner 6LW engine.
Note L:	172/173 (CBX54/141) Body refurbished by Bruce Coachworks, Cardiff in 1950, and retrofitted with Gardner 6LW engines.
Note M:	176-178 (UH8624/8626/8629) were new to Western Welsh Omnibus Co., 556/8/561 respectively.
Note N:	179-188 (CBX298/299/311/312/341/406/476/477/488/494). Their bodies were refurbished by Bruce Coachworks, Cardiff in 1951.
Note O:	194 (CTH 615) had its Burlingham saloon body removed and scrapped in 1955. The chassis was rebuilt to PD1 specification by Western Welsh Omnibus Company, and re-bodied by Metro-Cammell-Weyman with a new 'Orion' L27/28R body in 1955. After withdrawal in 1961, the M.C.W. 'Orion' body was transferred to James' 208 (FTH682) and the chassis subsequently scrapped.

Note P:	200 (DBX 260) was rebodied in 1957 with a second hand Burlingham B34F body (of 1946 manufacture) salvaged from withdrawn Leyland Tiger, 193 (CTH 490). In turn, the discarded Strachan body from 200 was fitted to the chassis of 193 for disposal as scrap. The body swop was carried out by Western Welsh O.C., at Ely works, Cardiff.
Note R:	201/3 (DBX637/DTH722) had their Strachan saloon bodies removed and scrapped in 1955. Their chassis were rebuilt to PD1 specification by Western Welsh Omnibus Company, at Ely Works, Cardiff, and re-bodied by Metro-Cammell-Weymann with new 'Orion' L27/28R bodies in 1955. After withdrawal of these vehicles in 1961, the M.C.W. 'Orion' bodies were transferred to James' 207/6 (FTH681/680) respectively.
Note S:	202 (DBX638) had its body overhauled by Longwell Green Coachworks, Bristol, in 7/1952.
Note T:	204/5 (EBX662/3) had their Strachan saloon bodies removed and scrapped in 1954. Their chassis were rebuilt to PD1 specification by Western Welsh Omnibus Company, and re-bodied by Longwell Green coachworks with new L27/26R bodies in 4/1954. After withdrawal of 204 (EBX662) in 1961, the Longwell Green body was transferred to James' 209 (FTH683) and the chassis subsequently scrapped.
Note U:	206-209 (FTH680-3) had their original Leyland L27/26R bodies removed and scrapped in 1961. In exchange they received second hand bodies salvaged from the withdrawn 'Leyland Tiger rebuilds'. 206(FTH680) received the 1955 M.C.W. 'Orion' L27/28R body from 203 (DTH 722) in 4/1961. 207(FTH681) received the 1955 M.C.W. 'Orion' L27/28R body from 201 (DBX 637) in 4/1961. 208(FTH682) received the 1955 M.C.W. 'Orion' L27/28R body from 194 (CTH 615) in 4/1961. 209(FTH683) received the 1954 Longwell Green L27/26R body from 204 (EBX 662) in 8/1961. All this work was carried out by Western Welsh Omnibus Company, at their Ely Works, Cardiff.
Note V:	227(RTH637) was exhibited on the Leyland Motors Ltd., stand, of the 1958 Commercial Motor Show, Earls Court, London, in October 1958. Numerically the fourth pre-production prototype chassis built by Leyland Motors, it was the very *first* Leyland Atlantean to enter passenger service in the world, on 4th December, 1958.

VEHICLE DISPOSALS

	BX234	Sold to E.E. Gape, Dillwyn Arms, Pontardawe, Glamorganshire 9/6/1920
	BX463	Sold to unknown Breconshire owner at unknown date.
	BX477	No trace.
	BX795	Replaced by Lancia 8/1924 with no further trace.
	BX1565	Sold to unknown owner at Bootle, Lancs; later to Liverpool owner.
1	BX1735	Sold by 1930 to unknown owner, converted to lorry and scrapped in 1939.
2	BX2237	No trace.
3	BX2725	No trace.
4	BX3280	Sold to unknown owner at Swansea as a lorry by 1928, and scrapped 1928.
5	??	No trace.
6	BX4914	Sold to unknown Breconshire owner 1/1925.
6	BX5196	Sold to J.M. Bacus & Co., Burry Port by 2/1927. To unknown Glamorganshire owner at unknown date.
7	BX5197	Sold to Cardiff owner, date unknown. No further trace.
8	BX5198	Sold to Watts (Factors) Lydney, Glos., as a lorry 12/1926. To: Holland, Oldbury, Worcs., as a lorry 5/7/1928 and last licenced 1931. No further trace.
9	BX5204	Sold to unknown Glamorganshire owner.
10	BX5205	Sold to unknown owner as lorry 9/1930. Last licenced 1931.
11	??	No further trace.
12	BX7333	Sold to Griffin Motor Co. Ltd., Brynmawr, Brecs. (39) as B31D by 3/1932. To: H. Joynson, Nantyglo, Mon., 10/1935 and last licenced 1940.
14	BX8220	Sold to Griffin Motor Co. Ltd., Brynmawr, Brecs, (43) 7/1932. Withdrawn 3/1935. To: T. Evans, New Tredegar, Mon., 3/1935. Last licenced 1938.
15	BX8221	Sold to T. Evans, New Tredegar, Mon., at unknown date. No further trace.
16	BX8222	Sold to T. Evans, New Tredegar, Mon., at unknown date. No further trace.
17	BX8400	Re-bodied & renumbered 40 in 1933. See details of vehicle number 140.
18	BX8530	Re-bodied & renumbered 42 in 1934. See details of vehicle number 142.
19	BX9119	No trace.
20	BX9850	Sold to Evans, Kenfig Hill, Glam., at unknown date. No further trace.
21	TH 120	Sold to W.G. Richards (Richards Bros) Moylgrove, Pembs, by 6/1947 as 35 seater. To: Harold & Huddlestone (J. & L. Coaches), Barking, Essex, 2/1950. To: J. Pascall, Ilford, Essex, 5/1951. To: M.L. Leader, (Maryland Coaches) Stratford, London, E.15, 6/1952. Registration obsolete 7/9/1956.
22	TH 260	Sold to B. Mitchell, Glyncorrwg, Glam., by 6/1947. No further trace.
23	TX5630	Sold to: Borough Services, Southend, Essex, 11/1930. To: Eastern National O.C. Ltd., 5/1933. To: H.C.Simmons, Dover, 3/1935 and scrapped in 1935.

124	TH 800	Sold to: V. Williams (The Richmond), Neath, Glam., by 7/1947. To: United Welsh Services Ltd., Swansea in 1951 – not operated.
125	TH 801	Sold to: L.C.W. Motors, Ltd., Llandilo, Carms., 3/1947. Withdrawn 1949. To: O.J. Williams (Haulier), St. Clears, Carms., to provide spare parts for a lorry. Remains scrapped – 3/1950.
26	TH1070	Withdrawn c.1951. No further trace. Registration obsolete 9/1956.
127	TH1280	Sold to: Evans (Express Motors) Kenfig Hill, Glam, 1947. Registration obsolete 11/1956.
128	TH1850	Sold to: Evans (Express Motors) Kenfig Hill, Glam, unknown date. Registration obsolete 9/1956.
29	TH2300	Sold to: S. Blackwell & Sons, Earls Colne, Essex, 8/1945. Withdrawn 11/1951. No further trace. Registration obsolete 9/1956.
30	TH2727	Sold to: C.G. Hill, Tredegar, Mon, 5/1947 and re-bodied by Groom & Llewellyn, Bridgend to B33F. To: Jones Omnibus Services Ltd., Aberbeeg, Mon., No37, 10/1949. To: Edmunds Bus Services, Rassau, Mon., by 1952, withdrawn by 6/1956, still at garage derelict 2/1959.
31	TH3060	Sold to: L.G. Potter, Skewen, Glam., 1/1947. Last licenced 1950.
	BX8638	Sold to: Jeffreys (Dealer) Swansea, 9/1933. No further trace.
	TH 396	Sold to: J. Evans & Sons, Als Garage, Bancffosfelin, Pontyberem, Carms. 5/1933. To:Hall-Lewis(Thorneycroft Dealer)Cardiff depot. Last licenced 1939. No further trace.
32	TH2515	Sold to: A.A. Woodbury, Wellington, Somerset, - 7/1934. To: M.N. Cruise, Warminster, Wilts., 12/1939. Last licenced 1947. No further trace.
133	TH3580	Requisitioned by War Department 18/7/1940 and Not returned. Sold to: H. Porter (Henry's Coaches) South Tottenham, London. N15 (No.16) 6/1946, where it was fitted with a new Duple 'A' C33F body in 1946 and hired to London Transport 1947-49. To: A. Oliver, Hawkhurst, Kent, 2/1956. To: E.H. Ive (John's Cross Garage) Robertsbridge, Essex, 8/1957. To: Cooks Coaches, Westwell Ashford, Kent, 6/1959. Withdrawn 10/1960.
134	TH3581	Sold to: E.P. John (Kenfig Motors) Kenfig Hill, Glam., (No.16) 10/1948, where it was re-bodied as B33F. Withdrawn 5/1955. Disposed of by 11/1960.
135	TH3636	Sold to: Rees Jones, Ystradgynlais, Brecs., 10/1951. Its identity was transferred by Jones to a Leyland TS7, chassis No. 9636 at unknown date. Withdrawn by 12/1955.
136	TH3637	Sold to: Rees Jones, Ystradgynlais, Brecs., 1951 and broken up 1951.
37	TH 256	Gone by 1935
38	TH2844	Sold to: Thomas & James, Port Talbot, Glam., 9/1938. To: J. Tulk, Brynhyfryd, Swansea, 6/1943. To: Showman 10/1949. Last licenced 1953.
39	TH2845	Sold to: Jones Bros., 'Brynawel', Penygroes, Carms, 31/7/1940. Re-acquired with the Jones Brothers business, 2/1945; and given fleet No.191.
140	BX8400	Sold to: unknown owner 8/4/1943 and converted into a lorry. To: James Thompson & Co. Ltd., Dumballs Road, Cardiff, for scrap 3/4/1952.
41	TH3030	Sold to: L.C. Williams (L.C.W. Motors), Llandilo, Carms, 7/1938. Requisitioned by War Department -/1940., returned after war and last licenced 1948.

142	BX8530	Sold to: E. Marsden & Sons., Mossley, Manchester, by 7/1946. Withdrawn 10/1950. No further trace.
143	TH4501	Sold to: T.D. & T.J. Edmunds (Edmunds Omnibus Services), Rassau, Mon., unknown date before 1951. To: Dobson, Ystrad Mynach, Mon., by 1951.
144	TH4502	Sold to: Starkey, Ton Pentre, Glam., -/1945, and converted to B32F by Starkey. To: G.H. Thomas (Thomas Motors) Barry, Glam. 7/1945. To: Smith (Showman) Cardiff, 7/1950. No further trace
145	TF7310	Sold to: Williams Bros., (Pioneer Buses), Laugharne, Carms. -/1945. To: S. Eynon & Sons, Trimsaran, Carms, 8/1949, and rebuilt by Jeffreys Commercial Motors, Swansea to L26/24R. Withdrawn 9/1956 and sold for scrap 1956.
146	TH8102	Requisitioned by War Department, 18/7/1940, and operated by U.S. Air Force. Not returned after war. Sold to: J.A. Whitmarsh (Avon Coaches), Netheravon, Wilts., -/1944. Withdrawn 11/1954. Sold to: Rawlings (Castle Coaches) Ludgershall, Wilts., (No.11) unknown date. No further trace.
147	TH8103	Withdrawn 1952. Sold to: Edwards (Showman), Carmarthen 2/1953. To: Immobile caravan at Gorslas, Carms, by 1963 and lived in until c.1982, remaining there derelict minus engine, gearbox and radiator until 10/1993 when it was cut up for scrap by M.R.J. Phillips (Scrap dealer), Gorslas, Carms., to make way for a housing development.
148	TH8104	Sold before 1952. Noted as a tar spraying lorry at Carmarthen – unknown date.
149	TH9902	Withdrawn 11/1951. Cannibalised for spares; remains sold to Mr. Austin, Baptist Lane, Ammanford 7/1/1952 for scrap.
150	TH9901	Withdrawn 11/1951. Sold to Dealer. To static caravan at Llanstephan, Carms.
151	BBX 500	Scrapped 1/11/1951
152	WN2785	Withdrawn 12/1944. No further trace.
153	WN2786	Sold to: J. Jones, Ystradgynlais, Brecs., -/1943. To: Seamarks Bros. (Seamarks Coaches), Westoning, Luton, Beds., 10/1946. Re-bodied as a coach C32F by 1950. Withdrawn by Seamarks 9/1955. To: Sir Robert McAlpine (National Contractor) London S.W.9. by 7/1956. No further trace.
154	RB4885	Sold to Arlington Motors (Dealer) Cardiff, 11/1944. To: T.D. & T.J. Edmunds (Edmunds Omnibus Services) Rassau, Mon., unknown date, last licenced by Edmunds 9/1945. No further trace.
155	TF3183	Withdrawn 7/1945. Sold to: H.G. Hooper, Crynant, Glam., unknown date. To: W. Carberry, Rishton, Lancs, by 4/1949, To: W. Barnes, Rishdon and last licenced 7/1952.
156	UF6469	Sold to: M.L. Leader (Maryland Coaches), Stratford, London E.15., 5/1952. Note – at an unknown date the double decker body had been removed and the cassis rebodied with a coach body, C - - F. To: E.W. Beldom, (Showman), London Colney, Herts., by 8/1953. Last licence expired 12/1956.
157	UF7408	No trace
158	UF7426	No trace.
159	FV1649	Sold to: Arlington Motors (Dealer) Cardiff, 2/1946. To: Rees Jones, Ystradgynlais, Brecs., at unknown date. To: Keelings Coaches, Kirkstall Rd, Leeds 4., 6/1953.

160	TH1418	Withdrawn 1945. Sold to: Ford & Reames (Alma Queen Coaches), Brynmawr, Brecs., at unknown date, To: Howells & Withers, Ynysddu, Mon., (No.11) 6/1948., withdrawn 6/1951 and scrapped.
161	AWN 753	No trace
162	AWN 766	Sold to: J.C. Hodgson, Preston, Lancs., No.33 at unknown date. To: J.Woodcock, Heskin, Lancs., 11/1946. To: A. & M. Foster, Dinnington, S. Yorks., 1/1948, later fitted with K.W. FC33F body. Withdrawn 12/1959 and scrapped.
163	DLT 20	Sold to: J. Woodcock, Heskin, Lancs, 3/1946. To: W.M. Armstrong (Redwing Coaches) North Shields, 5/1948, To: R. Armstrong, Westerhope, Newcastle-Upon-Tyne, 11/1951. Withdrawn 5/1956, To unidentified showman. No further trace.
164	BTH 174	Withdrawn 1953. Mechanical parts to Western Welsh O.C., Chassis and body to J.G. Evans, Llanelly 1/1954 for scrap.
165	BTH 175	Sold to: S. Eynon & Sons, Trimsaran, Carms (No.19) 9/1955, Later No.24. Withdrawn 10/1958. Sold to Birds (Dealer) Stratford-on-Avon, Warwickshire, 10/1958 and scrapped.
166	BTH 652	Sold to: C. W. Jordan (Maple Leaf Garage) Bristol, 4/1947 as B28F. To Wessex Coaches Ltd., Bristol, 4/1948 and withdrawn 1950. To Hale, Barnstaple, Devon, 6/1950 and withdrawn 6/1955.
167	BTH 854	Sold by 1947. To: I Pursey (Caerphilly Greys) Caerphilly, Glam., by 4/1955. Probably long before.
168	CBX 85	Sold to: J. Evans & Sons, Als Garage, Bancffosfelin, Pontyberem, Carms. 3/1946 and withdrawn 11/1955. No further trace.
169	BTH 813	Sold to: West Wales Motors Ltd., Tycroes, Ammanford, No.34, 12/1959. Withdrawn 4/1962 and scrapped by 8/1962.
170	BTH 910	Sold to: West Wales Motors Ltd., Tycroes, Ammanford. No.35, 12/1959. Withdrawn 11/1962 and scrapped.
171	CBX 7	Sold to unknown showman 19/4/1957. No further trace.
172	CBX 54	Sold to: T.H. Lewis (Scrap dealer) Swansea, 1960 and scrapped 11/1960.
173	CBX 141	Sold to: Unknown showman at Gloucester, 10/1957. No further trace.
174	CBX 86	Sold to: J. Evans (Express Motors), Kenfig Hill, Glam., 5/1947, withdrawn 11/1957 and scrapped 12/1957.
175	CBX 87	Sold to: V. Williams (The Richmond) Neath, Glam., 1/1947, and withdrawn by 1/1950. To: G.B. Smith, Cymmer, Glam., 5/1951., To: Thurgood (Dealer) Ware, Herts., 7/1957. To: Cowley (Dealer) Salford, Lancs., 11/1957. To: W. Whiteley, New Maldon, London, S.W.20 (Fairground) 11/1957.
176	UH8624	Sold to: S.J. Davies, Penygraig, Glam., 6/1946. To: Howells & Withers, Pontllanfraith, Mon., (No.2) and withdrawn by 1952. No further trace.
177	UH8626	Sold to: S.J. Davies, Penygraig, Glam., 4/1945. To: Jones Omnibus Services Ltd., Aberbeeg, Mon., (No.31) -/1947, withdrawn 1955. No further trace.
178	UH8629	Sold to: S.J. Davies, Penygraig, Glam., 6/1946., and withdrawn 5/1949. To: Priory Coaches, Christchurch, Hants., 12/1950 and withdrawn 1/1954. No further trace.
179	CBX 298	No trace.

180	CBX 299	To: Western Welsh O.C., Cardiff, for disposal 1955. To South Wales Motor Traders, Newport, Mon., 10/1955. No further trace.
181	CBX 311	Chassis only sold to Sir Alfred McAlpine (National Contractor) Hoxton, London, S.W.9., unknown date; Body scrapped.
182	CBX 312	Sold to: South Wales Motor Traders, Newport, Mon., 10/1955. No further trace.
183	CBX 341	To: Western Welsh O.C., for disposal by 12/1956. To: A.M.C.C. (Dealer) Stratford, London, E.15 by 1/1957. No further trace.
184	CBX 406	Sold to: E. Evans (Scrap dealer) Cwmgorse, Glam., 9/1958., and scrapped.
185	CBX 476	To: Western Welsh O.C. for disposal, 1/1959. Engine fitted to W.W.O.C., 383 (LDE601) in 1/1959. Remains scrapped.
186	CBX 477	To: Western Welsh O.C. for disposal 6/1957. To: Showman at Gloucester, 10/1957.
187	CBX 488	Chassis to: Sir Alfred McAlpine (National Contractor), Hoxton, London, S.W.9., unknown date. Body scrapped.
188	CBX 494	Sold to: Lancashire Motor Traders (Dealer} Altrincham, Cheshire, 1954. Exported to The South Western Omnibus Co., Sri-Lanka, Ceylon, 9/1954, re-registered IC2420.
189	AKE 884	No trace.
190	TH 2385	Sold to: T. Evans, New Tredegar, Mon., 7/1946. Withdrawn 6/1949. Sold to Thomas & Evans (Corona soft drinks) Porth, Glam., as a lorry.
191	TH 2845	Sold to: unknown showman 1/4/1946. Last licenced 1951.
192	WN 5629	Sold to: V. Williams (The Richmond Bus Co.) Neath, Glam. To: Rhymney Transport, Rhymney, Mon., Last licenced 12/1947.
193	CTH 490	After withdrawal in 1957, the body was removed and interchanged with 200 (DBX 260). The chassis, subsequently carrying the discarded Strachan body from 200 was disposed of for scrap. The body swap was carried out by Western Welsh O.C., at Ely works.
194	CTH 615	After withdrawal in 1961, the body was removed and fitted to James' 208(FTH682) by Western Welsh O.C., in 1961. The chassis was subsequently sold for scrap in 1962.
195	CTH 823	Withdrawn 4/1959. Sold to: McEwan, Lennoxtown, Scotland by 8/1960.
196	CTH 825	Withdrawn 4/1959. Noted derelict in scrap yard at Kirk O'Shots, Scotland, 6/1960.
197	CTH 826	Withdrawn 4/1959. Sold to: Clarke, Dumfries, Scotland by 7/1960.
198	CTH 827	Written off after serious accident on 5/1/1959, when it overturned on an icy road at Glanamman. Sold for scrap 1959.
199	DBX 259	To: Western Welsh O.C., for disposal 14/12/1956. To: A.M.C.C. (Dealer), Stratford, London, E.15 by 2/1957 and still there 7/1957. No further trace.
200	DBX 260	Sold to: Samuel Eynon & Sons, Trimsaran (12/1959). Withdrawn 4/1962 and sold for scrap.
201	DBX 637	After withdrawal in 1961, the body was removed and fitted to James' 207(FTH681) by Western Welsh O.C., in 1961. The chassis was subsequently sold for scrap.
202	DBX 638	Sold to: T.H. Lewis (Scrap dealer), Swansea, 1960 and scrapped in 11/1960.

203	DTH 722	After withdrawal in 1961, the body was removed and fitted to James' 206(FTH680) by Western Welsh O.C., in 1961. The chassis was subsequently sold for scrap in 1962.
204	EBX 662	After withdrawal in 1961, the body was removed and fitted to James' 209(FTH683) by Western Welsh O.C., in 1961. The chassis was subsequently sold for scrap in 1961.
205	EBX 663	To: South Wales Transport (205), 1/9/1962. Withdrawn by 3/1963. Sold to: S.J. Davies (Dealer), Penygraig, Glam., 1963. No further trace.
206	FTH 680	To: South Wales Transport (1106), 1/9/1962. Withdrawn 1963. Sold to: S.J. Davies, (Dealer), Penygraig, Glam., 1963. To: Wheatsheaf, Merthyr Tydfil, 10/1963, and withdrawn 7/1965. To: Way, (Scrap dealer), Cardiff by 5/1966 for scrap.
207	FTH 681	To: South Wales Transport (1107), 1/9/1962. Withdrawn 1963. Sold to S. J. Davies, (Dealer), Penygraig, Glam., 1963. To: Wheatsheaf, Merthyr Tydfil, 10/1963, and withdrawn 6/1965. To: Edwards, Joys Green, Glos., for spares 10/1965 and scrapped by 7/1966.
208	FTH 682	To: South Wales Transport (1108), 1/9/1962. Withdrawn 1964. Sold to: S.J. Davies, (Dealer), Penygraig, Glam., 1964. To: Wheatsheaf, Merthyr Tydfil 3/1964, and withdrawn 5/1965. To Leggatt (Contractor), Barrhead, Strathclyde by 7/1966. No further trace.
209	FTH 683	To: South Wales Transport (1109). 1/9/1962. Withdrawn 1963. Sold to: S.J. Davies, (Dealer), Penygraig, Glam., 1963. To: Daniel Jones, Abergwili, Carmarthen, (No.7), 10/1963. Withdrawn 4/1968 and sold for scrap.
210	FTH 717	To: South Wales Transport (210), 1/9/1962. Withdrawn by 2/1963. Sold to: S.J. Davies, (Dealer), Penygraig, Glam., 1963 for scrap. No further trace.
211	FTH 718	Withdrawn 7/1962 with fire damage. To: South Wales Transport (211), 1/9/1962 but not operated. To: S.J. Davies, (Dealer), Penygraig, Glam., for scrap by 10/1962. No further trace.
212	GTH 297	To: South Wales Transport (800), 1/9/1962. Withdrawn 1964. Sold to: S.J. Davies, (Dealer), Penygraig, Glam., 1964. To: Standard Box & Carton Co., (Non PS.V.) Merthyr Tydfil, Glam., by 3/1965.
213	HBX 60	To: South Wales Transport (801), 1/9/1962. Withdrawn 1964. Sold to: S.J. Davies, (Dealer), Penygraig, Glam., 1964. To: Maberly Parker (Contractor) Tongwynlais, Glam., (Non P.S.V.) by 1/1969. No further trace.
214	HBX 61	To: South Wales Transport (802), 1/9/1962. Withdrawn 1964. Sold To: S.J. Davies, (Dealer), Penygraig, Glam., 1964. To: John Morgan (Contractor), Cardiff. (Non P.S.V.) by 6/1964. No further trace.
215	JBX 940	To: South Wales Transport (1110), 1/9/1962. Withdrawn 1965. Sold To: S.J. Davies, (Dealer), Penygraig, Glam., 1965 for scrap. No further trace.
216	JBX 941	To: South Wales Transport (1111), 1/9/1962. Withdrawn 1965. Sold to: S.J. Davies, (Dealer), Penygraig, Glam., 1965 for scrap. No further trace.
217	JTH 291	To: South Wales Transport (217) 1/9/1962. Withdrawn 4/1963 on expiry of c.o.f. Sold to: S.J. Davies, (Dealer), Penygraig, Glam. To: D. Cronin, Co. Cork, Ireland, by 7/1963. (Shipped via. Liverpool Docks). To: Twomey, Coolea, Co. Cork, Ireland, c.7/1965. To: Glynns, Graigue-Na-Spiddogue, Ireland, by 8/1976, where it lay derelict, 8/1976.

218	KBX 997	To: South Wales Transport (803) 1/9/1962. Withdrawn 1967. Sold to: North (Dealer) Sherburn-in-Elmet, 2/1967. To: Bartle, Outwood, W.Yorks., 1967 and scrapped 3/1969.
219	KBX 998	To: South Wales (Transport (804) 1/9/1962. Withdrawn 1967. Sold to: North (Dealer), Sherburn-in-Elmet, 2/1967. To: Sheffield, Cleethorpes, Humberside, 3/1967. To: Eastern Counties Scaffolding (Non P.S.V.) by 3/1969. To: Cumberland Rydalmere, New South Wales, Australia, post 7/1970; Chassis only for spares.
220	NBX 77	To: South Wales Transport (805) 1/9/1962. Withdrawn 1967. Sold to: North, (Dealer), Sherburn-in-Elmet, 2/1967. To: Sheffield, Cleethorpes, Humberside, 3/1967. To: Scrap yard at Barnsley, 1/1971.
221	NBX 78	To: South Wales Transport (806) 1/9/1962. Withdrawn 1967. Sold to: North, (Dealer), Sherburn-in-Elmet, 2/1967. To: A. Jenkins, Pontardulais, Glam., 3/1967 and withdrawn 4/1968. No further trace.
222	NTH 33	To: South Wales Transport (1222) 1/9/1962. Withdrawn 1969. Sold to: P.V.S. (Dealer), Canvey Island, Essex, 1969. To: P.V.S. Contracts, Upminster, Essex, and withdrawn 12/1971. No further trace.
223	NTH 850	To: South Wales Transport (1223) 1/9/1962. Withdrawn 1969. Sold to: P.V.S. (Dealer), Canvey Island, Essex, 1969. To: City Coach Lines, Upminster, Essex, (515), 10/1969. To Lamcote, Radcliffe, Notts., 6/1970 and withdrawn 2/1972. Exported to America. Being restored 2011.
224	NTH 851	To: South Wales Transport (1224) 1/9/1962. Withdrawn 1969. Sold to: P.V.S. (Dealer), Canvey Island, Essex, 1969. To: City Coach Lines, Upminster, Essex, 10/1969. To: Rannoch, Haughley, Suffolk. (Non P.S.V.), 7/1970. To: Omnibus Promotions Ltd., London, E.C.1. (Non P.S.V.) 7/1974. To: Wombwell Diesels (Dealer), South Yorks., 10/1974, for scrap.
225	OBX 780	To: South Wales Transport (807) 1/9/1962. Renumbered 311 in 1970. Withdrawn 1972. To Sykes, (Dealer), Blackerhill, S. Yorks., by 5/1973 and scrapped 3/1974.
226	OBX 781	To: South Wales Transport (808) 1/9/1962. Renumbered 312 in 1970. Withdrawn 1972. To: Sykes, (Dealer), Blackerhill, S.Yorks., 5/1973. To: Sibley, Tangmere, W. Sussex, 7/1973 as mobile caravan. Later moved to Sompting, Sussex. Noted at Bristol, still in use as mobile caraven with Mr. Sibley 3/2002. Last licenced 2002, the vehicle is currently out of use, awaiting restoration in Bristol.
227	RTH 637	To: South Wales Transport (1227) 1/9/1962. Withdrawn 1970. To: City of Oxford M.S. (208), 10/1970; withdrawn 4/1975. To: Twell, (Dealer and breaker), Ingham, Lincs., 4/1975. No further trace.
228	RTH 638	To: South Wales Transport (1228) 1/9/1962. Withdrawn 1970. To: City of Oxford M.S. (210), 11/1970; withdrawn 8/1975. To: F.Cowley, (Dealer), Salford, 6/1976 for scrap.
229	RTH 639	To: South Wales Transport (1229) 1/9/1962. Withdrawn 1970. To: City of Oxford M.S. (212), 11/1970; withdrawn 8/1975. To: Derby Borough Transport (63) 3/1976, known as Derby City Transport after 6/1977; withdrawn 1/1982. To: Rollinson, (Dealer), Barnsley, 5/1982. No further trace.
230	RTH 640	To: South Wales Transport (1230) 1/91962. Withdrawn 1970. To: City of Oxford M.S. (211), 11/1970; withdrawn 8/1975. To: F. Cowley, (Dealer), Salford, 6/1976 for scrap.

231	RTH 641	To: South Wales Transport (1231) 1/9/1962. Withdrawn 1970. To: City of Oxford M.S. (207) 10/1970; withdrawn 12/1970 with severe accident damage. To: Anderson, (Dealer), Eynsham, Oxford, for scrap 8/1971.
232	UBX 45	To: South Wales Transport (1232) 1/9/1962. Withdrawn 1970. To: City of Oxford M.S. (202) 4/1970; withdrawn 6/1972 with fire damage. To: Barraclough, (Dealer), Barnsley, W. Yorks, 9/1972 for scrap.
233	UBX 46	To: South Wales Transport (1233) 1/9/1962. Withdrawn 1970. To: City of Oxford M.S. (201) 4/1970; withdrawn 10/1974. To: Twell, (Dealer and breaker), Ingham, Lincs., 5/1975.
234	UBX 47	To: South Wales Transport (1234) 1/9/1962 and was the first ex. James vehicle to receive S.W.T. livery in 11/1962. Withdrawn 1970. To: City of Oxford M.S. (203) 5/1970; withdrawn 7/1974. To: Hayward, Coventry, 12/1975. To: T. Wigley, (Scrap Dealer), Carlton, S. Yorks, by 12/1979 for scrap.
235	UBX 48	To: South Wales Transport (1235) 1/9/1962. Withdrawn 1970. To: City of Oxford M.S. (204) 7/1970; withdrawn 8/1975. To: Derby Borough Transport (61) 2/1976, known as Derby City Transport after 6/1977, withdrawn 5/1978 after accident. To: P. Sykes, (Dealer), Barnsley, 12/1978 for scrap.
236	UBX 49	To: South Wales Transport (1236) 1/9/1962. Severely damaged in collision with a river bridge at Ponthenry 13/12/1962. The extensive rebuild in 1963 included a new chassis frame. Withdrawn 1970. To: City of Oxford M.S. (209) 10/1970; withdrawn 1973. To Pickersgill & Laverick, (Dealer), Carlton, S. Yorks., 4/1973 for scrap.
237	WTH 113	To: South Wales Transport (1237) 1/9/1962. Withdrawn 1970. To: City of Oxford M.S. (206), 10/1970; withdrawn 8/1975. To: Derby Borough Transport (62) 2/1976, known as Derby City Transport after 6/1977 and withdrawn 2/1979. To: P. Sykes (Dealer), Barnsley, 8/1979 for scrap.
238	WTH 114	To: South Wales Transport (1238) 1/9/1962. Withdrawn 1970. To: City of Oxford M.S. (207), 12/1970; replacing accident damaged – RTH641 (207) in 12/1970; withdrawn 10/1973. To: T.P.E. (Dealer), Macclesfield, Derbyshire, 10/1973. To Jowitt, Middleton-in-Teesdale, Durham, 10/1973. To: Andertons, Keighley, West Yorks. To: Autospares (Scrap Dealer), Bingley, W. Yorks, by 3/1980.
239	YTH 805	To: South Wales Transport (1239) 1/9/1962. Withdrawn 1970. To City of Oxford M.S. (205), 8/1970; withdrawn 7/1974. To: North, (Dealer), Sherburn-in-Elmet, 7/1974.

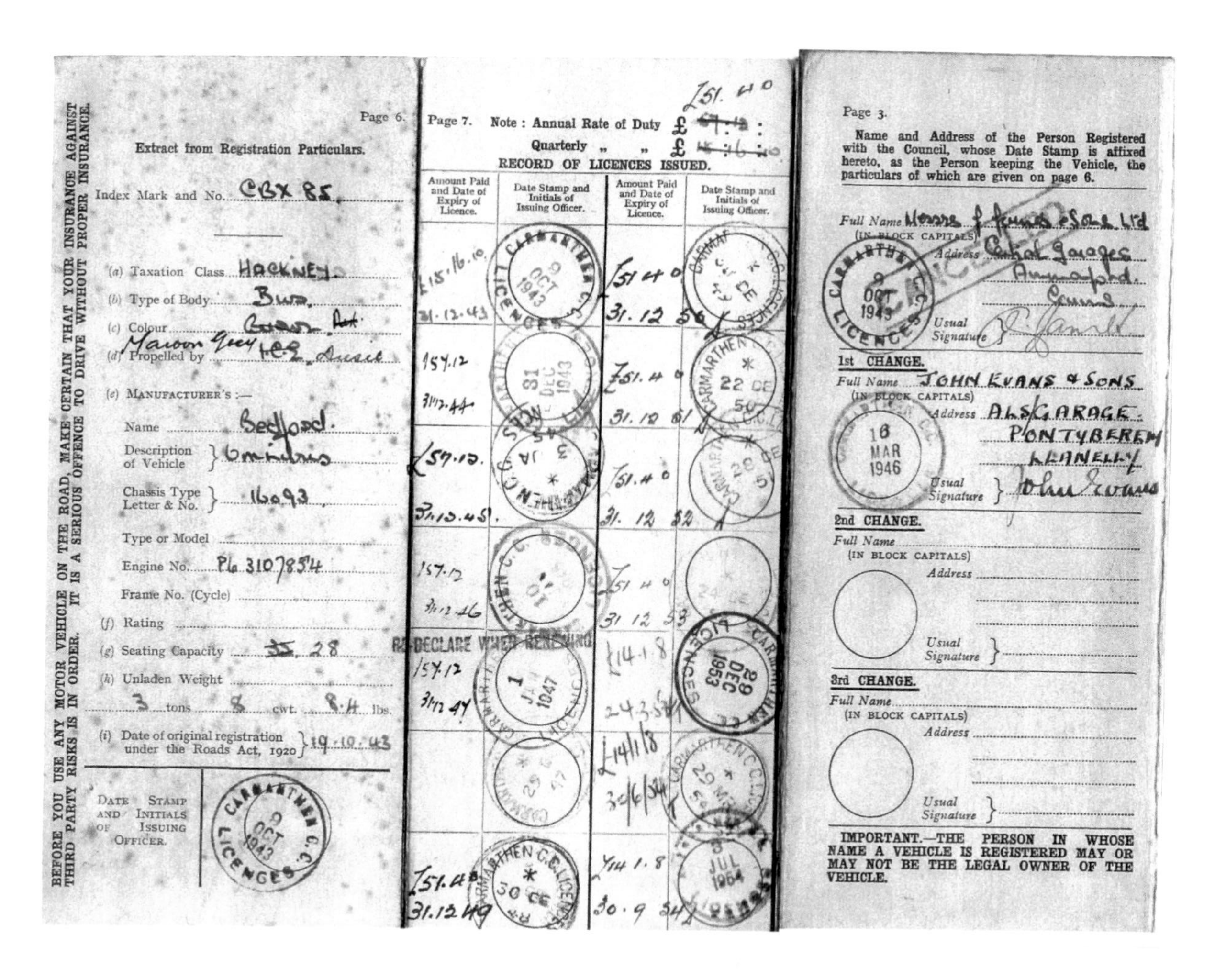

BEFORE YOU USE ANY MOTOR VEHICLE ON THE ROAD, MAKE CERTAIN THAT YOUR INSURANCE AGAINST THIRD PARTY RISKS IS IN ORDER. IT IS A SERIOUS OFFENCE TO DRIVE WITHOUT PROPER INSURANCE.

Page 6.

Extract from Registration Particulars.

Index Mark and No. CBX 85.

(a) Taxation Class HACKNEY.

(b) Type of Body Bus.

(c) Colour Maroon Grey

(d) Propelled by H.C. Diesel

(e) MANUFACTURER'S :—

Name Bedford.

Description of Vehicle Omnibus

Chassis Type Letter & No. 16093.

Type or Model

Engine No. PL 3107854

Frame No. (Cycle)

(f) Rating

(g) Seating Capacity ~~35~~ 28

(h) Unladen Weight 3 tons 8 cwt. 84 lbs.

(i) Date of original registration under the Roads Act, 1920 19.10.43

DATE STAMP AND INITIALS OF ISSUING OFFICER. CARMARTHEN C.C. 9 OCT 1943 LICENCES

Page 7. Note : Annual Rate of Duty £ ~~47.12~~ £51.4.0

Quarterly „ „ £ ~~13.6.0~~

RECORD OF LICENCES ISSUED.

RE-DECLARE WHEN RENEWING

Amount Paid and Date of Expiry of Licence.	Date Stamp and Initials of Issuing Officer.	Amount Paid and Date of Expiry of Licence.	Date Stamp and Initials of Issuing Officer.
£15.16.0 31.12.43	CARMARTHEN C.C. 9 OCT 1943 LICENCES	£51 4 0 31.12.56	CARMARTHEN C.C. LICENCES
£57.12 31.12.44	31 DEC 1943	£51.4.0 31.12.51	CARMARTHEN C.C. 22 DE 50
£57.12. 31.12.45	CARMARTHEN C.C. 3 JA 45	£51.4.0 31.12.52	CARMARTHEN C.C. 28 DE 51
£57.12 31.12.46	CARMARTHEN C.C.	£51 4 0 31.12.53	24 DE
£57.12 31.12.47	CARMARTHEN C.C. 1 JAN 1947 LICENCES	£14.1.8 24.3.54	CARMARTHEN C.C. 29 DEC 1953 LICENCES
	CARMARTHEN C.C. 29 47	£14.1.8 30.6.54	CARMARTHEN C.C. 29 MR 54
£51.4.0 31.12.49	CARMARTHEN C.C. LICENCES 30 DE 48	£14 1.8 30.9.54	3 JUL 1954

Page 3.

Name and Address of the Person Registered with the Council, whose Date Stamp is affixed hereto, as the Person keeping the Vehicle, the particulars of which are given on page 6.

Full Name (IN BLOCK CAPITALS) Messrs J. James & Sons Ltd

Address Central Garages Ammanford Carms

Usual Signature

CARMARTHEN C.C. 9 OCT 1943 LICENCES — CANCELLED

1st CHANGE.

Full Name (IN BLOCK CAPITALS) JOHN EVANS & SONS

Address ALS GARAGE. PONTYBEREM LLANELLY

Usual Signature John Evans

CARMARTHEN C.C. 16 MAR 1946

2nd CHANGE.

Full Name (IN BLOCK CAPITALS)

Address

Usual Signature

3rd CHANGE.

Full Name (IN BLOCK CAPITALS)

Address

Usual Signature

IMPORTANT.—THE PERSON IN WHOSE NAME A VEHICLE IS REGISTERED MAY OR MAY NOT BE THE LEGAL OWNER OF THE VEHICLE.

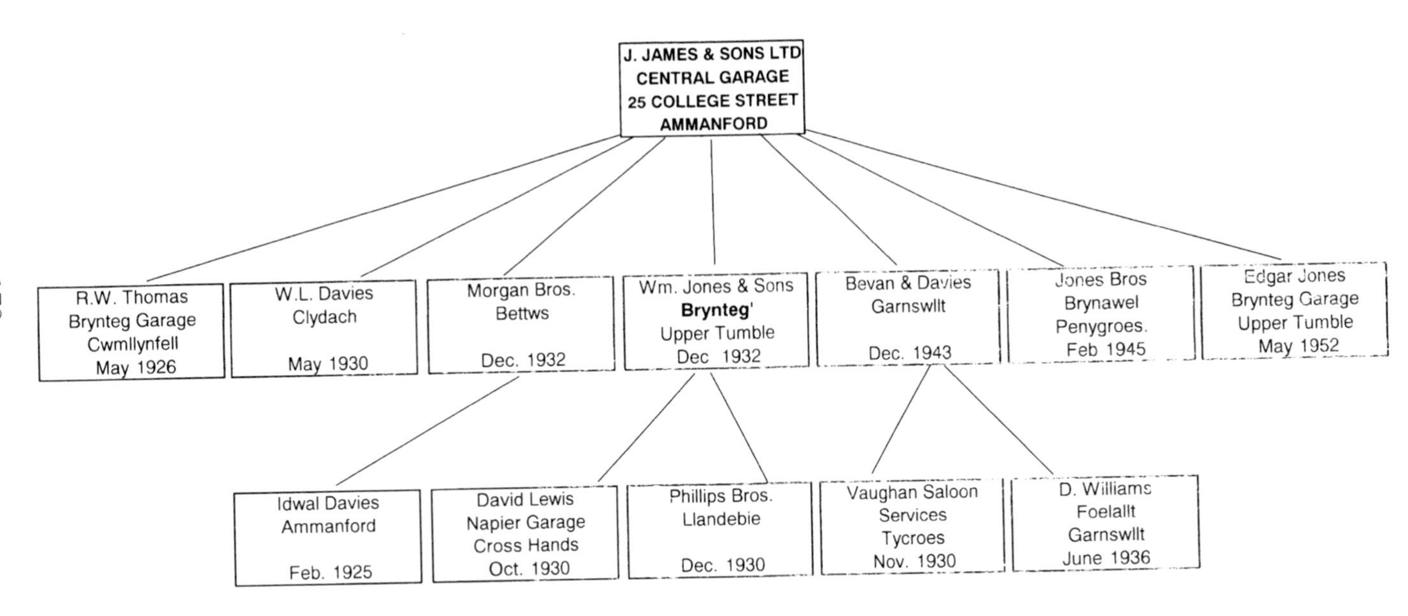

J. JAMES & SONS LTD.
FAMILY TREE
J. JAMES & SONS LTD
CENTRAL GARAGE
25 COLLEGE STREET
AMMANFORD
R.W. Thomas
Brynteg Garage
Cwmllynfell
May 1926
W.L. Davies
Clydach
May 1930
Morgan Bros.
Bettws
Dec. 1932
Wm. Jones & Sons
Brynteg'
Upper Tumble
Dec 1932
Bevan & Davies
Garnswllt
Dec. 1943
Jones Bros
Brynawel
Penygroes.
Feb 1945
Edgar Jones
Brynteg Garage
Upper Tumble
May 1952
Idwal Davies
Ammanford
Feb. 1925
David Lewis
Napier Garage
Cross Hands
Oct. 1930
Phillips Bros.
Llandebie
Dec. 1930
Vaughan Saloon
Services
Tycroes
Nov. 1930
D. Williams
Foelallt
Garnswllt
June 1936

JONES BROS (BRYNTEG)
UPPER TUMBLE
CARMARTHENSHIRE

'Brynteg', home of the Jones brothers, was originally a farm smallholding, situated alongside the busy A476 Llanelly – Llandilo trunk road at Upper Tumble in Carmarthenshire. From here the ambitious Jones brothers started operating passenger vehicles during World War 1, mysteriously running as three separate enterprises!

The intricate history of this fascinating company begins in April 1915 with:

Enterprise 1 - When John Jones, the second eldest brother, purchased his first motor vehicle. Forming a company called **'Tumble Motor Transport'** he confusingly used his home address of 'Arfryn', Llannon Road, Upper Tumble, and the garage address 'Brynteg', Llannon Road, Upper Tumble.

Originally a collier at the Great Mountain Colliery, Tumble, John borrowed £100 from his uncle, Tom Evans (a bus operator at Fforestfach), to buy this first vehicle, a Ford model 'T' motorcar registered BX514. With mechanical help from his father, a colliery engineer, they converted the car into a 12 seater to carry children to school at Llanelly. Additionally, John Jones became involved in transporting miners to several collieries in the community, and utilised his charabancs as ambulances whenever necessary, to take injured miners to hospital after accidents. The first passenger service officially started in 1916 with a licenced service from Cross Hands Square to Llanelly Railway Station via Upper Tumble, in direct competition with the (G.W.R.) Great Western Railway Company's bus service.

Enterprise 2 - A month after the formation of Tumble Motor Transport in April 1915, John Jones' eldest brother David left Tumble Colliery and founded the **'Jones Bros.'** company in partnership with brother Tom, operating three model 'T' Fords from the family home at Brynteg. Hampered by the wartime fuel shortage, the brothers slowly started a network of services by firstly joining their brother John on the busy Cross Hands to Llanelly route. Later, joined by brothers William, Gomer and Trevor, with sister Mary Ann as a 'clippie' (conductress), their business venture expanded rapidly to become Carmarthenshire's largest passenger vehicle operator by 1923.

Enterprise 3 – commenced after W.W.1 ended in 1918, when motor engineer Robert Johnson from Co. Tyrone in Northern Ireland became closely involved with the Jones brothers. Johnson, in partnership with John Morris from Tumble, formed his own company known as **'Johnson & Morris'**. Purchasing their own bus in November 1918, a dark green 40 h.p. Straker-Squire (BX849), they also plied the Tumble – Llanelly route jointly with the Jones brothers, and operated from Jones' premises at Brynteg! Johnson & Morris' little enterprise however, was short lived; it was swallowed up by the expanding Jones Bros., business in 1923. Johnson remained with Brynteg for some time afterwards, but eventually left to become a motor engineer with rivals, the Great Western Railway Co., at Ammanford, becoming depot superintendent under Western Welsh ownership.

In April 1919 however, Jones Bros., started a new 'un-licenced' daily service from Tumble to Ammanford via Cross Hands, Penygroes and Llandebie, with connections at Tumble for Llanelly on Thursdays and Saturdays (Llanelly's market days). At the same time they inaugurated another new service between Pontyberem and Llanelly, which also ran un-licenced. The Tumble to Ammanford service however, was soon amended to run daily between Llanelly (Railway Station) and Ammanford Square without connections.

During this period, Jones Bros., were operating a fleet of Straker-Squire, Dennis, Selden and Thames buses. The model 'T' Fords had been disposed of soon after W.W.1 ended, as they became too small for the company's requirements. Simultaneously, Llanelly Borough Council's licencing committee had imposed new safety regulations which rendered charabancs unsuitable for stage carriage operation, and to comply with the authority's new regulations, all stage carriage passenger vehicles operating within the Borough after 1920 had to be constructed with a rear entrance doorway. As a result, the Jones brothers purchased a motley collection of surplus, cheap, ex. W.W.1 Army lorry chassis, which were bodied into buses for further use. Sending drivers to collect these chassis from Slough in Buckinghamshire, they were driven back to Tumble at 12 m.p.h., (the speed limit of the day), without any protection from the elements, with drivers sitting on wooden boxes or the petrol tank.

Nevertheless, the ambitious Jones brothers had their share of troubles, ranging from serious accidents to crucial financial problems, but most of their troubles were self-imposed as revealed in the following text.

To begin with, in January 1923, it was stated at a meeting of the Llanelly licencing committee that Jones Bros., and their associate company Tumble Motor Transport, were not providing passengers with fare tickets. They were formally warned of the conditions attached to their operators licence, regarding the issue of tickets, and consequently almost lost their annual licence renewal.

Fourteen months later, a vehicle examiner engaged by Llanelly Borough Council, placed immediate prohibition orders on three buses licenced to Tumble Motor Transport and one bus licenced to Jones Bros., owing to their poor mechanical condition. At the same time the G.W.R. company complained to the council about Jones Bros' irregular running between Tumble and Llanelly. Taking a very serious view of this, the authority suspended renewal of their annual licences, reviewing the situation regularly and issuing short period licences at monthly intervals.

PUBLIC NOTICE!

TEMPORARY TIME TABLE OF

New 'Bus Service

— BY —

Messrs. JONES BROS., Brynteg Garage,

BETWEEN

CWMMAWR STATION (Burry Port & Gwendraeth Valley Railway) and TUMBLE, CROSS HANDS, PENYGROES, LLANDEBIE & AMMANFORD

Commencing APRIL, 1922, until further notice.

Mondays, Tuesdays, Wednesdays, Thursdays & Fridays:—

		a.m.	a.m.	p.m.	p.m.
Cwmmawr Station	Dep.	7.15	10.45	2.20	5.45
Cross Hands	„	7.35	11.10	2.40	6.10
Penygroes	„	7-45	11.20	2.50	6.20
Llandebie	„	8.0	11.30	3.0	6.30
Ammanford	Arr.	8.10	11.40	3.10	6.40

Ammanford	Dep.	11.20	4.30	8.30
Llandebie	„	11.35	4.45	8.40
Penygroes	„	11.50	5.0	9.0
Cross Hands	„	12.0	5.10	9.15
Cwmmawr Station	Arr.	12.20	5.30	9.45

Saturdays:—

Cwmmawr Stn.	Dep.	7.15	10.45	3.15	7.0	10.0
Cross Hands	„	7.35	11.10	3.35	7.20	10.20
Penygroes	„	7.45	11.20	3.45	7.35	10.30
Llandebie	„	8.0	11.30	4.0	7.50	—
Ammanford	Arr.	8.10	11.40	4.10	8.0	—

Ammanford	Dep.	11.20	2.30	5.30	8.45
Llandebie	„	11.35	2.40	5.40	9.0
Penygroes	„	11.50	2.55	5.55	9.15
Cross Hands	„	12.0	3.5	6.10	9.25
Cwmmawr Station	Arr.	12.20	3.25	6.30	9.45

All 'Buses from Cwmmawr Station wait for Trains and run through to Ammanford. Also 'Buses from Ammanford meet Trains at Cwmmawr for Gwendraeth Valley. Also 'Buses meet Trains at Llandebie for Llandilo.

'The crew of this 'Brynteg' Straker-Squire omnibus resemble a pair of 'gangsters' as they pose for the camera at Llanelly railway station in the early 1920's. Jones Bros., were loyal supporters of the rare and notorious Straker-Squire products in the early years, which may have attributed to their eventual downfall. This 35 seater 40.h.p. 'A' type; registered BX 2399, was one of a pair delivered in January 1922, and is pictured here about to depart for Ammanford via: Cross Hands, Penygroes and Llandebie.

Straker-Squire fitted a very impressive radiator badge to all their products, as shown here reproduced on publicity material.

PUBLIC NOTICE.

TEMPORARY

TIME-TABLE

Commencing

MONDAY, AUGUST 20th, 1923,

UNTIL FURTHER NOTICE,

OF

Brynteg's Buses

BETWEEN

CWMMAWR STATION, TUMBLE, CROSS HANDS, PENYGROES, LLANDEBIE, AMMANFORD, LLANDILO, LLANWRDA, PUMPSAINT, AND LAMPETER STATION.

		a.m.	a.m.	p.m.	p.m.
Dep.	Ammanford..	8.0	11.30	4.20	7.0
,,	Llandilo ...	8.45	12.15	5.0	7.40
,,	Llanwrda ...	9.10	12.40	5.40	8.10
Arr.	Lampeter ... (About).	10.0	1.30	6.20	9.0

		a.m.	a.m.	p.m.	p.m.
Dep.	Lampeter ...	8.15	11.15	2.40	7.2
,,	Llanwrda ...	9.5	12.5	3.15	8.15
,,	Llandilo ...	9.45	12.45	3.45	9.0
Arr.	Ammanford...	10.15	1.15	4.40	9.20

Dep. TUMBLE connection for LLANDILO and LAMPETER direct at LLANDEBIE.

a.m.	a.m.	p.m.	p.m.
7.45	10.45	3.30	6.30

Direct Bus or connections from Lampeter to all above-mentioned places.

JONES BROS.

Brynteg Garage, Upper Tumble.

In the meantime, the adventurous Jones' inaugurated another new service. Their enterprising new service from Ammanford to Lampeter in Cardiganshire commenced in August 1923. This lengthy 32 mile route through the rural countryside of North Carmarthenshire had previously never been served by public transport between the towns of Llandilo and Lampeter. This was a remarkable achievement for the company taking into consideration the appalling road conditions over the 1000ft. Pencarreg Mountain, coupled with the primitive vehicles of the era. Furthermore, the service made connections at Llandebie Square with their Llanelly to Ammanford service, enabling a through journey from the Llanelly, Tumble and Cross Hands areas to Lampeter. The service, however, ran un-licenced due To the fact that the Ammanford, Llandilo, and Lampeter councils had not commenced licencing omnibuses. Complexity of the timetable, coupled with the length of this route, called for one vehicle to remain at Lampeter overnight, and manned by crews living in that area.

On the other hand, whilst researching the company's history a very sobering story was retrieved from a local newspaper dated 26th August 1926. The article highlighted the company's disregard towards public safety, and briefly read:

The driver and conductor of a 'Brynteg' bus were fined £2-10-0 each for dangerously overloading their vehicle. The bus, on route to Lampeter, was seen by a policeman at Llandilo Square already over crowded, with 6 people riding in the luggage rack on the roof of the bus. More people were being 'crammed' into the bus until the policeman intervened and approached the driver and conductor telling them they could go no further with such a load, and ordered the men on top of the bus to come down. After getting them down, the driver told them to get back on again as there would be more room when the bus reached Manordeilo. The crew were then warned of prosecution if they continued, to which the conductor replied:- 'you are the only one that has ever stopped us' and continued on their journey to Lampeter, 24 miles away carrying 53 passengers; 32 seated, 15 standing, and 6 on the roof of their solid tyred 32 seater bus.

In July 1925, the Jones brothers absorbed 'Tumble Motor Transport', the associate company owned by their brother John Jones, discarding his fleet name altogether. John however, left the bus business at this point and purchased a farm at Llanddarog. At the same time the company began modernising the fleet, purchasing a batch of lightweight W & G (Willie & George du-Cros) 33.5 h.p. buses through the dealership of William Jeffreys, 2–9 Wassail Place, Swansea, who later became known as Jeffreys Commercial Motors Ltd.

One of the W & G 'L' type lightweight buses purchased by the company in 1926 is pictured here before delivery, outside the W & G (Willie & George du-Cros) factory at Acton Vale, London. Its 26 seater rear entrance bodywork, also built at Acton by Strachan & Brown, boasted a low loading line of 22 inches. Its 6 cylinder W&G engine had the R.A.C. rating of 33.5 h.p., yet the actual b.h.p. developed was 70 b.h.p. at 2,200 r.p.m.

The next major event in the Company's history took place in February 1926, when the Jones brothers borrowed £6,000 from colliery agent James Nicholas to purchase a business known as the 'LLANELLY EXPRESS MOTOR SERVICE CO. LTD'., previously owned by D. Thomas of 1 Market Street, Llanelly. Three Leyland buses were acquired with the business along with 2 stage carriage services:- Llanelly to Ammanford via Llangennech and Pontardulais; and Llanelly to Pontardulais via Tumble, Drefach and Cross Hands. The latter service connected with Lewis Bros., of Pontardulais' service at Pontardulais, for onward journeys to Swansea. After the takeover, Jones Bros., surprisingly adopted the Llanelly Express name and consequently traded as **'Llanelly Express Motor Service Co. Ltd'.,** from their own premises at Brynteg Garage, Upper Tumble. The 'Brynteg' title then became redundant.

This 1924 solid tyred Leyland A9, with a Leyland 22 seat body was one of three Leyland buses acquired with the Llanelly Express undertaking in 1926. In this official view taken before delivery in 1924, it is clearly visible that Llanelly Express used the fleetname 'Llanelly & District' long before the Llanelly trolleybus undertaking: Llanelly & District Traction Company!

By August 1926, the re-labelled company modified their Llanelly – Drefach – Cross Hands – Pontardulais route. The original service was split into two, making two separate services: (1) Llanelly to Drefach Square, via Tumble. (2) Pontardulais to Newcastle Emlyn and Cardigan via: Cross Hands, Drefach and Carmarthen. This service maintained its connection at Pontardulais with Lewis Bros' Pontardulais to Swansea service enabling a through service from Swansea to Cardigan with through fares.

The Pontardulais to Cardigan service was another ambitious long distance service launched by the Jones family, running through 49 miles of rural West Wales countryside.

At this time, the 1926 'General Strike' had commenced and was causing serious financial problems. Coupled with this, the Company's first competitor appeared on the Ammanford – Lampeter route. J. D. Evans (Inglis) of Llanybyther began a daily *indirect'* route from Ammanford to Lampeter via: Talley and Llanybyther, which was very short lived.

Llanelly Express Motor Service Co., Ltd.

TIME TABLES.

Daily.—Pontardulais, Cross Hands, Drefach, Carmarthen, Newcastle-Emlyn, Cardigan Route.

	a.m.	a.m.	a.m.	p.m.	p.m.	p.m.	p.m.
Pontardulais dep.		8 45	10 45		3 0	5 30	9 30
Cross Hands ...	8 0	9 40	11 15	1 15	3 45	6 25	10 0
Drefach ...	8 15	9 55	11 30	1 30	4 0	6 40	10 15
Carmarthen ...	9 15	10 30	12 0	2 0	4 30	7 30	Up to Garage.
Conwil ...	9 45	11 0	12 30	2 30	5 0	8 0	
Newcastle-Emlyn ...	10 45	12 0	1 45	3 45	6 15	9 15	
Cardigan ...							

	a.m.	a.m.	a.m.	p.m.	p.m.	p.m.	p.m.
Cardigan ...							
Newcastle-Emlyn ...		7 40	10 35	12 5	2 0	4 15	6 15
Conwil ...		8 45	11 45	1 15	3 15	5 30	7 25
Carmarthen ...		9 10	12 15	1 45	3 40	6 0	8 0
Drefach ...	7 10	9 50	12 45	2 15	4 15	6 30	8 30
Cross Hands ...	7 30	10 5	1 0	2 30	4 30	7 0	9 0
Pontardulais ...	8 0	10 30		2 55	4 50		9 20

Daily.—Drefach, Tumble, Llannon, Llanelly Route.

			T	T & S				T & S		
	a.m.	a.m.	a.m.	a.m.	a.m.	p.m.	p.m.	p.m.	p.m.	p.m.
Drefach dep.		7 45	8 40	9 0	9 55	12 20	1 20	3 55	5 50	8 30
Tumble (Police Stn.)	6 30	8 5	8 55	9 15	10 10	12 40	1 35	4 10	6 10	8 45
Llannon ...	6 40	8 15	9 5	9 25	10 20		1 45	4 20	6 20	8 55
Llanelly arr.	7 10	8 45	9 35	9 55	10 50		2 15	4 50	6 50	9 25

				T	T & S		T & S		S	
	a.m.	a.m.	a.m.	p.m.	p.m.	p.m.	p.m.	p.m.	p.m.	p.m.
Llanelly dep.	7 15	9 0	11 15	1 40	2 40	3 55	5 15	7 15	8 30	9 30
Llannon ...	7 45	9 30	11 45	2 10	3 10	4 25	5 45	7 45	9 0	10 0
Tumble (Police Stn.)	7 55	9 40	11 55	2 20	3 20	4 35	5 55	7 55	9 10	10 10
Drefach arr.		9 55	12 10	2 35	3 30	4 50	6 5	8 10	9 20	

T—Thursdays only. S—Saturdays only. T & S—Thursdays & Saturdays only.

Buses leaving Llanelly at 7-15 a.m. and 9 a.m. have connections at Drefach for Newcastle-Emlyn and Cardigan.

On the other hand, in February 1927, the Llanelly Licencing Authority refused renewal of Llanelly Express' licence for the Llanelly – Pontardulais –Ammanford service after receiving numerous complaints about the service. Competitors of the jointly operated service, Rees & Williams and South Wales Transport however, were granted renewal of their licences and equally shared the journeys previously operated by Llanelly Express.

Despite this, the undaunted partnership applied for a new licence to operate a direct through service from Llanelly to Lampeter via Llandilo, in December 1927. This was immediately refused and after a second application three months later, was again refused. Nevertheless the Lampeter service continued to operate in its usual way, making the necessary connections at Llandebie Square.

Seven months later, J.D. Evans of Llanybyther, in conjunction with Jones Bros., (Red Bus Services) of Aberystwyth, commenced a summer only service: Ammanford to Aberystwyth via Lampeter. This was inevitably soon followed by other operators, namely, L.C. Williams (L.C.W. Motors) of Talley; Gough's of Mountain Ash; South Wales Transport Co., (Saturdays only); and the Great Western Railway Co., (with a daily service Ammanford to Lampeter only). The sudden increase of operators plying the Lampeter route was a serious blow to the company during these lean times. This was a reflection of the lackadaisical attitude of local authorities along the route, for not exercising the powers vested in them under the provision of the Town Police Act – to licence all passenger services. In addition to this, the Great Western Railway Co., deviously adjusted the train times at Lampeter to suit their own bus service to Ammanford, leaving Llanelly Express to run empty half an hour later. Sympathetic Lampeter Borough Council met to discuss the matter, stating that as Llanelly Express were the first operator on the route, they should have the advantage. This did not materialise and as the industrial recession worsened in 1928, the Company experienced serious financial problems coupled with their bad reputation for unreliability – due to bad maintenance.

In the meantime, Swansea based South Wales Transport heard of their troubles and prematurely applied to the Llanelly Licencing Authority on 16th October, 1928, for the licences they held. They were refused!

Nevertheless, on 31st October, 1928, the Llanelly Express Motor Service Co., Carmarthenshire's largest bus operator, running 25 buses, fell into the hands of a receiver and two days later ceased trading. Consequently the Llanelly Licencing Authority met to discuss alternative arrangements to maintain the services. The licences were revoked nine days later, with temporary arrangements made for the G.W.R. Co., to operate most of their services.

Promptly taking advantage of the company's misfortunes were Lewis Bros., of Pontardulais. Lewis Bros., having an arrangement to connect their Swansea to Pontardulais service with Llanelly Express' Cardigan service at Pontardulais, decided to continue running the abandoned Cardigan service themselves; un-licenced. They were inevitably caught by Carmarthen Borough Council and prosecuted.

Llanelly Express' failure, however, created a 'stampede', as the following companies all applied for the licences:-
G.W.R. Co.; S.W.T. Co.; David Lewis, Cross Hands; David and Tom Jones (Brynteg) Tumble; J.M. Bacus & Co., Burry Port; J. D. Evans, Llanybyther; and a syndicate involving James Nicholas (Colliery Agent), Edward Howell, John Jones (Brynteg); T. E. Williams and C. B, Williams (Rees & Williams, Tycroes).

The licences were distributed as follows:-

(1) Llanelly – Cross Hands – Llandilo – Lampeter route to J. D. Evans, Llanybyther.

(2) Pontardulais – Carmarthen – New Castle Emlyn, - Cardigan route to David Lewis, Cross Hands.

(3) Llanelly – Cross Hands – Ammanford route shared between the G.W.R. Co., and the syndicate mentioned above, which emerged as a new operator trading as 'West Wales Motors Ltd'., Llanelly. (Moving to Tycroes in December 1930).

Applicant David Lewis of Cross Hands however appealed to the Ministry of Transport against the Llanelly Council's unfair sharing of the Llanelly – Ammanford licences, which resulted in a complete re-organisation of the service in May 1929, to include Lewis. Lewis received a share of the service, operating journeys between Llanelly and Cross Hands only, extending to Ammanford, Lampeter and Aberystwyth soon afterwards. Additionally, Lewis purchased numerous vehicles from the defunct Llanelly Express and engaged most of their staff, but after a difficult year David Lewis' business also collapsed in bankruptcy in June 1930. His licences were then *temporarily* shared between Western Welsh Omnibus Co., (the re-organised G.W.R. Co.), and West Wales Motors Ltd., who were joint operators of the Llanelly to Ammanford service.

In the meantime, Llanelly Express shareholder James Nicholas of Ravelston, Tumble, ended up in the Carmarthenshire Bankruptcy Court with gross liabilities estimated at £8,887.

Nicholas, a colliery agent, (freelance agent marketing coal) attributed his failure to advancing large sums of money to the Jones brothers without security and becoming guarantor to their motor transport company.

Receiving approximately £8,700 of shares in the company, Nicholas became heavily involved with the brothers in a desperate attempt to keep the company afloat. Foolishly, he advanced in various amounts £13,400 without security, just I.O.U.'s and promissory notes, which included £6,000 to purchase the original Llanelly Express Company in 1926.

However, when the company assets were sold off, by the official receiver, Nicholas received absolutely nothing, leaving him completely bankrupt!

'BRYNTEG' PHASE II

In the meantime, William Jones, a partner of the ill-fated 'Llanelly Express' Company, restarted the **'Brynteg'** business trading as **Wm. Jones & Sons, 'Brynteg'** from the same family owned premises, Brynteg Garage, Upper Tumble. Purchasing a new 20-seater bus in July 1929, it was followed by a new G.M.C. T60 Duple 26 seater four months later.

On 16th June 1930 however, William Jones & Sons applied to the Llanelly Licencing Authority for a licence to continue running the Llanelly – Cross Hands – Llandilo route, which had become available due to the failure of David Lewis, Cross Hands and J. D. Evans of Llanybyther's abandoning of the service. They were unsuccessful, but a month later the 'new' Brynteg company started running an unlicenced service from Ammanford to Aberystwyth via Lampeter. The service latterly operated by David Lewis, was a service inaugurated by the original Brynteg company in 1923, which ran from Ammanford to Lampeter only in those early days.

Making a second application, in October 1930, the company obtained the licence they desperately wanted for the Llanelly – Cross Hands – Ammanford – Lampeter – Aberystwyth route, which was operated as two separate services making connections at Ammanford. Furthermore, the Llanelly to Ammanford section of this route was still operated jointly with Western Welsh Omnibus Co., and West Wales Motors, and the Ammanford to Aberystwyth route ran jointly with Western Welsh between Ammanford and Lampeter only. (Western Welsh followed them into Aberystwyth from July 1932 onwards).

During this period, several operators were looking for extra licences to increase their network of services before the 1930 Road Traffic Act was implemented in April 1931. One operator concerned with the prospect of obtaining extra licences to expand his territory was William Jones, who set up another company in December 1930, with the intention of gaining extra licences.

Abandoning the Brynteg title again he formed a 'new' company registered as **'Llanelly & District (Carmarthenshire) Transport Company Ltd'**., which was actually an amalgamation of bus companies in the area, namely:

J. D. Evans	(Inglis) Inglis Garage, Llanybyther
John Jones	(Pontyberem & District Services) Danyrhiw, Pontyberem
Wm. Jones & Sons	(Brynteg) Brynteg Garage, Upper Tumble
Phillips Bros.	(Amman Valley Bus Service) Hawthorn Garage, Llandebie.
Thomas Taylor & Son	(Taylors Motor Service) Central Garage, Llandilo Road, Cross Hands.

Directors of the new concern, Wm. Jones (Brynteg) and Harry Taylor (Taylor's Motor Service), were financed with £2,000 from the National Provincial Bank in April 1931, to pay off liabilities of *'alleged'* various businesses taken over.

However, when the 1930 Road Traffic Act was implemented in April 1931, the new company Llanelly & District (Carmarthenshire) Transport Co., Ltd., applied to the Traffic Commissioners (the new licencing authority) for nine Road Service Licences allocated under their operator reference/application number, TGR 363. The services applied for were:-

TGR 363/1:	Ponthenry to Llanelly, via: Pontyberem and Llannon.
TGR 363/2:	Tumble to Ammanford, via: Cross Hands, Penygroes and Llandebie.
TGR 363/3:	Drefach to Llandilo, via: Tumble, Penygroes and Carmel.
TGR 363/4:	Tumble to Aberystwyth, via: Penygroes, Saron, Ammanford, Llandilo, Llangadock, Llanwrda, Lampeter and Aberayron.
TGR 363/5:	Llanelly to Llandilo, via: Tumble, Drefach, Cross Hands, Penygroes and Carmel.
TGR 363/6:	Trimsaran to Ammanford, via: Pontyates, Pontyberem, Tumble, Cross Hands, Penygroes and Capel Hendre.
TGR 363/7:	Pontyberem to Burry Port, via: Pontyates, Trimsaran, Pinged and Pembrey.
TGR 363/8:	Carmarthen to Cardigan, via: Conwil Elfed, New Castle Emlyn and Cwmcoy.
TGR 363/9:	Ammanford to Llandrindod Wells, via: Llandilo, Llangadock, Llandovery and Llanwrtyd Wells.

Williams Jones' plan failed, the new concern obtained only three of the licences they applied for. The licences granted to them in July 1931 were:- TGR 363/1, previously John Jones' route; TGR 363/4, previously Wm. Jones' route, and TGR 363/7, previously Phillips Bros' route. This put the amalgamated group in a very serious position; unable to repay their creditors. With the exception of Phillips Bros., the group hastily split up in October 1931, and continued to operate on their own separate licences and identities.

On 1st December, 1931, the bank made a winding up order against the Llanelly & District (Carmarthenshire) Transport Co., Ltd., and their Road Service Licences were revoked. Eighteen months later in June 1933, directors of the company, William Jones and Harry Taylor, appeared at Carmarthen Assizes for non-payment of their £2,000 bank loan and the interest accrued £202!

'BRYNTEG' PHASE III

William Jones reverted to his former identity; **Wm. Jones & Sons, 'Brynteg',** re-applying for his licences under that title in October 1931. The road service licences he applied for, to continue running his own services, were given a new operator reference/

application number; TGR 370. The services were:

TGR 370/1:	Llanelly to Aberystwyth, via: Tumble, Cross Hands, Saron, Ammanford, Llandilo, Llanwrda, Lampeter and Aberayron.
TGR 370/2:	Llanelly to Llandilo, via: Tumble, Drefach, Cross Hands, Penygroes and Carmel.
TGR 370/3:	Tumble to Ammanford, via: Cross Hands, Penygroes, Caerbryn and Llandebie.
TGR 370/4:	Ammanford to Burry Port, via: Saron, Capel Hendre, Penygroes, Cross Hands, Tumble, Cwmmawr, Pontyberem, Pontyates, Carway, Trimsaran, Pinged and Pembrey.

The Ammanford to Burry Port service listed above had previously been operated by Phillips Bros., of Llandebie. Surprisingly, Phillips Bros., had been absorbed by Wm. Jones & Sons, eleven months earlier, during the formation of Llanelly & District (Carmarthenshire) Transport Company. This accounted for Wm. Jones' mysterious bank loan! On the other hand Joseph Trevor Phillips, former partner of Phillips Bros., transferred to 'Brynteg' with the 'Amman Valley Bus Service' business.

Despite this, Wynford Arnold Phillips of the Phillips Bros., concern re-applied for the Ammanford to Burry Port licence which inevitably led to a public enquiry in February 1932. At the enquiry a document produced by Phillips proved that the Jones' had agreed to pay Phillips £350 for disposing of any right to run the Ammanford to Burry Port route, and that Jones were to waive their rights and interest in the route if there was any delay in payment. Foolishly, Jones had only paid one instalment of £20 for the route!

Nevertheless, the Traffic Commissioner granted the licence to Wm. Jones & Sons., because they had operated the route on their own over the past seven months and was issued subject to condition 1 below.

At the same public enquiry, licence TGR 370/1 was granted as applied for, subject to conditions 2 and 3; TGR 370/2 was granted with a modification to their application:-
To operate the service as originally authorised i.e.:-

Llanelly (Railway Station) to Ammanford (Square)
via : Felinfoel, Llannon, Tumble, Drefach, Cross Hands, Penygroes and Llandebie.

Issued subject to condition 2 below, and to operate jointly with Western Welsh O.C., and West Wales Motors.

The licence application TGR 370/3 above was refused after the compulsory alteration of application TGR 370/2.
Condition 1: *Not entitled to pick up any passengers after leaving Butchers Arms on*

journeys into Burry Port, and shall not on journeys from Burry Port to Ammanford take up any passengers before reaching Butchers Arms, except passengers bound for a destination beyond Butchers Arms.

Condition 2: *This licence is granted without prejudice and subject in all respects to the provisions of the Llanelly & District Traction Act 1930, (which did not allow passengers to be picked up and set down between Felinfoel vicarage and Llanelly railway station, on inward and outward journeys).*

Condition 3: *Not entitled to pick up and set down passengers between Lampeter and Aberystwyth, on inward and outward journeys except passengers bound for a destination beyond Lampeter, on journeys returning to Ammanford.*

Furthermore, licence TGR 370/1 was modified five months later, with respect that condition 3, the boundary of Lampeter, was extended to Temple Bar.

Meanwhile, in January 1932, the company were prosecuted for 'a breach of the Road Traffic Act'. The offence was - using a passenger vehicle on the highway 19 days after its certificate of fitness had been suspended. The case was *'the first of its kind'* brought in front of the Traffic Commissioners.

Taking into account that the new licencing Act had been in force for over a year, the Jones' were still desperately looking for ways to expand their small network of services and in May 1932 three more stage carriage licences were sought after, each one being refused. They were:-

TGR 370/5:	Swansea to Cardigan,	via: Pontardulais, Cross Hands, Tumble, Drefach, Carmarthen, Conwil Elfed, (Drefach, Henllan), New Castle Emlyn and Cwmcoy. (Daily including Sundays)
TGR 370/6:	Ponthenry to Swansea,	via: Pontyberem, Cwmmawr, Tumble, Llannon, Hendy, Pontardulais and Penllergaer. (To run on Saturdays and Sundays and Bank Holidays only). This application was afterwards retracted.
TGR 370/7:	Llandilo to Swansea,	via: Carmel, Penygroes, Cross Hands, Pontardulais and Penllergaer. (Daily including Sundays).

The above service, TGR 370/7, had latterly been operated by Taylors Motor Services of Cross Hands. Taylor, at one time involved with Wm. Jones and the Llanelly Express (Carmarthenshire) Transport Co., had this – his only Road Service Licence revoked in

May 1932 due to illegal fare cutting, putting him out of business. The licence however, passed to joint operator of the service; Bassetts' of Gorseinon.

Failing to obtain the above licences was a serious blow to the Jones' as they experienced more financial problems combined with their bad reputation. Furthermore, four local operators knew of their troubles and hastily applied to the Traffic Commissioners for Brynteg's Burry Port to Ammanford Road Service Licence. One of the applicants, W. A. Phillips (Phillips Bros) was still frantically trying to retrieve his former service.

In a desperate attempt to change the company's image, Brynteg ordered three new Tilling Stevens (T.S.M.) coaches, which they could ill-afford at the time!

Consequently, bus proprietors J. James & Sons Ltd., of Ammanford stepped in with financial assistance in October 1932, taking full control of Brynteg's finances, and two months later registered a new subsidiary company:- **Wm. Jones & Sons (Brynteg) Ltd., Central Garage, Ammanford,** which was James' legal address. The new limited company continued to trade as 'Brynteg' but were issued with a new operator reference / application number, TGR 1678 in January 1933, due to change of identity and address.

The three Road Service Licences held by the Brynteg company were then given new numbers:-

TGR 1678/1: Ammanford (Square) to Aberystwyth (Railway Station).

TGR 1678/2: Ammanford (Square) to Llanelly (Railway Station).

TGR 1678/3: Ammanford (Square) to Burry Port (Railway Station).

With the company under James' control, several operational changes were made, including the introduction of weekly and season tickets, interchangeable return tickets on the Aberystwyth service with Western Welsh O.C., and interchangeable returns on the Llanelly service between themselves, W.W.O.C., and West Wales Motors.

On the other hand, two more applications were made for services into Swansea town. The first one applied for in May 1933 was:-

TGR 1678/4: Pontyberem to Swansea via: Cwmmawr, Tumble, Cross Hands, Pontardulais and Fforestfach. (To operate daily including Sundays).

This application was inevitably refused after receiving objections from seven competitors.

The second application, made in November 1934 was:

TGR 1678/5: Swansea to Aberystwyth via: Penllergaer, Pontardulais, Cross Hands, Drefach, Carmarthen, Conwil Elfed, Llandyssul, Synod Inn, New Quay, Aberayron and Llanon.

To operate one trip daily in each direction, Monday to Saturday, from July to September only.

This application, however, was retracted in February 1935, when J. James & Sons Ltd., applied for all the licences held by the subsidiary company W. Jones & Sons (Brynteg) Ltd., finally absorbing the company.

With the inevitable absorption of Brynteg's services taking place in June 1935, the remaining Brynteg vehicles were taken into stock six months later, marking the end of the **'Brynteg'** fleet name? The staff however, transferred to James and remained in their employ for several years afterwards, many of them were 'Brynteg' family members i.e. William; David; Gomer; Trevor; Tom; Mary Ann; Hiram; Edgar and William David Jones. Tom Jones received the position of Garage Foreman with James, whilst David Jones became an inspector and Mary Ann a 'clippy' (conductress). Driver William Jones remained in James' employ until his death in July 1955.

'BRYNTEG' PHASE IV

More than a decade later, the Brynteg title re-appeared under the name of:

EDGAR JONES 'BRYNTEG BUS Co' UPPER TUMBLE

Edgar Jones was a 'second generation' of the aforementioned Jones Bros., 'Brynteg' family: the son of David Jones, a former director of the erstwhile Jones Bros., concern.

Cutting his first tooth on a steering wheel, Edgar was previously a bus driver employed by J. James & Sons Ltd., at Ammanford.

With a capital of £400, he left the armed forces in 1946 to start a taxi business from the same family owned premises 'Brynteg Garage' at Upper Tumble. Ably assisted by his brother Hiram, the business moderately expanded to include buses and coaches with school contracts and a workers contract service carrying construction workers from Ammanford and the Gwendraeth Valley to the construction site of Carmarthen Bay Power Station at Burry Port.

In 1948 however, Edgar's father, David Jones, took early retirement from his employment as an inspector at J. James & Sons Ltd., Ammanford, to take full financial control of the new company, by now trading as 'Brynteg Bus Company'.

In the meantime, residents of Hopkinstown, a small district of the Amman Valley, were plaguing the Ammanford council for public transport, especially transport for their children attending Bettws primary school. Their request had been ignored for 3 years until April 1949 when Edgar Jones decided to apply for a licence to operate a daily service to the district, and accommodate the school children. The licence application was:-

TGR 3844/1: Ammanford (YMCA., Iscennen Road) to Hopkinstown. via: Bettws Square, Iscoed Road, Waungron Road and Maesquarre Road.

This created quite a stir at the James' establishment, resulting in their immediate objection and public hearing. Nevertheless, the licence was obtained in July 1949.

Two months later he applied for a modification to this service, asking to extend the service into Llanelly on Llanelly's market days, Thursday and Saturday only via: Saron, Capel Hendre, Gorsddu Square, Cwmgwili Square, Bryncelyn Bridge, Llannon and Felinfoel (with limited pick up points). Objections were received from all five major Ammanford bus operators and the licence was refused, yet three weeks later an application by J. James & Sons Ltd., for a similar Llanelly market day service from Ammanford was granted.

In February 1950 another modification to Edgar's new service was sought after, this time to extend it beyond Ammanford (Iscennen Road) to the Pullman Springfilled Company's factory at Pantyffynnon. Permission for the extension was granted in April 1950.

At the same time, a special late night licence was applied for and granted in April 1950:

TGR 3844/2: Ammanford (Dance Halls) to Upper Tumble (Brynteg Garage), via: Saron, Capel Hendre, Penygroes Square., Gorslas, Cross Hands and Upper Tumble. To depart from Ammanford Drill Hall at 12.00 midnight on Saturdays only, all year round.

In an attempt to expand the business further, two Excursions and Tours licences were sought after in August 1951:-

TGR 3844/3: Excursions and Tours starting from Tumble (Police Station), with pick up points at Drefach, Cefneithin, Cross Hands, Gorslas, Penygroes, Saron, Blaenau and Llandebie.

TGR 3844/4: Excursions and Tours starting from Hopkinstown (Waungron), with pick up points at Bettws and Garnswllt.

EDGAR JONES, Brynteg Garage, Upper Tumble

NEW 'BUS SERVICE

Time-Table between Ammanford (Y.M.C.A.), Bettws, Waungron, Maesquarre Road and Hopkinstown

								S.O.	S.O.
	a.m.	a.m.	p.m.	p.m.	p.m.	p.m.	p.m.	p.m.	p.m.
Ammanford (Y.M.C.A.) dep.	8 35	9 40	12 45	3†45	4 30	6 30	8 30	9 30	10 30
Bettws Square ..	8 38	9 43	12 48	3 48	4 33	6 33	8 33	9 33	10 33
Waungron ..	8 42	9 47	12 52	3 52	4 37	6 37	8 37	9 37	10 57
Maesquarre Rd. ..	8 45	9 50	12 55.	3 55	4 40	6 40	8 40	9 40	10 40
Hopkinstown arr.	8 50	9 55	1 0	4†0	4 45	6 45	8 45	9 45	10 45

								S.O.	S.O.
	a.m.	a.m.	p.m.	p.m.	p.m.	p.m.	p.m.	p.m.	p.m.
Hopkinstown dep.	8†55	10 0	1 5	4 10	5 0	6 45	9 0	10 0	11 0
Maesquarre Rd. ..	9 0	10 5	1. 10	4 15	5 5	6 50	9 5	10 5	11 5
Waungron ..	9 3	10 8	1 13	4 18	5 8	6 53	9 8	10 8	11 8
Bettws Square ..	9 7	10 12	1 17	4 22	5 12	6 57	9 12	10 12	11 12
Ammanford (Y.M.C.A.) arr.	9†10	10 15	1 20	4 25	5 15	7 0	9 15	10 15	11 15

NOTE.

† denotes Schoolchildren when Bettws Schools open, and Passengers during School Holidays

S.O. Saturdays only

December 5th 1949.

Phone Tumble 58
Ammanford 211

LUXURY COACHES FOR HIRE

After objections from Western Welsh O.C., and West Wales Motors Ltd., both licences were refused in October 1951. A month later, Edgar's father David Jones sadly passed away at the early age of 62. His unfortunate death inevitably left Edgar to control his own finances – resulting in financial disaster. The company ceased trading five months later on 30th April, 1952.

At the Carmarthen bankruptcy court it was stated that the business had been profit-able until 1950, but afterwards, despite additional cash advances which amounted to £3,146, Jones was seriously overburdened with hire purchase commitments and his affairs had shown a deficiency of £2,881.

NOTICE

AMMANFORD–
HOPKINSTOWN
'BUS SERVICE

The above Service, run by Mr. Edgar Jones, Brynteg 'Bus Co., WILL CEASE TO OPERATE AFTER THE 30th APRIL NEXT.

Five vehicles reverted to the owners in default and J. James & Sons Ltd., picked up the abandoned Hopkinstown service along with a school service, Penygroes to Llandebie Secondary Modern School.
After his business venture collapsed, Edgar Jones never returned to the bus industry, he made a complete change and drove coal lorries.

Other Companies Mentioned

Abbey Services, Neath
Ammanford and District Bus Services
Amman Valley Bus Service (Phillips Bros., Llandebie)
Amman Valley Road Motor Bus Service
J.M. Bacus & Co., Burry Port
Bassett Bros., Gorseinon
Bevan & Davies, Garnswllt
Blue Bird Motors, Neath
S. Bowen, Llandebie
Brynteg Bus Company, Upper Tumble
Idwal Davies, Ammanford
D.J. Davies, Garnswllt
J.W. Davies, Pontardawe
L. J. Davies, Swansea Valley
W. L. Davies, (Cambrian Express) Clydach
Davies & Williams, Trebanos
Eclipse Saloon Services, Clydach
O.D. Edwards, Cross Inn Hotel, Ammanford
Enterprise Motor Services, Gorseinon
J.D. Evans (Inglis M.S.), Llanybyther
T. Evans, Fforestfach
Gough Motor Services, Mountain Ash
Gower Vanguard Motors
Great Western Railway Company (G.W.R.)
W. H. Hughes, Ystalyfera
Johns Bros., Grovesend
Johnson & Morris, Upper Tumble
Daniel Jones, (Abergwili Express) Carmarthen
Edgar Jones, Upper Tumble
John Jones, (Pontyberem & District Services)
E. Isaac Jones, Brynamman
Rees Jones, Tirydail
Wm Jones, Brynteg, Upper Tumble
Jones Bros., (Red Bus Service), Aberystwyth
Jones Bros, Brynawel, Penygroes
Jones Bros, (Brynteg), Upper Tumble

Dd. Lewis, Cross Hands
Dd. Lewis, Tirydail
Lewis Bros, Pontardulais
L.C.W. Motors (L.C. Williams), Talley & Llandilo
London & North Western Railway Company, (L.N.W.R.)
Llanelly Express Motor Service Company
Llanelly & District Traction Company
Llanelly & District (Carmarthenshire) Transport Company
Morgan Bros., Bettws
Mumbles Electric Railway Company
N & C Luxury Coaches, Neath
Neath Omnibus Company
Osbourne Bus Service, Neath
Petters, Carmarthen
Phillips Bros., (Amman Valley Bus Service), Llandybie
John Rees, Ystalyfera
Rees & Williams, Tycroes
Richmond Services, Neath
South Wales Transport Company
South Wales Commercial Motors
Swansea Bus Services
Swansea Improvements & Tramways Company
Jack Smith, Garnant
Albert Thomas (M.M.T. Services), Tirydail
R.W. Thomas, Cwmllynfell
Thomas Taylor& Sons (Taylors Motor Service), Cross Hands
Tumble Motor Transport, Upper Tumble
United Welsh Services, Swansea
Vaughan Saloon Services, Tycroes
West Wales Motors, Llanelly/Tycroes
Western Welsh Omnibus Company
Windsor Bus Serice, Neath
Willmore Motors, Neath
Dd. Williams, Garnswllt